SCHOLARS AND GENTLEMEN

Scholars and Gentlemen

UNIVERSITIES AND SOCIETY
IN PRE-INDUSTRIAL BRITAIN
1500–1700

HUGH KEARNEY

CORNELL UNIVERSITY PRESS

First published 1970

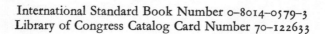

International Standard Book Number 0-8014-0579-3
Library of Congress Catalog Card Number 70-122633

PRINTED IN GREAT BRITAIN
BY LATIMER TREND AND CO. LTD., PLYMOUTH

For Kate

Contents

Introduction   *page* 11

I The Changing Social Function of the Universities   15

    1. The Tudor Revolution   15

    2. The Gentry   22

    3. The Clergy   28

II Court and Country Humanists   34

III The Ramist Challenge   46

IV The Radicalism of the Sectaries   71

V The Revival of Scholasticism   77

VI Clerical Offensive and Country Reaction   91

VII The Cromwellian Decade   110

VIII Scotland   129

IX Social and Intellectual Trends after the Restoration   141

X 1700: Ancients and Moderns   157

    Conclusion   167

XI A Comparative Postscript: the Nineteenth Century   174

    Bibliography   193

    Index   207

Diagrams

page

1. Graph showing the relative numbers of students at
   Oxford and Cambridge, 1540–1850   40–1
2. Graph showing the relative numbers of students at
   different colleges at Cambridge, 1544–1740   56–7

Reproduced by kind permission of the President and fellows of Queens' College Cambridge from J. A. Venn, *Oxford and Cambridge Matriculations 1544–1906* (Cambridge, 1908), and *A Statistical Chart to Illustrate the Entries at the Various Colleges in the University of Cambridge 1544–1907* (Cambridge, 1908).

Introduction

This book was originally planned as an examination of the curriculum in European universities during the seventeenth century with the idea of tracing such changes as followed in the wake of the Scientific Revolution. After some time, it became clear to me that a work on this scale was beyond the capabilities of a single scholar. In 1550, there were over fifty universities in Western Europe. In addition, the history of university education, which had attracted the attention of many scholars for the medieval period, had been relatively neglected by twentieth-century European historians. There was no equivalent for the early modern period of Rashdall's classical study of the medieval universities.

I also began to realize, again rather belatedly, that a university curriculum did not exist in a vacuum but formed part of a wider social picture. Changes in the curriculum could take place for social, political or religious reasons as much as intellectual ones. The university, in other words, was a social as much as an intellectual institution.

This is, no doubt, a self-evident truth but it is often hidden from view in the histories of individual universities. As a general rule, the history of a university has been written as a piece of 'official' history by specially appointed historians. In such circumstances, the portrait normally appears without the warts. Scholars who are a credit to the universities may be mentioned but not their indifferent colleagues who may have been more powerful in academic politics. Successes are highlighted but not failures. It would seem 'bad form' on the occasion of a university centenary to mention that certain classes of people are excluded, formally or informally, from the university because of religion, colour or income. In my experience, the history of particular universities often resembles 'old-style' business history commissioned as subtle pieces of advertising. There are many exceptions to the general rule, but the tendency is there, none the less.[1]

In this book I have tried to discuss the curriculum of the universities of England, Scotland and Ireland (and, very briefly, Harvard) against the social background of the sixteenth and seventeenth centuries. One of my major sources has been students' notebooks, many of which have survived in private and public collections. This type of material is very useful since it shows the historian what was actually being taught in a particular college at a particular date. Unfortunately, as will become clear, there are many gaps, though undoubtedly more notebooks exist than I have come across.

Though I have confined my attention to these islands, I would like to think that my study has certain wider implications. The universities under discussion were European in the sense that they used European textbooks drawn from Spain, Portugal, France, Holland, Germany and the Spanish Netherlands. From this point of view, we may regard the English, Scottish and Irish universities as case studies of European universities generally during the period. There is good reason to think that they were typically European rather than specifically English.

I have also tried, however inadequately, to consider these universities as fulfilling varied social functions in particular societies. Trinity College, Dublin, for example, seems to me to fall into place as a type of 'colonial' institution which had many parallels in seventeenth-century Europe, as the expanding nation states attempted to control restive minority groups. Similarly, the colleges of Oxford and Cambridge, catering for gentry and clergy, had their parallels in the colleges of the University of Paris. Over Europe generally, the universities were the educational organs of a ruling *élite*, and in this as in so much else, the universities of these islands were characteristic institutions.

Finally, I regard my book as a contribution to a discussion about the nature of English education and society which has gathered pace during the last decade. The debate may be said to have begun with the publication of Mark Curtis's book *Oxford and Cambridge in Transition* (1959). It has continued with contribu-

[1] For a similar comment on American university histories, see B. D. Karl, 'The Power of Intellect and the Politics of Ideas', *Daedalus* (summer, 1968), p. 1032.

tions by Lawrence Stone, Hugh Trevor-Roper, Christopher Hill, Kenneth Charlton, Mrs. Joan Simon and Jack Hexter. The discussion of statistical evidence has been important in the debates, but it would be a pity if statistics dominated them wholly when so much of what is at stake, the significance of social and educational ideas, is not susceptible to statistical examination.

I am extremely grateful to the Culbenkian Foundation for a generous grant which enabled me to begin work on the book. I must also thank Louis B. Wright and his staff at Folger Library for the magnificent facilities which I enjoyed in 1964 and 1967. University College, Dublin, and the University of Sussex each granted me a term's sabbatical leave, in 1958 and 1964 respectively. Like other scholars, I am in the debt of my friends and colleagues in many universities and libraries. For early encouragement in this field, I must thank Aubrey Gwynn, Herbert Butterfield, Peter Laslett, Rosalie Colie, Hugh Trevor-Roper, Mark Curtis and John Cooper. On my visits to Scotland, I greatly enjoyed conversations with R. G. Cant, G. E. Davie and John Durkin. Finally, I thank Barry Supple, Rosalie Colie, Peter Burke, James Shiel and Asa Briggs, and especially Keith Thomas, for reading the manuscript in its various forms and making many helpful suggestions.

Ditchling
30 January, 1969

CHAPTER I

The Changing Social Function of the Universities

1. *The Tudor Revolution*

Oxford and Cambridge in 1500 fulfilled the same social function as they had done two centuries earlier. They provided the means for educating a clerical intelligentsia. This was an *élite* within the church, separated from the rank and file of parish clergy; it was also an *élite* within the state, from the ranks of which were drawn many of the members of the royal bureaucracy. Clerical importance was reflected in the dominating place held by the clergy within the King's Council, not least during the period of Thomas Wolsey's domination (1512–29). It was also displayed in the landed wealth of the Church, reckoned at one-third of the land of England. Essentially the universities were the educational organs of a vast ecclesiastical corporation, looking to the Papacy as its head.[1]

Sociologically, the medieval Church may be regarded as a distinct sub-culture with its own social hierarchy, its own law, its own view of politics, its own ideology, its own *raison d'être*. In this scheme of things, the practice of Church law (i.e. canon law) had become the dominating clerical profession, a dominance which was reflected within the universities themselves. The majority of those engaged in higher studies at Oxford and Cam-

---

[1] The indispensable guide for Oxford is E. H. Cordeaux and D. H. Merry, *A Bibliography of Printed Works referring to the University of Oxford* (Oxford, 1968). For short 'official' histories of the various colleges, and much else, see *Victoria History of the County of Oxford*, ed. H. E. Salter and M. D. Lobel, vol. III (London, 1954), and *A History of the County of Cambridge and the Isle of Ely*, ed. J. P. C. Roach, vol. III (London, 1959). The volumes published by the Oxford Historical Society contain a great deal of useful material and are conveniently listed in E. L. C. Mullins, *Texts and Calendars* (London, 1958). There is no Cambridge equivalent. The classical account of the history of Oxford is Anthony Wood, *The History and Antiquities of the University of Oxford* (Oxford, 1792–6). J. B. Mullinger, *The University of Cambridge from the Earliest Times*, 3 vols. (Cambridge, 1873–1911), is extremely valuable. I found G. G. Coulton, *Medieval Panorama* (Cambridge, 1938), chap. 21, very illuminating.

bridge spent their time in the study of canon law. Of the sixty halls at Oxford in 1450, thirty were halls of legists, namely canon lawyers. At Oxford there were many more legist halls than there were colleges. The real university was the halls not the colleges.[1] At Cambridge in 1489, the number of those taking a baccalaureate of canon law numbered twenty-two, as against thirty taking a B.A. In both universities, the popularity of canon law was so great that certain colleges prohibited, or limited by statute, canon law studies.[2]

The influence of law was also felt beyond the strictly legal sphere. There was an extraordinary emphasis in the medieval world upon the place of law in the universe and the role of law in ethics. The legal mind pervaded almost every corner of the medieval Church. Scholastic theology itself has been described as the application of legal methodology to the Bible. The episcopate of the medieval Church was dominated by canon lawyers, and the theory of indulgences reflected a lawyer's concern with the problem of divine rewards. The administration of wills and other matters of probate fell within the sphere of canon law.

The attraction of studying canon law at the university may be seen by examining the lists of cathedral livings for the diocese of Exeter. A quick analysis shows that the number of cathedral prebendaries holding higher degrees rose from one-fifth in the early fourteenth century to two-thirds in the early sixteenth century. Obviously a higher degree was considered essential as a qualification in the Church. Even more illuminating is the fact that two-thirds of these degrees were in canon law. The incentive behind the study of canon law is revealed in these figures. It lay in a growing insistence upon legal expertize as a qualification for ecclesiastical office.[3]

---

[1] H. E. Salter, *Medieval Oxford* (Oxford, 1936), p. 95. A list of Oxford halls is to be found in Anthony Wood's *Survey of the Antiquities of the City of Oxford*, ed. A. Clark (Oxford, 1889), vol. I, Appendix K, pp. 638–41. Unfortunately most halls left no records, but see A. B. Emden, *An Oxford Hall in Medieval Times* (Oxford, 1927), and H. E. Salter, 'An Oxford Hall in 1424', in *Essays Presented to Lane Poole* (Oxford, 1927).

[2] At Oxford, New College, Jesus and Queen's; at Cambridge, Jesus and St. Catherine's. King's restricted to M.A.s studying canon law to four. Mullinger, *Cambridge*, vol. I, pp. 211, 307–20.

[3] J. Le Neve, *Fasti Ecclesiae Anglicanae 1300–1541*, vol. IX, 'Exeter diocese', ed. Joyce M. Horn (London, 1964).

Another aspect of the medieval Church reflected in the organization of the universities was the importance of the monastic and mendicant orders. The leading place in size and wealth among the colleges was held by monastic foundations such as Canterbury College, Durham College and Gloucester College, at Oxford. The mendicant foundations were more significant in size than wealth but nonetheless they were important.[1]

In contrast, most of the colleges catering for the secular clergy were small and impoverished institutions,[2] the academic equivalent of the collegiate foundations which covered England and which provided the material basis for clergy to live a life in common without being confined to any particular rule. In some cases, colleges had been founded at the instance of a local bishop to provide accommodation for his clergy. Exeter was founded in 1314 for scholars from Devon and Cornwall. Merton gave preference to the diocese of Winchester and other dioceses where college estates were situated. Brasenose preferred natives of the diocese of Coventry and Lichfield or of Lancashire and Cheshire.[3] In general there is good reason to believe that the endowment of colleges was bound up with the spread of ecclesiastical reforms in particular areas, with the propagation of the gospel into the dark corners of the realm, or even with the effective centralization of Church and State.

Thus the universities reflected in 1500 certain aspects of the social and political structure of England; first, the great power enjoyed by the Church, and then within the Church the dominance of the canonists and the monastic orders. It was a situation which was to change in a drastic and revolutionary manner within the next half century. By 1540 the profession of canon lawyer had ceased to exist and the monastic orders had been dissolved.

Signs of an impending change are plain enough. Tension had existed between canon and common lawyers since the thirteenth century, but bad feeling increased in the early sixteenth century. One reason for this was the growing prestige of Roman Law as a

---

[1] See W. Pantin, *Canterbury College, Oxford*, Oxford Historical Society, new series (Oxford, 1947–50).

[2] H. E. Salter, *Medieval Oxford*, p. 96. Salter thought that if all the colleges had been dissolved in 1400, it would not have been a crushing blow to the university, ibid., p. 97.

[3] *Registrum Collegii Exoniensis*, ed. W. Boase (Oxford, 1894), p. iii.

by-product of the Italian Renaissance. Customary law, of which English common law was a characteristic example, was placed on the defensive against Roman Law, on which canon law was based.

The common lawyers were well placed to defend themselves or to attack, when the time came. The Inns of Court, which were in effect colleges offering a legal education, were situated in the heart of London.[1] The common lawyers were also sure of reasonable representation in the House of Commons whenever Parliament met. The occasion arose in 1514 over the case of Richard Hunne, a layman who was alleged to have been murdered in a clerical prison.[2] From then onwards, inside and outside Parliament, the cause of the common lawyers was backed by a strong current of anti-clericalism. Friction between the two legal systems also reflected the current state of politics, since anti-clericalism could be used as a weapon against the King's minister, Wolsey.

The culminating point of the crisis, which was to decide the future of canon law, was of course, the question of the King's divorce. From 1527 onwards the personal future of Henry VIII, and as it seemed the political future of the realm, rested with the canon lawyers. This was their supreme moment. Given success in the labyrinthine machinery of the Papal courts, the future of the canon lawyers seemed assured. Failure brought with it the permanent displeasure of the King and in its turn, the abolition of the system of appeals to Rome, on which canon law was based.

Equally exposed to criticism were the monastic orders, and the regular clergy generally. There is little doubt that much of the criticism of the monks derived from social bitterness among the secular clergy. The Benedictine monks in particular were a wealthy corporation whose individual wealth increased as their numbers dropped. They drew upon the higher social groups for their membership, which made them even more of a target for clerics of uncertain social origin such as Erasmus. But the monks were also exposed to criticism from those lay families whose sons had been excluded from the wealth of local monastic houses. It is unrealistic to think of the great estates of Ramsey or Glastonbury

---

[1] On the Inns of Court, see W. Prest, 'The Legal Education of the Gentry at the Inns of Court', in *Past and Present*, vol. 38 (Dec., 1967), pp. 20–39.
[2] K. Pickthorn, *Early Tudor Government* (Cambridge, 1934), p. 112–14; A. G. Dickens, *The English Reformation* (London, 1964), chap. 5.

as islands of monastic independence in the countryside. They were controlled by local families in the interests of their sons and nephews, and the only way in which outsiders could break into the magic circle was to beat the anti-monastic drum.

The monks were also exposed to serious intellectual criticism. As is well known, the humanists directed their strictures against the technicalities of the canonists and the abuses of monasticism with equal impartiality, or lack of it. Erasmus was both the hammer of the monks and the scourge of the scholastics.[1] But humanism would have had little social impact if it had not become, in a sense, the ideology of those who were badly off in the ecclesiastical world. The new learning attracted the support of the alienated intellectuals among the secular clergy and the mendicant orders. It made next to no headway among the Benedictines and the orders who were well endowed. There was also a touch of the revolt of one generation against another. The group of dissidents who met at the White Horse in Cambridge were drawn from the less fashionable religious orders, from the lower social groups, and from the new generation.

During the 1530s a revolution occurred which radically changed the relationship between the English universities and English society. The first and perhaps most important changes affected the status of canon law in England. A succession of statutes culminating in the Act of Supremacy created a situation in which the corpus of canon law as built up since the twelfth century became totally irrelevant. The picture was completed by Thomas Cromwell's decision in 1535 to forbid the teaching of canon law within the universities, and the awarding of canon law degrees.[2]

At one stroke a whole profession was abolished, and with it the *raison d'être* of the most important branch of higher studies within the universities. It was this change rather than the better-known turning away from scholasticism, symbolized by the joke of putting Duns in Bocardo (Duns being the best-known schoolman

---

[1] For contrasting interpretations of Erasmus, see M. D. Knowles, *The Religious Orders in England* (Cambridge, 1959), chap. 9; and H. R. Trevor-Roper, *Historical Essays* (London, 1957).

[2] Mullinger, *Cambridge*, vol. I, p. 630. On Thomas Cromwell, see, of course, G. R. Elton, *The Revolution in Tudor Government* (Cambridge, 1953). Professor Elton tells me that there is no satisfactory discussion of Cromwell's policy towards the universities (18 Dec., 1966).

and Bocardo the university prison), which changed the social and intellectual character of the universities.

Along with the disappearance of the legists went the decline of the halls. By 1550, only eight halls survived. This was a sudden transformation, not the evolution beloved of so many historians. The so-called rise of the colleges was not really a rise at all. The disappearance of so many halls inevitably left the colleges enjoying a lonely, and it appeared for a time at least, a dangerous isolation. The real victors were the Inns of Court, which now became the dominant institutions for legal education in the realm. The triumph of the common lawyers was complete.

This change in itself would have been sufficient to transform the character of the universities. It was, however, accompanied by a revolution of almost equal magnitude, namely the dissolution of the monasteries (1535–40). The monastic colleges were dissolved along with the other houses. The monks and friars, for so long a dominating feature of university life, disappeared completely, a change which took the strength from scholastic theology as much as any decree of the government. The beneficiaries were the secular clergy. In some cases the secular colleges were granted property which had originally belonged to the monks. For example, Sir Thomas White founded St. John's, Oxford, in 1555 on the basis of a grant from Christ Church of buildings which had belonged to the Cistercian college of St. Bernard.[1]

But the dissolution of the monasteries was not an event which occurred in isolation from the rest of society. It was one of the side effects of a movement of social change, which brought new social groups into prominence. The Reformation would have been inconceivable without pressure from important sections of the laity, who were drawn into a movement of anti-clericalism and anti-monasticism.

Anti-clericalism was not new in England, nor was criticism of the monks. They were already present at least as early as the fourteenth century in the Lollard Movement and the Peasants' Revolt. What was new about anti-clericalism was firstly its strength in Parliament and by inference among the legal profes-

[1] W. H. Stevenson and H. E. Salter, *The Early History of St. John's College, Oxford,* Oxford Historical Society, new series (Oxford, 1939), p. 93. See also *Letters and Papers of Henry VIII, 1539* (London, 1894), vol XIV, i, p. 404.

sion, the gentry and the London merchants, and secondly the support it received from the Crown in the time of Cromwell, but its causes lie buried in the complex social history of the fifteenth century still largely unexplored.[1] Into the consequent social revolution, the most important single social change since the Norman Conquest, the universities were drawn willy-nilly. It was inevitable that change should be thorough-going and violent. What is surprising is that the universities survived at all at Oxford and Cambridge, when the obvious place for higher education was London, near 'the third university', the Inns of Court.

The most important decisions taken about the future of the universities were the establishment of Regius professorships in 1540, and of royal colleges in 1547, Trinity College at Cambridge and Christ Church at Oxford. These decisions were in theory royal, but there is no need to attribute them, as is often done, directly to royal enthusiasm for learning. The first decision, to establish Regius professorships, was clearly due to the influence of Thomas Cromwell. His nominees were first appointed, in the persons of Sir John Cheke and Sir Thomas Smith, and it seems likely that Cromwell's idea was based upon the practice of Francis I of France. Regius professorships in both countries offered a means of controlling appointments in sensitive academic areas. We may also assume that the example of the universities in Lutheran Germany was not far from Cromwell's mind.

But the decision to endow royal colleges at Oxford and Cambridge was an even more novel departure. The endowments were on so generous a scale as to transform the traditional image of the college. Trinity and Christ Church were academic palaces, where Peterhouse and Corpus had been poor hostels. The royal colleges were clearly intended to dominate the universities in a way without precedent. They also broke new ground in providing encouragement for laymen to take up university education. Whose was the final decision it is hard to say. Henry VIII was dying when the decisions were taken late in 1546, but there was a reforming group in power which included Thomas Cranmer, Archbishop of Canterbury.[2]

[1] There are some interesting comments on social change in A. R. Bridbury, *Economic Growth; England in the Later Middle Ages* (London, 1962), though the author takes the foundation of colleges as a sign of economic prosperity.
[2] In 1539, Cranmer seemed to envisage a college at Canterbury itself; *Letters and Papers of Henry VIII, 1539*, vol. II, p. 212.

The collegiate foundations which survived the crisis of the 1530s, or were founded later in the century, were essentially different from what they had been in the fifteenth century. The new model was based upon Reformation assumptions about the greater role of laymen within the Church. There was also a fresh emphasis upon the moral role of education. Finally, the colleges provided a degree of social and intellectual control which had been impracticable in the looser system of halls but which in the changed circumstances of the sixteenth century seemed imperative to official eyes. The college, in short, was the educational equivalent of the centralizing institutions which formed the basis of Tudor monarchy.

Within the college, the student, lay or clerical, was provided with a controlled intellectual and religious environment. The tutorial system, in which a single tutor was responsible for twenty or so students, replaced the hurly-burly of the lecture-room. Tutorial supervision, which in the twentieth century aims at creating a critical attitude of mind, was in the sixteenth century a form of intellectual and moral discipline. The college reproduced in little the social and intellectual assumptions of the Tudor state. Social divisions among the student body between fellow commoners and sizars reflected those of society at large. The object of education within the colleges was to produce intellectuals and gentlemen who could be relied upon in a world constantly threatened, it was thought, by revolution.

Thus the rise of the colleges was a mixed blessing. It provided the universities with new wealth and prestige and architectural benefits on the grand scale. It brought a rise in entry numbers at each university from 150 a year in 1500 to 400–500 by 1600. It made possible the creation of an educated gentry. On the other hand, the object of the colleges was not freedom but control and to lose sight of this fact amid the splendours of college architecture is to risk being blinded by sentimental nostalgia.

2. The Gentry

The changes which followed upon the collapse of canon law and the disappearance of the regulars from the universities were both social and intellectual. On the one hand, there was a social change which is hard to measure statistically, in the absence of admission registers. Sometime between 1530 and 1570 laymen from the gentry class began to go up to Oxford and Cambridge in large numbers. The universities ceased to be merely the educational organs of the Church. They began to cater in part at least for the educational needs of the lay ruling *élite*. At the same time, numbers at the universities rose until by the 1630s there were several times more students than in the middle ages, perhaps half or more of them lay.[1]

At the same time the circles which supported humanism enjoyed a dramatic victory. As will be seen below (p. 34), classical studies and the textual study of the Bible came to dominate the curriculum, as Erasmians had always hoped. Elyot's *The Governor* exercised considerable influence.[2] These changes began under Cromwell and were completed by university visitors appointed under Edward VI. The universities lost a good deal of the professional character which had been so marked a feature of the pre-Reformation period. They continued to train the secular clergy, but the emphasis was upon intellectual formation, not technical training in law.

The significance of the changes, however, is still very much a matter for debate. For those who follow the views of Lawrence Stone (who elaborates and develops the thesis of J. H. Hexter and Mark Curtis),[3] the answer, in a word, is modernization:

> This was one of the really decisive movements in English history by which the propertied classes exploited and expanded the higher educational resources of the country. By doing so they fitted themselves to rule in the new conditions of the modern state and they turned the intelligentsia from a branch of the clergy into a branch of the propertied classes.[4]

In other words, the universities were the decisive instrument in transforming England from a society in which the lay military

[1] See L. Stone, 'The Educational Revolution', *Past and Present*, 1964, pp. 41–80.
[2] See below, p. 34.
[3] J. H. Hexter, 'The education of the aristocracy during the Renaissance', in *Reappraisals in History* (London, 1961); M. Curtis, *Oxford and Cambridge in Transition* (Oxford, 1959), is the standard work on this period, though his conclusions have not gone unchallenged.
[4] Stone, op. cit.

aristocracy left national administration to the clergy, into one in which the laity had the whiphand, thanks to improved education. On this view, the code of honour by which the fifteenth-century gentleman lived, was replaced by one which stressed the importance of technical skills to be used in the service of the monarchy. A *noblesse de l'épée* transformed itself rapidly into a *noblesse de la robe*.

Professor Curtis tells us that secular learning now came into its own:

> The arts course which had once been training in secular learning consecrated to religious ends, became . . . secular learning justified for its own sake.[1]

The impulse for the change, he argues, came from the flood of young gentry who came up to the universities in the second half of the sixteenth century. Under this pressure the universities were transformed from the essentially clerical institutions of 1500 into the lay institutions of 1600.

Professor Stone has termed the period of rapid change 'the educational revolution', and there is, to be sure, a great attraction in looking on the sixteenth century as an age of modernization in education, as well as in other fields. The difficulty with this view, however, is that the universities never seem to have lost their function as seminaries for the training of the clergy. If anything, that aspect of the universities increased in importance in the course of the sixteenth century. Attempts made at Cambridge to 'modernize' the university by extending the scope of civil law studies there, even in a minor way, were decisively defeated. Sir Thomas Smith's plans to turn Clare Hall into a legal foundation met with determined and successful opposition on the part of Ridley, the future Marian martyr, on the ground that it would affect the teaching of the divine word.[2] The 'reforms' of Edward VI's reign rested upon attempts to bring over continental theologians to England, and culminated in the arrival of Peter Martyr and Martin Bucer.[3]

When we turn to the second half of the sixteenth century, the clerical impression upon the universities does not seem to

---

[1] Curtis, *Oxford and Cambridge in Transition*, p. 123.
[2] M. Dewar, *Sir Thomas Smith* (London, 1964), p. 41.
[3] A. G. Dickens, *The English Reformation* (London, 1964), p. 232.

diminish. It is true that the chancellors of the university were laymen, like Leicester and Cecil, but the heads of the colleges and the tutors were clergy. The day-to-day teaching was in the hands of the clergy, and the dominant senior faculty was theology. To ignore this side of university life, and to stress the lay aspect, distorts the picture. Moreover, the opportunities of service in the modern Tudor state do not seem to have been particularly great. We have heard a great deal in recent years about the Tudor administrative revolution of the 1530s and it is no doubt true that the civil service was more efficient at the end of the century than at the beginning. But these civil servants were not very numerous. By comparison with France or Spain, the proportion of office holders per head of population was much lower.[1] If men did flock to the universities in such large numbers it was hardly the chance of becoming a crown official which attracted them. Even if state offices had been more plentiful, it was by no means clear, on the assumptions of the sixteenth century, that a university education offered the best approach to them.

One of the features of Elizabethan England was the growth of the court, with a complex system of patronage, and the rise of London as a centre of social life. The backing of an influential patron was as important as the possession of technical skills. As one Elizabethan remarked to Cecil:

My good lord, advancement in all worlds be obtained by mediation and remembrance of noble friends.[2]

William Cecil himself drew a distinction between the life of the university and the life of the court. In 1561, he wrote to Throgmorton, the English envoy in Paris, about his eldest son Thomas:

I mean not to have him Thomas scholarly learned but civilly trained . . . if he might without corruption be in that Court France three months, I think he should learn more both in tongue and knowledge than otherwise in double space.[3]

[1] G. E. Aylmer, *The King's Servants* (London, 1961), pp. 439–53. See also W. T. McCaffrey, 'Place and patronage in Elizabethan politics', in S. T. Bindoff, J. Hurstfield, C. H. Williams (eds.) *Elizabethan Government and Society* (London, 1961), pp. 95–126.
[2] C. Read, *Mr. Secretary Cecil and Queen Elizabeth* (London, 1962), p. 212.
[3] Ibid., p. 213.

Throgmorton thought that Thomas should learn to ride, play the lute, dance, play tennis and 'use such exercises as are noted ornaments to courtiers'. These arts were more likely to be required outside the university than in it. There were, it would seem, two systems of education, that of the court and that of the universities, each with their own code of values, the one based upon the traditional code of honour and loyalty to one's patron, the other based on a system of religious and academic values.

If these remarks on the social situation are justified, the sure-footedness of the 'English propertied classes' becomes open to question. Why should so many wish to enter the universities when it was by no means clear that this was the best method of surviving in the more competitive world of the sixteenth century? Life in a college in a small country town like Oxford, redolent of its ecclesiastical past, was not self-evidently the path to success. A smoother road would appear to have been via a tutor in London, a short stay at the Inns of Court and an early start at court with the chance of catching the eye of an influential courtier, or the prospect of a successful military career in one of Elizabeth's innumerable campaigns.

In fact, there seem to be several reasons behind the influx of so many into the universities in the second half of the sixteenth century. One reason, without a doubt, was connected with reasons of status. In the sixteenth century, the division between gentleman and non-gentleman became the most important social distinction in English life. This was not a merely academic or snobbish criterion, but one that affected almost every aspect of existence, marriage, punishments, religious worship.[1] There was a gentlemanly pattern of life from which the great majority of Englishmen were excluded, and the barriers and boundaries to it seem to have been drawn in the sixteenth century. For those in the half world of yeoman, agriculture and trade, the decision whether to become a gentleman or not was one which affected the future life-chances of a family. At issue was a question of *status* rather than *power*, though of course an acceptable social status did mean the general opening of possibilities in politics and elsewhere. This is perhaps what is meant by the rise of the gentry in the sixteenth

[1] Cf. L. Stone, *Crisis of the Aristocracy* (Oxford, 1965).

century, namely the process by which thousands of prosperous yeomen and merchants chose to adopt the life-style of the gentleman.

Several ways were open by which this could be achieved. The army was one route, the court another, but for most a year or two at the university and the Inns of Court became the cheapest and the easiest route. The self-made men of the fifteenth century became the gentlemen of the sixteenth. There are numerous examples of this process. Nicholas Bacon's father was a yeoman, but after going up to Cambridge in 1523, Nicholas looked upon himself as a gentleman. Of the 102 Yorkshiremen who purchased entrance into the gentry between 1558 and 1642, half were yeoman farmers, and the remainder lawyers or merchants.[1]

Thus the expansion of the universities and the appearance of the English gentlemen were two aspects of the one development. It is for this reason that the rise of a gentry is so difficult to date. The decisive stage in the social history of many families was reached not when they reached a certain income, but when they decided to adopt the style of life associated with a gentleman. Some families did not take this step, which would explain why so many non-gentry even in 1600 were as wealthy or wealthier than gentlemen. The crucial decision could be taken at any time during the period after about 1400. The Brudenells and the Treshams took it around 1500, the Ishams in the fifteenth century, the Spencers and the FitzWilliams around 1500.[2] Others did not take it until the seventeenth century by which time the trickle into universities had become a flood.

This process also applied to the merchant class. A successful merchant often preferred to buy an estate and send his son to the university. On the other hand, a hard-pressed country gentleman might well send his younger son directly into business. John Isham, mercer of London, bought his estate of Lamport in 1560, took up residence in 1572, and sent his second son to Christ's, Cambridge and the Middle Temple.[3] (John's eldest son, Thomas,

---

[1] A. Simpson, *Wealth of the Gentry 1540–1660* (London, 1961), p. 29; J. T. Cliffe *The Yorkshire Gentry from the Reformation to the Cival War* (London, 1969), p. 190.
[2] M. Finch, *The Wealth of Five Northamptonshire Families, 1540–1640* (Oxford, 1956).
[3] Finch, op. cit., p. 24.

in his turn sent his son to Queens', Cambridge.) Sir William FitzWilliam went up to King's in 1564, and he in turn sent his sons William and Walter to Emmanuel.[1]

Of course, desire for social advancement was not the only reason for the increase in the numbers of those going to universities. Some allowance must also be made for those who regarded the colleges of Oxford and Cambridge as a means of ensuring a godly education for their sons. The Reformation had brought the layman into the forefront of Christian society. The Marian exiles included many gentlemen, and Lawrence Humphrey was making a familiar point to reformed ears when he denied the distinction between clerical and lay. Without some such religious enthusiasm among laymen, it is difficult to explain the great increase in numbers at colleges which were well known for their religious radicalism. Emmanuel College, Cambridge and Magdalen College, Oxford, were among the largest in point of size and they attracted many godly laymen. Yet by going to colleges like these, young men might in fact be doing themselves harm in the eyes of Elizabeth or Whitgift.

3. The Clergy

Another reason why young men went up to university was their wish to enter the Church. A substantial proportion of those who entered Oxford and Cambridge stayed on to take an M.A., an almost certain indication of a desire to become a clergyman. This trend may appear odd if we accept the view that there was little future in being a parson, at least in this world. If we are to accept the conclusions of recent commentators, the social and economic status of the clergy dropped in the course of the century.[2] Whitgift told the Queen that less than one-twentieth of the benefices in the country provided a living minimum of £30 a year.[3] Others maintained that only 600 livings were adequate financially. Here is a paradox indeed. Hundreds of men were flocking to be ministers at a time when the economic prospect facing the average parson was grim.

Clearly the clerical profession could not have been in so de-

[1] Op. cit. Ibid., p. 124.
[2] C. Hill, *Economic Problems of the Church* (Oxford, 1956), chap. 9.
[3] Ibid., p. 205.

pressed a condition as its many critics made out. Of course, there were poorly endowed livings and decayed parsonages. But a good deal of the complaint derived from a higher expectation of what the parson had a right to. In social history all is relative, and in the sixteenth century the parish priest helped by pluralities was better off in general than his fifteenth-century predecessor.

In the first place, the abolition of the regular clergy with the Dissolution led to a rise in the status of the secular clergy. Before the Dissolution the regulars had enjoyed a certain superiority. Their men attended and taught in the universities. The monastic houses in many cases were extremely wealthy corporations, dominating the surrounding countryside and exercising more influence than the isolated and often poorly-educated parish priest. Many parish livings had been under monastic control. Thus the Dissolution of the monasteries was an event of immense significance within the Church itself as well as on society without. Attention has been largely concentrated upon the fate of the monastic lands. Of equal, perhaps of greater, importance, was the effect within the Church of the disappearance of the regular orders.

In Catholic countries, the victory in education went to the Jesuits and the revivified orders. In England, it went to the parish clergy. Relatively speaking, therefore, the status of the parish ministry rose, and this played a part in attracting university graduates. The notion that university graduates were appropriate material for the ranks of the parish clergy was a novel one. It may be interpreted partly as a sign of rise in status in the second half of the sixteenth century. To some eyes, the parson's life was still menial and degrading and suitable only for the lower orders. But to others, perhaps the majority, it was a form of social mobility. If not a gentleman himself, a parson was often literally next door to one.

In addition, the sixteenth century saw the rise of the notion of seminary education for the clergy. Whitgift's notion that one graduate in twenty ministers was not enough, was in itself revolutionary by the standards of his pre-Reformation predecessors. In medieval times, the local bishop was the judge of a candidate's fitness for holy orders. Seminary education in a fixed place did not exist and the potential cleric might well pick up his Latin in a dozen possible ways. In Counter-Reformation countries, the Council of Trent in its third phase (1562–3) encouraged the setting up of local seminaries. A similar policy was already being tried in England, with the object of raising the educational standards of the clergy. In this there was more than a hint of the social conservatism induced by fear of the anabaptists. In Europe generally, the activities of John of Leyden and the revolutionary visions of the millenarian sects in the 1530s drove the ruling groups into renewed support for a learned and amenable clergy. The alliance between religion and society was as strong as that between religion and the state. Toleration was a luxury which no landowner could afford for fear of the social evils which might attend it.

Thus Oxford and Cambridge retained, indeed developed, their chief medieval function. England passed through many political and religious changes in the course of the sixteenth century but none of its revolutionaries succeeded in abolishing the clerical profession. The vested interest of the Church stood four-square. The parson took a wife or married his mistress in the course of the Reformation, but socially speaking this brought no violent change. The oldest profession of all remained, along with that of the lawyers, each with its own arcana and its own training.

It was precisely because the universities achieved this position as training-grounds for the parish clergy that the government took so great an interest in them, since sixteenth-century states increasingly equated religious orthodoxy with political loyalty. In England, as in France and Spain, the clergy were regarded as providing additional support for the secular power, and hence it was essential that the universities should be a loyal and sound source of loyal and sound clergy. The close watch which the government maintained upon Oxford and Cambridge illustrates clearly the extent to which the universities remained seminaries. The Chancellors of both universities were prominent politicians who took a keen interest in their charges. Fellowships and college headships were frequently obtained by government patronage and if ever the gentry had threatened to turn the universities completely into finishing-schools, the state would have blocked the way.

The professional character of the universities was also reinforced by the generosity of professional donors, including merchants. Professional men proper, lawyers and clergy, put the endowment of university education highest on their scale of priorities. They gave two-thirds of their charitable benefactions to this cause. Merchants as a whole did not share this enthusiasm but those who did provided generous benefactions. London merchants spent more on poor relief than upon university endowments but even so they gave £135,000 to Oxford and Cambridge during the period 1480–1640, at a time when the cost of endowing a college was in the region of £8,000.[1] The interest of the merchants formed part of a wide pattern of religious revival from the 1590s onwards, and the number of fellowships and scholarships was a substantial counter to the opposite trend for turning the universities into institutions for the gentry. There was indeed considerable pressure from many quarters in Elizabeth's reign to raise the educational standard of the clergy. As a result the number of graduates among the clergy steadily increased. By 1640 in the diocese of Worcester over four-fifths of the clergy were graduates. In the diocese of Oxford the figure was even higher.

Finally, the attraction of the ministry lay in its being something more than a profession. Up to 1640 the Church exercised power; the cleric was as powerful in his own way as the gentleman, much as the parish priest was in nineteenth-century Ireland. At the top of the scale lay the quasi-political rewards open to Whitgift, Bancroft and Laud. In each diocese, a modest replica of this could be found in the Church courts. A clerical career had something to offer for a variety of ambitions, academic, political or even, for the few, spiritual.

It may also be suggested that economic as well as religious reasons made a professional career more attractive in the second half of the sixteenth century. In the first half when the English cloth trade was booming, a commercial career had an obvious attraction. Prospects were bright when the Isham brothers entered the cloth trade in the 1540s. Twenty years later, the outlook was bleak and the second generation of the family had to accept a

---

[1] For the original endowments made to the colleges, see W. K. Jordan, *The Charities of London* (London, 1960), p. 252. The list includes (1511) Brasenose, 5,000; (1505) Christ's, 5,000; (1508) St. John's, Cambridge, 8,000; (1557) St. John's, Oxford, 13,000; (1557) Caius, 6,500 + 2,000; (1583), Emmanuel 3,000; (1583) Sidney, 5,000.

reduced standard of living in the country. For these and for many others, the security offered by the clerical profession had become more attractive than the hazards of commerce.

The economy had in fact entered a prolonged slump. A rising population led to rising food prices and therefore to the greater content of many landlords, but the merchants had much less to look forward to. The great voyages of exploration were less epic adventures than panic measures of a depressed economy. The Statute of Apprentices, far from being a landmark in social legislation, was a milestone in the history of restrictive practices, an attempt to limit entry into the now over-crowded cloth industry. In the economic doldrums of Elizabeth's reign, the attractions of a professional career, whether in law or divinity, were greatly increased. This state of affairs persisted well into the seventeenth century, until it seemed to some observers that the supply of university graduates had far out-stripped the demand. To the generation of the 1580s and 1590s some other careers were possible, which may explain why the numbers entering the universities levelled off. Some became soldiers in the Netherlands and in Ireland. Others such as Richard Boyle, later Earl of Cork, took the desperate step of seeking a fortune in the Irish administration. In the early seventeenth century, emigration to America offered another way out.

The financial rewards of the Church were never as great as in other professions, but in a half-century of commercial stagnation, the average rector benefitted from the rise in agricultural earnings. It is true that the rise in ecclesiastical revenues was not equally spread. Vicars and curates often came off badly compared to rectors. Some parts of the country were better off than others. But, relative to other careers, the Church offered a reasonable hope of an adequate income. Wealth which had been concentrated in monastic hands was more evenly spread. The average increase in over ten counties for rectors ranged, except in one case, from 400 per cent to nearly 700 per cent which more than kept pace with the rise in prices.[1] A young man in 1550 could do a lot worse than take up an ecclesiastical career.

We may conclude that social changes reinforced the clerical element in English society in the period 1560–1640. We speak

[1] Hill, op. cit., p. 111.

easily of the rise of the gentry; it would be equally accurate to speak of the rise of the parish clergy.

If we try now to sum up the social function of the universities in the second half of the sixteenth century, the conclusion seems clear. Above a certain level in society—say that of prosperous yeomen—the universities were instruments of social mobility. But there was a price to be paid for it. By 1600, England was sharply divided into two nations, the 'gentlemen' and the rest, the great majority. In creating this social division the universities were a major instrument. Medieval society had been a social hierarchy with many steps in the ladder. By 1600, the complexities of this traditional society were rapidly disappearing, if they had not gone already. There were now only two social groups, each with its own role and almost indeed its own system of laws. The antithesis was made sharper by the fact that the parish clergy were ranged increasingly on the upper division of the social split. The medieval priest had been a peasant among peasants. The parson in 1600 was a gentleman among gentlemen.[1]

This was a situation which was bound to create a combination of religious and social discontent. The appearance of the religious sectaries in the later decades of the sixteenth century was a logical development arising from a situation in which the 'natural' leaders of the people, the priests, were alienated from them by receiving a gentleman's education. New spokesmen for the oppressed were needed and these were to come from outside the ranks of the established Church.

In sociological terms, the universities between 1500 and 1600 underwent a change of social functions. They were transformed from being institutions geared to training for a particular profession into institutions which acted as instruments of social control. 'Going up to university' meant something very different in 1600 from what it meant in 1500, though even in 1600 it did not mean the same for every undergraduate.

---

[1] Thomas Wilson in his survey of 'The State of England 1600' placed the clergy with gentlemen and esquires among the lesser nobility: *Camden Miscellany*, vol. XVI (1936), p. 23.

CHAPTER II

Court and Country Humanists

Intellectual changes within the universities accompanied these social changes. The tone given by scholastic theology and canon law was replaced by an emphasis on classical studies, which by mid-century dominated the curriculum in a way which they had never done before. It is true that some infiltration of the classics had already taken place before the Reformation. John Dorne, an Oxford bookseller, offered a wide range of classical texts to students and a good selection of the works of Erasmus, although the staple fare of scholastic works and canon law tracts were still prominent on his shelves.[1] Thomas More's well-known letter defending the 'Greeks' against the 'Trojans' at Oxford was another sign that the new learning was making headway at the time he wrote, in 1518.[2] But the pace of change quickened under Cromwell and became very rapid indeed under Edward VI, when Royal Commissioners laid down the lines of a new curriculum, based on classical authors.[3] The humanists were beginning to exploit their victory.

But the day has gone when humanism could be described merely as the study of the classics. Professor Baron has shown that social and political implications may be seen in apparently innocent choices of classical authors. Thanks to his work, we are invited to make a distinction between court humanism and civic humanism, the one looking to the patronage and support of the social hierarchy, the other to a wider involvement in political life with the classical republicans as their inspiration. In Florence the contrast lay between the broader intellectual life of the early fifteenth-century

---

[1] 'The daily ledger of John Dorne, 1520', ed. F. Madan, in C. R. L. Fletcher (ed.) *Collectanea, First Series*, Oxford Historical Society (Oxford, 1885), p. 78.
[2] E. F. Rogers (ed.), *Correspondence of Sir Thomas More* (Princeton, 1947), pp 111–20; E. F. Rogers (trans.), Thomas More, *Selected Letters* (London, 1961), pp. 94–103.
[3] Joan Simon, *Education and Society in Tudor England* (Cambridge, 1966), chap. 10.

republic and the more confined conditions under the Medici.[1]

In the English universities from the 1530s on there seems little doubt that it was humanism of a court type which dominated, at least initially. The key feature of the period of change was the way in which university reforms were sponsored by the state. The prizes were great, as the endowments of Trinity College, Cambridge, and Christ Church, Oxford, showed. The Regius chairs, established in 1540, were a generous contribution to humanist scholarship. But, as with the Regius chairs of history established later under the Georges, the price was high in terms of the conformity demanded. The royal colleges and the royal chairs left the Crown with a great say in the running of the universities. As in Florence under the Medici, the type of intellectual most likely to flourish under these conditions was the court humanist, all too conscious of how much he owed to his patrons, and all too anxious to prove his loyalty.

There was another type of humanism, exemplified in Thomas More's *Utopia*, in which the inspiration of the classics gave rise to criticism of the social and political conditions of early Tudor England. *Utopia* was a devastating attack upon the place of the aristocracy in political life. It implied that political power should be much more widely spread than it was and it condemned by implication the life of conspicuous consumption.[2] This was the nearest England came to civic humanism. By 1540, More was dead and the ideas of *Utopia*, at least in government circles, were of merely speculative interest. Much more influential was the exposition of court humanism made by Sir Thomas Elyot in *The Governor*, a treatise which was reprinted many times in the course of the century. Elyot saw the social and political role of the gentleman as being to serve the king. The gentry were to form an educated ruling *élite* drawn up solidly behind the Crown. There is no hint of criticism, still less of resistance to the Crown. Elyot saw education as necessary, but it was to be education with service in view, and with obedience as the prime virtue.[3]

The arguments in favour of intellectual conformity, if we may

---

[1] H. Baron, *Crisis of the Early Italian Renaissance* (Princeton, 1955).

[2] E. Surtz, S. J., and J. H. Hexter (eds.), *Utopia* (London, 1965), pp. li–liv.

[3] Thomas Elyot, *The Book Named the Governor*, ed. S. E. Lehmberg (Everyman edition, 1962).

so describe court humanism, had assumed a new force by 1540. In particular, the crucial factor was the threat to social order, conjured up by the anabaptist risings in Münster in 1534–5. The success of the Münster risings haunted the imagination of the ruling groups in England, as elsewhere. Henry VIII burnt thirteen anabaptists in 1535 immediately after the rising and several more in the years following. In 1543, Bible-reading was confined to the gentry, in an attempt to keep the spark of new doctrine from spreading to more inflammable material. There was also renewed emphasis upon orthodoxy within the Church.[1] The climax was the panic created by Kett's rebellion in 1549, which in its Protestantism and its appeal to Christ's blood as a liberating force, seemed to many to smack of anabaptism. The universities were exposed to the pressures of these years, and we should not hesitate to see Regius chairs and the royal colleges as in part at least defensive measures by which a secure clergy was to be a bulwark of English society. Learned clergy seemed necessary to counteract the social threat of religious radicalism.

This social conservatism was implied in the *Book of Homilies*:

Take away kings, princes, rulers, magistrates, judges and such states of God's order, no man shall ride or go by highway unrobbed . . . all things shall be common and there must needs follow all mischief and utter destruction. . . .[2]

And it is to be seen also in Parker's letter to Grindal of 1560 asking him not to admit into the ministry people who were untrained in learning, or who followed base occupations.[3] In short, we may see much of the Tudor preoccupation with learning and a learned clergy, and hence with universities, as part of a general social unease. Take but degrees away, and hark what discord follows! Seen against this background, a university curriculum dominated by court humanism seems almost inevitable.

Sir John Cheke was a typical court humanist who became Regius Professor of Greek at Cambridge in 1540, and repaid his debt to the court by writing a pamphlet, *The Pricke of Sedition*, in which he attacked the social irresponsibility, as he saw it, of Kett's re-

---

[1] Dickens, *The English Reformation*, pp. 189–90.
[2] Reprinted in G. R. Elton, *The Tudor Constitution* (Cambridge, 1960), pp. 15–16.
[3] Ibid., p. 328.

bellion (1549).[1] In Cheke and his fellow professor, Thomas Smith,[2] we may see the beginning of the alliance between Crown and some at least of the university intellectuals, which continued throughout the century and beyond.

Another Cambridge court humanist was Andrew Perne who retained his mastership of Peterhouse under Mary and Elizabeth. Perne managed to accept all the theological changes which occurred at court without much intellectual difficulty. For example, he preached the sermon, in 1556, when the dead Bucer was condemned as a heretic, and four years later presided over the Senate which restored him to honour. Perne carried the principle of conformity to a pitch which few Peterhouse men, before or since, have rivalled.[3]

But for a detailed example of how this alliance between the court and humanism worked out in practice, we must turn to John Whitgift, Archbishop of Canterbury (1583–1601), who was protected by Perne at Peterhouse during Mary's reign. Under Elizabeth, he became Master of Trinity, a 'plum' among court academic appointments, where he led a court-sponsored attack upon Puritan dons.[4] This culminated in his revision of the Cambridge statutes which placed much greater power in the grip of the heads of colleges. Whitgift was the model of a successful court intellectual who, in a position of power, was able to harass dissident intellectuals.

In his new statutes of 1570, Whitgift attempted to press a court-orientated curriculum upon the university.[5] A notebook of his, dating from the 1570s,[6] also shows that during his period as Master of Trinity, Whitgift carried forward into Elizabeth's reign the Elyot tradition of court humanism. At each point, the curriculum which his pupils followed recalls Elyot's *Governor*. The course of study was dominated by Cicero. Whitgift's pupils bought various

---

[1] On Cheke, see A. B. Ferguson, *The Articulate Citizen and the English Renaissance* (Durham, Duke U.P., 1965), pp. 274–8, where a more sympathetic viewpoint is adopted than mine.

[2] M. Dewar, *Sir Thomas Smith*. (London, 1964)

[3] *D.N.B.*

[4] H. C. Porter, *Reformation and Reaction in Tudor Cambridge* (Cambridge, 1964).

[5] J. Heywood and T. Wright, *Cambridge University Transactions*, p. 5.

[6] S. R. Maitland, 'Original Papers relating to Whitgift' in *The British Magazine*, vols. XXXII–XXXIII, Oct., 1847–Feb., 1848.

works of Cicero, *De Officiis, Quaestiones Tusculanae, Epistolae ad Atticum* and the *Rhetorica*. This emphasis on rhetoric was accentuated by the orations of Demosthenes and Isocrates. There was also some logic, confined in the main to Seton's little textbook, some history, in the shape of Livy and Caesar, and poetry, in Homer. This was a curriculum in which rhetoric occupied the preponderant position, with 'history' included as part of the rhetorical pattern of study. The role of history as rhetoric formed one aspect of the general inheritance which the English universities took over from the Renaissance. The classical historians provided a fund of analogies and examples which a writer or speaker could rely upon to produce an emotional response among an educated audience.[1]

Whitgift does not seem to have had different reading requirements for lay and clerical students. There was no distinction between the kind of books which a gentleman commoner read over two or three years in college and those which a future minister read. George Clifford, Earl of Cumberland, read Erasmus's *Colloquies*, Castellio, Cicero's *Orations* and Justinus. The course of study followed by the Bacon brothers revolved around rhetoric (Cicero and Demosthenes), history (Caesar, Livy, Sallust and Xenophon), poetry (Homer's *Iliad*) and moral philosophy (Aristotle's *Ethics* and Plato's *Laws*). It is possible that the clerical students paid more attention to books which would stand them in good stead when they came to their M.A. But Francis Dalton, who became a B.D. in 1586, studied Plato, Demosthenes, Aristotle's *Ethics*, and Sophocles, in his early years under Whitgift.

There is little doubt that the tradition of court humanism which Whitgift represented was strong at Cambridge. There is a hint of its strength in Gabriel Harvey's statement that many of the students were reading Castiglione's *The Courtier*, which like Elyot's *Governor*, was a treatise expounding the court humanist position. (*The Courtier* was first published in English translation in 1561.) But there was another contrasting tradition which, for want of a better term, we may call 'country humanism'. For insight into this tradition we must turn to the writings of Lawrence Hum-

---

[1] Henry Peacham's *The Complete Gentleman*, first published in 1622, carried the Elyot tradition into the seventeenth century. For a convenient edition, see V. B. Heltzel (ed.), *The Complete Gentleman* (Ithaca, 1962).

phrey, a university teacher who occupied a position at the heart of the academic world, but was not and never became a courtier. Humphrey was President of Magdalen from 1560 to 1589 and Vice-chancellor of the university of Oxford on several occasions. He was influential and well connected, numbering the Earl of Bedford among his friends. Humphrey was a product of the Edwardian Reformation. He received his academic training at Oxford during the reign of Edward VI, and went into exile under Mary, first to Strasburg and then to Basle and Geneva. He was a correspondent of Peter Martyr and John Sturm. He knew the Strasburg of Sturm at first-hand, he knew John Foxe the martyrologist and may even have helped in writing the *Book of Martyrs*. When he returned to England in 1559, he was disappointed with the ungodly turn of events, but he finally agreed to serve the Church as a university don, not as a bishop.

Humphrey's treatise on education, *The Nobles* (1563), is at the opposite pole from Elyot's *The Governor*.[1] Where Elyot turns to the classics for his models with only an occasional mention of Biblical heroes, Humphrey places the Bible first and the classics decidedly second. Humphrey devotes one of the three books in his treatise to explaining that the true model for a gentleman was Christ. He thought the gentleman should be 'good, godly, wise and learned'—the order is illuminating—if he wished to be respected, because it is hard for 'a free and learned man to obey an ignorant slave of sin'. This adoption of Christ as the model brought the Christian virtues as Humphrey saw them into a central position:

> Christ ought be the crest, the fame and type of nobility, without whom nothing is noble in this inferior circle below the moon.

Fear of the Lord was essential, but this was a Jewish virtue, not a Greek or Roman one. The scriptures took precedence over the classics.

> The sound and onlye proof of good religion is the conference and examining of divine scriptures.

Humphrey also denied any division between sacred and secular worlds:

[1] L. Humphrey, *The Nobles* (1563), passim.

Wickedly therefore who termed some spiritual, some laymen, some temporal, some secular.

In fact, Humphrey took as his model not the Italian courtier but the Marian exile who, in the storm of Mary's reign, took refuge in the Church and Christian congregation then dispersed abroad. The Marian martyrs themselves were also to be thought of as a model to follow 'in this our England', 'marching towards the skie':

> But we (say they) are no priests, teachers, nor pastors. So great perfection is not required of nobility. But sith they be Christians, they ought not to shrink to die for Christ.

Humphrey emphasizes virtues which are at the other end of the scale from that of the Renaissance Court. He puts humility high on his list:

> Philip of Macedon had one of his servants remind him every morning thou art a man. Would our nobles in like manner charge herewith some one of their servants.

He makes much of temperance, modesty and continence, expounding at length on these virtues, where Elyot is content with a brief mention. He praises thrift:

> We must imitate and express the thrift of the ancients.

In apparel, all superfluity should be shunned. Nobles should imi-

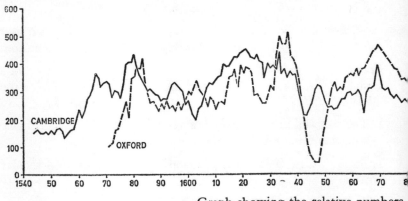

Graph showing the relative numbers

tate those kings who for the baseness of their apparel were hardly discerned from the common sort.

The difference between the two men comes out clearly in their attitude to dancing. Elyot saw dancing as in some way analogous to the virtue of prudence and devoted many pages of his work to an exposition of this idea.[1] Humphrey, on the other hand, merely tolerated dancing 'for the health and exercise of body' so long as 'lascivious and wanton gesture' was avoided. In this contrast, we may see the difference between the court and the country tradition.

Humphrey's values recall at many points the ideal type of Puritan sketched by Weber in *The Protestant Ethic*. Humphrey saw no reason why the true noble should not engage in husbandry or any other lawful activity. He calls in Jewish example to support this argument, as well as the more obvious classical models, like Cincinnatus. Of husbandry he said:

> I thinke but know and have red antiquity thought nought more liberal, nought worthier a nobleman.

What he reacted violently against was the life of the court and the courtier who

> licentiously roams the street in ryot, coasting the streets with wavering plumes, hanged to a longside blade and pounced in silks . . . haunting plays, feats, baths and banquetings.

[1] Elyot, *Governor*, pp. 69–88.

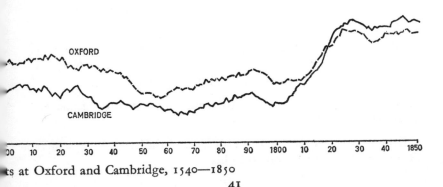

ts at Oxford and Cambridge, 1540—1850

To Humphrey, idleness of this kind was anathema:

> For we are all charged to labour. . . . In the sweat of thy brow
> thou shalt eat thy bread.

History teaches us that there was no idle nobility among the Jews
or in Plato and Aristotle, and even the natural universe preaches
the same lesson:

> Yet leapeth the Sonne forth as a Giant to runne his course.
> The moon taketh charge of the night and serveth men, planets,
> living creatures. The stars rise and set. To conclude, every
> creature labours and travails.

Humphrey and Elyot also differed in the choice of books which
they recommended for study. They overlapped to some small
extent in pressing the importance of the classical historians, Livy,
Caesar, and the historical books of the Bible, but in general they
took a very different line. Humphrey included far more sacred
history than Elyot. He mentioned Josephus in particular, and the
chronicles of that other chosen race, the English—'our England
marching to the sky'; and though he excluded Homer, Horace,
Lucian, Ovid and Virgil's *Aeneid*, all of which Elyot praised, in
compensation he brought in the writings of Seneca and the works
of John Calvin. He included Terence for the simple reason that
Cicero thought highly of him. Of course, censorship was necessary:

> If any filth be intermingled let the trusty diligence of the teacher
> remedy it.

Elyot on the other hand was much more tolerant in his attitude
to literature. He criticized the

> false opinion that now reigneth of them that suppose that in
> the works of poets is contained nothing but bawdy (such is
> their foul word of reproach) and unprofitable learning.

He defended Ovid, Catullus, Martial and others against the charge
of being

> lascivious poets that wrote epistles and ditties of love which
> contained but incitation to lechery.

He concluded

> although I do not approve the lesson of the wanton poets to be taught unto all children, yet when maturity comes none ancient poet would be excluded from the lesson of such one as desireth to come to the perfection of wisdom.

The contrast between the two also comes out in their attitude to Virgil. Humphrey objected to Homer and Virgil on the grounds that they presented too eloquently the values of the traditional aristocratic culture, which he was attempting to criticize. He would accept the *Georgics* with its implicit approval of duties and work of country life, but he rejected the *Aeneid*. (Perhaps the differences between court and country parties may be summed up in this distinction.) Elyot, on the other hand, praised the *Aeneid*:

> If the child have delight in hunting, what pleasure shall he take in the hunting of Dido and Aeneas, which is described in his book of *Aeneid*. . . . If he take solace in hearing minstrels, what minstrel may be compared to Jopas which sang before Dido and Aeneas?

Here are two contrasting ideals of what a humanist education should be, the one drawing its inspiration from the values of the Italian courts, the other from the city states of Strasburg, Geneva, Basle and Zurich. One was lay, the other clerical. One looked to the court, the other to the country. One stressed the values of display, magnificence and sexual prowess, the other the virtues of restraint and godliness. In the first we see the reflection of the Renaissance and in the second the influence of the Reformation. And it was the second outlook which seems to have been dominant in the universities during the first three decades of the reign of Elizabeth.

Humphrey, in contrast to Elyot, was an active and influential university don, probably the most important single person at Oxford during his lifetime. As President of Magdalen, he exercised a great deal of power within his own college. It was to Humphrey that Protestant gentlemen like Francis Knollys entrusted their sons.[1] Thomas Bodley, son of a Marian exile, was educated at Geneva and Magdalen. John Field, the Puritan leader

[1] J. E. Neale, *The Elizabethan House of Commons* (London, 1949), p. 304.

of the 1570s and 1580s, was another protegé of Humphrey's. Humphrey's influence was also responsible for the placing of Swiss Protestant students in Broadgates Hall.

If we look further for the influence of Humphrey and Puritans like him, in university studies, we find it in an Oxford diary for the 1570s.[1] The diary was kept by two young Cornishmen, the Carnsew brothers, who came up to Broadgates Hall in the early 1570s. They came from an area of the south-west in which the influence of the Earl of Bedford was strong, and Bedford was a friend of Humphrey. (Onè of the brothers was later to sit for a Bedford pocket borough.) Like good Puritans they kept a record of their studies, perhaps a unique document for the period, in the details of which we may see the day-to-day working of the curriculum.

During the hard grind of their years at Oxford, the two boys found themselves translating Foxe's sermons into Latin. Their guided course of reading was unrelieved by any poetry or flights of fancy. They read a good deal of history—Sallust, Caesar or Jewish history. They translated parts of the New Testament, including the Lord's Prayer, or read elevating tracts. They noted when the routine of their life was enlivened by the sermons of Doctor Humphrey, or those of another Oxford Puritan, Richard Kingsmill. The nearest they got to the profane literature of the classical world was Cicero's *De Officiis*. Some of their studies were not obviously religious in tone, for example, the study of the cube and the quadrant; but in the main there is little doubt that they moved and studied in a stringently Protestant religious atmosphere. They read the notorious Puritan pamphlet, the *Admonition* of Cartwright and Wilcox, and they noted that the Principal of Broadgates Hall went up to Parliament in 1572, the assembly dominated by Puritan issues.

How typical was this form of Protestant education? The amount of evidence is scanty, but what there is tends to confirm it. A notebook for Christ Church dated 1576 shows us a student taking notes from Beza and Calvin, attacking Ramists and non-Ramists alike, and showing no interest in classical literature.[2] In

[1] P.R.O. SP.46/15. I am indebted to Dr. N. J. Williams of the Public Record Office for drawing my attention to this document, which has also been used to some effect by Dr. A. L. Rowse, *Tudor Cornwall* (London, 1941), pp. 430-1.
[2] B. M. Harleian 4048.

1581, another student, also from Christ Church, combined notes of his reading in grammar and astronomy (the treatise of the medieval commentator John of Hollywood) with a record of sermons preached by Puritan ministers at Balliol and Lincoln.[1] It was also at this time that Humphrey himself launched violent attacks against Popery at Oxford.[2] The picture is rounded off by the fact that the Puritan colleges, Exeter, Brasenose, Magdalen, Queen's, Christ Church, were those which increased in numbers most remarkably during the Elizabethan period.

Historians have often noted the existence of Puritanism at Oxford, but they have confined its significance to the purely religious spheres. They have dealt with Puritan divines but not with Puritan gentlemen. The Carnsew diary throws light upon the education of the Puritan gentleman, a social ideal which was to exercise a revolutionary influence on the course of English history during the next half century. The universities acted as seminaries for the education of godly laymen as well as godly divines.

The significance of the two intellectual traditions within the universities surely provides us with some clue towards explaining the divisions within the English ruling *élite* during the late sixteenth and early seventeenth centuries. Hitherto these have been explained on largely economic grounds. Perhaps we should pay as much attention to the intellectual formation of the gentry as to rent rolls, and in this way throw some light on the difficult problem of the intellectual origins of the English Revolution.

[1] Bodleian MSS. Rawlinson D.273.
[2] F. Madan, *Oxford Books* (Oxford, 1895), vol. I, p. 26.

CHAPTER III

The Ramist Challenge

I.

In the 1570s a new academic influence made its appearance in England, the attempted revolution in logic known as Ramism—from the name of its most prolific writer, Pierre de la Ramée (1515-72). The keynote of Ramism was its practical, anti-metaphysical emphasis, in which it was poles apart from the traditional curriculum of the universities. In some ways, it was a form of humanism, but a humanism with a difference. Humphrey's Puritan humanism appealed to the godly gentry. Ramism appealed to the godly merchant.[1]

There was, perhaps, a split at the heart of the Puritan movement between town and country, between the merchant and the gentleman. The social values which were associated with trade and urbanization contrasted with those associated with the country house and the social hierarchy of the country, a contrast perhaps most obvious in the field of education. It was difficult to see what a merchant's son could hope to gain from an arts course at Oxford and Cambridge unless he were aiming at a career in the Church. The attraction of Ramism lay here. It provided a practically-orientated alternative to the education which gentlemen received at the universities.

In this chapter I will suggest that demands for drastic reform of the university curriculum were not purely academic gestures but were part of a movement which aimed at radical social and

[1] The most substantial treatment of Ramism is by Walter J. Ong, S.J., *Ramus: Method and the Decay of Dialogue* (Harvard, 1958), though in my opinion, it exaggerates the importance of Ramism by placing it in an interpretation of history, popularized by Marshall McLuhan, in which Ramism is seen as a key to the Renaissance trend away from oral to visual culture. Another approach may be found in R. Hooykaas, *Humanisme, science et reforme: Pierre de la Ramée (1515-72)* (Leyden, 1958) and C. Hill, *Intellectual Origins of the English Revolution* (Oxford, 1965), where Ramism is seen as a precursor of modern science. There is much on Ramism in Perry Miller, *The New England Mind: the Seventeenth Century* (New York, 1939).

religious change. On this interpretation, Ramism appears as the intellectual aspect of the urban wing of Puritanism, which came into conflict with the country wing. There was a social division within the Puritan movement, which Ramism helped to make more explicit. If this were not the case, it would be difficult to explain the attention which Ramism aroused. No purely academic movement could have aroused so great a measure of satirical attention or emotional hostility. When Ramism began to infiltrate into the universities, it was regarded by conservatives as an immensely dangerous development. Yet to twentieth-century eyes there can be scarcely anything duller than a Ramist textbook.

2.

The influence of Ramism was first felt in the English academic scene in the 1570s. Ramus, the author and inspiration of textbooks in logic, rhetoric and other subjects in the school and university curriculum, at this date represented the intellectual attractions of France and the French Huguenots for the second generation of English Puritans. Ramus produced between fifty and one hundred books or pamphlets during his lifetime; in the century after his death there were about three hundred editions of his logic and one hundred and fifty editions of his rhetoric. He was an educational revolution in himself.[1] In Lawrence Humphrey's period of exile, the Puritans turned to Geneva, Basle or Strasburg. But by the later decades of the century, French Calvinism had emerged as the great hope for the future. Ramus was something more than a former professor of the Sorbonne; he was a Protestant martyr who had been killed in the bloodshed of St. Bartholomew's day.

The most obvious characteristic of Ramism was an attitude to the classics which emphasized content as much as style, matter as much as form, logic as much as rhetoric. It was to be found, for example, in the English Ramist, Gabriel Harvey, fellow of Pembroke Hall, Cambridge, and university praelector in rhetoric. In his inaugural lecture, Harvey told how he once had been completely under the spell of a false approach to Cicero, in which the

[1] Ong, *Ramus and Talon Inventory* (Cambridge, Mass., 1958).

student was urged to follow Cicero's style to the letter—'one formed one's style according to Cicero in the same way that one formed one's soul according to the Evangelist'. After reading Ramus, however, he came to realize that content was equally if not more important:

> From Cicero's pleasant Gardens I began to pluck the fruits of reason as well as the flowers of oratory.

And he went on to urge his listeners to follow his example:

> Do you wish to be honoured with the glorious and magnificent appellation of Ciceronianus? . . . Consider not merely the flowering verdure of style but much rather the ripe fruitage of reason and thought.

As commentators, he praised Ramus, Erasmus and Freigius (another Ramist) above Sturm and Ascham.

Harvey's enthusiasm is revealing, but he does not go into detail about the method which Ramists applied to Cicero and other classical authors in order to separate real content from flowers of style. Ramus claimed to be able to paraphrase an author whose thought moved on rational lines, by laying it out in the form of a table, or perhaps more appositely a family tree, in which the logical development of the thought could be understood visually. Conclusions which appeared unrelated at one end of the table could be traced to their origins at the other. Indeed, one of the special features of the Ramist method was its emphasis on a dialectic of opposites.

Ramism had certain attractions as an educational method. It brought clarity to complex problems by its ruthless simplification, or as its defenders would say, by its cutting away the verbiage of centuries. It was anti-Ciceronian in the sense that it emphasized logic at the expense of rhetoric. It was anti-Aristotelian in the sense that it found only a small proportion of the philosopher's works of any value. Thus it appealed to those who thought Ciceronian eloquence overvalued by such educators as John Sturm, or to those who considered that far too much of Aristotle had survived the Reformation. Inevitably, it antagonized the Ciceronians and the Aristotelians. It was not surprising that so eloquent an English Ciceronian as Richard Hooker should make a sharp passing reference to Ramism in his *Laws of Ecclesiastical Polity*.[1]

But Ramism was something more than a novel approach in educational method. It was, or claimed to be, part of an intellectual revolution, and much of the significance of Ramism lies in this fact. Ramus launched a thorough onslaught on almost every aspect of Aristotelian thought. He took as much of Aristotle's *Organon* as was necessary for his purpose, which amounted in practice to the *Topics*. He rejected the *Categories* which, though theoretically part of Aristotle's logic, contained a strong metaphysical strain. Ramus also rejected the *Physics* on the grounds of its metaphysical content and gave his approval only to works like the *Historia Animalium* in which Aristotle had confined himself to observing and classifying. He saved his worst strictures for the *Metaphysics* themselves:

> Wherefore students of true theology, its lovers, patrons and defenders, stand by with open minds and know well the greatest and most noble of controversies. I declare the fourteen books of [Aristotle's] metaphysics to be a mountain of fourteen logical tautologies . . . I declare indeed its theology (such as they call it) to be a most detestable and hateful mass of impiety upon impiety and I denounce the inexpiable crimes in certain Christian scholastics . . . to whom the metaphysics of Aristotle is a veritable pillar of the Christian religion. Indeed their physics text-books teach the physics of Aristotle stuffed with an impious theology of infinity and eternity. Their metaphysics text-books will go on teaching impieties deriving from the physics and full of other foul things. I hope shortly in the future that Christians will be ashamed of such foul theology and will repent and in their change of heart, not only repudiate that pagan theology, scarcely worthy of satyrs and fauns, but will embrace the Gospel purer and more holy after cleansing from such miserable filth.[2]

[1] R. Hooker, *Laws of Ecclesiastical Polity*, Book I, chap. 6: 4. 'Of marvellous quick dispatch it is and doth show them that have it as much almost in three days, as if it dwell threescore years with them.'

[2] 'P. Rami Scholarum Metaphysicarum . . . Praefatio', in *Scholae in liberales artes* (Basle, 1578), p. 933.

Where Saint Thomas baptized Aristotle, and the Jesuits canonized him, Ramus exorcized him.

The Ramist attack upon Aristotle's metaphysics and physics also carried with it important theological implications. The post-Lutheran reformers rejected Aristotelian terms of 'substance' and 'accident' to describe the Eucharist, but they still retained an Aristotelian outlook upon the universe and this undoubtedly influenced their modes of thought. Joseph Hall, later Bishop of Norwich, used Aristotelian concepts to discuss spiritual matters:

> There is no vacuity in nature, no more is there in spirituality.

> I see that in natural motions, the nearer anything comes to an end, the swifter it moveth. . . . A Christian's motion after he is regenerate is made natural to Godward and therefore the nearer he comes to heaven the more zealous he is.

> I see nothing stande still but the earth; all other things are in motion.[1]

An attack upon the Aristotelian world system undermined the traditional language of theology. Ramists turned from the world of nature to God's word as revealed in the Bible. Perkins advised his students to 'proceed to the reading of the Scriptures in this order, using a grammatical, rhetorical and logical analysis'.[2] And the anonymous author of a university play in 1598 made the same point by implication in poking fun at a Ramist character whom he named 'Stupido'.

> I have (I praise god prosper my labours) analised a peece of an homelie according to Ramus and surelie in my minde and simple opinion Mr Peter maketh all things verie plaine and easie.[3]

Stupido, a true Ramist, advised his hearers against studying the 'vaine artes' of Rhetoric, Poetrie and Philosophy:

---

[1] P. Hall (ed.), *The Works of Joseph Hall*, 10 vols. (London, 1808), vol. VI, pp. 4, 5, 107.

[2] For example of Perkins's tabular analyses, see W. Perkins, *Works* (Cambridge, 1603), pp. 1, 77, 79, 104, 131.

[3] J. B. Leishman (ed.), *The Three Parnassus Plays 1598–1601* (London, 1949), pp. 112, 115.

You shall not see a rhetorician, a rimer, a poet (as you call it) but he wears such diabolical ruffs and wicked great breeches full of sin . . . Mr Wigginton and Mr Penorie never wore such prophane hose but such plaine apparell as I doe.

The mention of John Penry and the well-known Puritan divine Giles Wigginton (fl. 1569–92) in this passage links up the Puritans with Ramism.[1]

In their Biblical emphasis, English and Scottish Ramists introduced a note not found explicitly in Ramus himself.[2] The Ramist logic textbooks of MacKilmaine published in 1574 and of Fenner published in 1584 replaced examples from the classics with short extracts from the Bible, and this turning to the Scriptures continued to be characteristic of Ramism during the century or so of its existence. This is another example, if one were needed, that the educational world did not become markedly more secularized in the course of the sixteenth century.

Ramist biblicism may be seen in the general tone of William Perkins's writings. Perkins (1558–1602), Fellow of Christ's, and one of the most influential Puritan divines of this period, relied exclusively upon the Bible in his writing.[3] Except in the logical form which his argument takes, there is no hint of Aristotle or the Great Chain of Being. His discussion of the angels takes place in a cosmological vacuum. He never mentions the schoolmen, and in dealing with the Early Fathers he is very critical, especially of Dionysius, the source of traditional views on the angels. Perkins replaces the notion of a natural hierarchy with the idea of 'the Calling', or rather two callings, the general and the particular. Every Christian must follow his general calling of godliness, a precept which implied a fundamental equality among the elect. In addition every man 'must join the practice of his personal calling with the practice of the general calling'. 'They profane their lives and callings that employ them to get honours, pleasures, profits, worldly commodities, etc.'.[4]

The anti-hierarchical aspect of English Ramism is clearly ex-

---

[1] John Penry was executed in May, 1593. *D.N.B.*
[2] W. S. Howell, *Logic and Rhetoric in England 1500–1700* (Princeton, 1956), p. 187.
[3] Perkins, *Works*, p. 911; on Perkins, see H. C. Porter, *Reformation and Reaction in Tudor Cambridge* (Cambridge, 1954), chap. 12.
[4] Ibid., pp. 913–15.

pressed in this discussion of 'callings'. The doctrine of the calling undermined the concept of hereditary social status by demanding that every man should not *inherit* position but *choose* a calling. In the Ramist commonwealth, there was to be no room for a leisured class, whether of monks or aristocrats. Perkins condemned the practice of employing servants. The three estates of his society were not King, Lords and Commons but Church, Commonwealth and Family, and the highest calling by his standard was the academic:

> If gifts will serve [he wrote] a choice must be made of the calling of a prophet or teacher; and that above all other, Academical callings must have the first place.

In current terminology, Perkins stressed achievement above inherited status.

Along with the revolutionary intellectual and theological implications of Ramism went overtones of social and political radicalism.[1] The English Ramists of the 1570s and onwards belonged to a younger generation of dissent. We may think of them as spelling out, in a more extreme way, the critical attitudes of Humphrey. They were in a sense the left-wing of the country party and their social radicalism was implied in part in their social origins. Cartwright and Travers were of common birth and this seems to have been true of Ramists in general. But their social radicalism also emerged in the assumption that logic was not a highly abstruse secret for an intellectual *élite*, but a simple tool which could be placed at the disposal of the artisan. Ramist emphasis on the practical utility of knowledge as against the contemplative trends of Aristotelians smacked of social radicalism during a period when the gentleman was held up as the social ideal.

Michael Walzer has recently drawn attention to the revolutionary strain among the Puritan intellectuals. But he has, in my opinion, tended to lump together two different generations. There was little of the alienated intellectual about men like John Jewell, Bishop of Salisbury. For the really radical criticisms of Elizabethan society we must turn to the hard-core of English Ramists

---

[1] M. Walzer, *Revolution of the Saints* (Princeton, 1965).

Cartwright, Perkins, Alvey and Penry who found an intellectual basis for their criticisms of the social assumptions of their time. It was this type of Puritan who rejected the optimistic approach of Aristotle's *Politics*, as they did so much of Aristotle. They also rejected Aristotle's *Ethics* which more than one historian has described as the textbook of the English gentleman, enshrining the values of the court.[1] Ramism provided an intellectual cutting-edge which made this rejection much easier.

Ramism was thus something more than an educational movement concerned with reforming the curriculum and teaching methods. Its sponsors, its implications, its general background had radical overtones, and the appearance of Ramism in the curriculum or in a student's notes is tantamount to finding revolutionary doctrines being taught in a religious seminary. Walzer found 'it hard to discover anything in the subject matter of an academic education in the seventeenth century which would have turned a careless young man into an ardent Puritan'. But, as we have seen, Magdalen under Humphrey was quite capable of doing so. And what was true at Oxford under the Puritan elder statesmen was equally if not more true of Ramists at Cambridge.

3.

There was another factor involved. From the mid-1570s the Ramist programme was being put into practice in Scotland under the aegis of Andrew Melville.[2] Melville had come under the influence of Ramus in France during the 1560s and on his return to Scotland in 1573, he was soon in a position to undertake university reform on Ramist lines. At Glasgow, Aberdeen and St. Andrews in turn, he was responsible for drastic changes. But Melville was something more than a new academic broom. Socially, he presented an attack upon the position of the Scottish aristocracy in the name of a truly godly ministry and of the burghers.

[1] C. B. Watson, *Shakespeare and the Renaissance Concept of Honor* (Princeton, 1960). See also Keith Thomas, 'The social origins of Hobbes's political thought' in K. C. Brown (ed.), *Hobbes Studies* (Oxford, 1965).

[2] The standard, pro-Melville biography is by T. McCrie (Edinburgh, 1856). On Buchanan, see H. Trevor-Roper, 'George Buchanan and the ancient Scottish constitution', *E.H.R.* Supplement 3 (London, 1966).

Scotland was an aristocracy in which the power of a few great lords counted for much, and the power of the King for little.[1] Essentially, this was the basis on which the Reformation under John Knox made so much headway in a short time. Knox relied upon the backing of one group against another—broadly speaking, the south and west against the north and east. The Catholic cause found itself allied with the Huntleys and their allies of the North-East and the Gaelic chieftains further to the West. The Protestants found a leader in the Earl of Argyll.

Melville's coming offered a further challenge to the accepted assumptions of this society. He stood for the establishment and extension of a presbyterian system, which at every point challenged the principles of a military aristocracy. The ministers of his Church would be chosen not by the local nobility but by a group of ministers (the presbytery) liable to inspection from the synod and the general assembly. His main support lay in the towns. Melville stood for central government by the urban godly against the local control of the rural aristocracy.

The urban character of Melville's movement needs to be emphasized. He was able to use the university of Glasgow precisely because it was established in a commercial centre of growing importance. He extended his urban bases with a new town college, Marischal College at Aberdeen. This last foundation was particularly significant since King's College, Aberdeen, already existed. The contrast between old and new could scarcely be more marked. St. Andrews was the only college not in a major town. Melville was also able to bring this under control, but we may note that it was from St. Andrews that the counter attack against him got under way.

James Melville, his nephew, describes the nobility as the chief enemy of the new movement in a brief commentary which he drew up in 1584, while exiled in England.[2] He criticized the gentleman tenants for not supporting the colleges of theology and he accused the nobility themselves of being unlearned and of having no interest in educating their children. Many noblemen, he pointed out gave their friends and servants control of estates which rightfully belonged to the Church.

[1] D. Mathew, *Scotland under Charles I* (London, 1955), p. 25, and passim.
[2] *The Diary of Mr. James Melville 1556–1601* (Edinburgh, 1844), p. 130.

To criticize these arrangements was tantamount to rejecting the basis on which Scottish society had been organized since the Middle Ages, if not before. It was a challenge issued by a group of urban intellectuals to a society which accepted the code of a military aristocracy as the highest value. In Scotland the clash between the two was as sharp as it was ever to be in Western Europe.

On Melville's principles, the Church was completely independent of secular society. This view in a centralized society such as England implied a clash with the government. In Scotland, however, Melville's chief enemy was the aristocracy and his system of presbyterianism was designed to reduce the power of the aristocracy to a minimum. Government of the Church was in the hands of ministers who preached the word of God, of 'doctors' who taught in schools and universities, and of 'elders' who kept a close watch on the spiritual welfare of their flocks ('discipline'). All this was a complete contrast with the prevailing system. If Melville had his way, there was no scope for aristocratic influence as such. A local gentleman would have no influence in the Church unless he was accepted as a 'godly person', judged by Melvillian standards. The Church governed itself at the top by means of the General Assembly, a representative body of elected ministers, doctors and elders, which was far more representative of the middle ranks of Scottish society than the Scottish Parliament had been, dominated as it was by the nobility.

Melville's system was based upon support in Glasgow, Edinburgh and Aberdeen. It met with most resistance in the rural north-east, where the Gordons defended the traditional system, and where the ecclesiastical hierarchy was so convenient a social counterpart of the established nobility that it could not be allowed to disappear without a fight. To the Gordons and their allies it appeared that Melville was acting as the agent for the *bourgeoisie* and smaller lairds of the south striving to free themselves from the influence of their natural overlords. The most dramatic moment in the struggle was September 1593, when Melville's power was at its highest. The General Assembly at St. Andrews, following Melville's lead, excommunicated the leaders of the nobility, William Douglas, Earl of Angus, George Gordon, Earl of Huntley, and John Home, Lord Home.[1]

[1] Ibid., p. 207.

In all this, Melville regarded the urban universities as occupying a key position. Duly reformed on godly principles, the universities would educate godly ministers, who would act as a leaven in the countryside. Unlike the students who emerged from the seminaries of the Counter-Reformation, Melville's students were trained to challenge the social assumptions of the society in which they found themselves, not to reinforce them.

Melville became Principal of Glasgow in 1574 and within five years had introduced changes along Ramist lines:

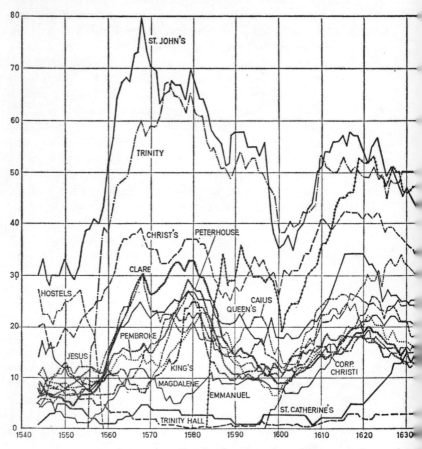

Graph showing the relative numbers of st

Sa falling to wark with a few number of capable heirars, sic as might be instructars of uthers thereafter, he teatched them the Greik grammer, the Dialectic of Ramus, the rhetoric of Taleus, with the practise thereof in Greik and Latin authors. . . . From that he enterit to the Mathematicks and teached the elements of Euclid, the Arithmetic and Geometrie of Ramus. . . .[1]

[1] Ibid., p. 38. See also C. Innes and J. Robertson (eds.), *Monumenta Almae Universitatis Glasguensis* (Glasgow, 1854), vol. II, p. 45.

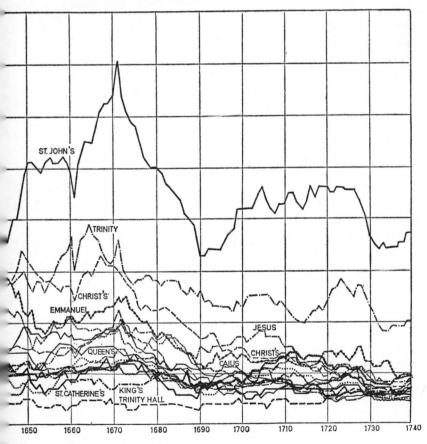

lifferent colleges at Cambridge, 1544—1740

During his six years at Glasgow, Melville also took his students through the Bible. But it was not until he moved to St. Andrews that the full extent of his Ramism brought him into opposition with the established Aristotelians. They saw 'their Aristotle mightily confuted' by Melville in his theology lectures, and according to Melville's nephew, James, they saw their livelihood being destroyed:

> Grait Diana of the Ephesians, thair bread winner, thair honour, thair estimation, all was gean, giff Aristotle should be sa awirharled [overhurled] in the heiring of thair schollars. . . .

Melville met their attempts at reaction with the 'force of truth, evidence of reason and spiritual eloquence'.[1]

Melville also seems to have successfully introduced a curriculum along Ramist lines at the newly-founded town college of Edinburgh, and at the new Marischal college in Aberdeen.[2] James Melville betrayed the Ramist view of philosophy when he described the restoration of true learning at Edinburgh which

> the Bishop haid altered and turned from theologie to philosophie, *ab equis ad asinos*.[3]

At Aberdeen, the high-water mark of Melville's influence in the north-east was the foundation of a town college in Aberdeen, Marischal College, to combat the influence of King's College, which lay just outside the town and had resisted reformation along Melvillian and Ramist lines. By 1595, Ramism was the dominant influence in all but one out of the colleges of Scotland.

But none of this was merely educational history in the narrow sense of the word. To the Presbyterian, Melville, the universities were part of the Church order and university teachers were doctors, a scriptural rank on a par with priests and elders. Thus the universities became a battleground in the running fight which developed in Scotland in the last two decades of the sixteenth century between Church and State, in which the balance went first in favour of Melville and then of James VI. Melville's years

---

[1] Ibid.
[2] A. Grant, *The University of Edinburgh During its First Three Hundred Years* (Edinburgh, 1884), p. 148.
[3] *Melville's Diary*, p. 162.

of exile in 1583–5 marked a depression between two periods of great influence in which Melville talked down to James as to an inferior. In 1587 when James visited St. Andrews, Melville humiliated him by discoursing in his grandest manner about 'the right government of Christ', and in 1597 when Melville's influence was on the decline, he rebuked the King most sharply

threatening him with feirful judgments if he repented nocht.[1]

Melville's Ramist innovations formed part of a general picture of change, with godliness extending into all fields, even logic. For their part Melville's opponents could not view Ramism in a neutral manner. It was associated with a man who called to order king and aristocracy alike.

Melville's fall was gradual. It began with a trial of strength over his position at St. Andrews. James was able to remove him from his rectorship and install a candidate of his own as Vice-chancellor, George Gladstanes.[2] Gladstanes had shown himself as a king's man in the General Assembly and a critic of Melville, and the next ten years was to witness his rise at the expense of Melville. The crucial event was the succession of James to the English Crown. Melville could not match the power and prestige which this brought the Scottish king and he was forced into exile in 1606. The story of Scottish Ramism was over.

4.

It was Melville's success in Scotland which helped to discredit the English Ramists in the eyes of Whitgift and Bancroft, the twin pillars of the later Elizabethan establishment. Cartwright had close links with Melville, indeed he was offered a chair at St. Andrews in 1580, almost as soon as Melville had been appointed Chancellor there.[3] Scotland was not a remote country. It provided an example close at hand as to what might happen if the English radicals ever obtained power. This was a point which Richard Bancroft made a good deal of when he attacked the Puritans in 1593 in his pamphlet *Dangerous Positions*. He denounced the Scottish Reformers for undermining the social hierarchy:

[1] Ibid., p. 274.   [2] *D.N.B.*   [3] *D.N.B.*

They threatened the greatest men of the lande, with God's heavy punishments if they should reject that discipline. . . .

But then he went on to denounce the English Puritans for being more dangerous than the Scots:

Master Penry exhorteth the Lord President of Wales by the example of Moses, David, Solomon, etc, to take in hand their pretended reformation in that country; proving that he hath authority thereunto because he is a governor under God. . . .[1]

Significantly, the suspected author of *Marprelate*, John Penry, possessed a notebook containing logical definitions on Ramist lines, and Nashe referred to him as 'a new fangled friend unto Ramus'.[2]

Officially, Cartwright's career at Cambridge had been terminated after his clash with Whitgift in 1570, which cost him the Lady Margaret chair of theology and, in 1572, his fellowship at Trinity. But as Bancroft noted, his influence remained immense. He was in fact the Calvin of the English Puritan movement. Cartwright's links with Melville were enough to suggest his Ramist sympathies, but the main piece of evidence linking him up with Ramism is to be found in a Cambridge notebook which contains jottings from Cartwright covering in the main the years 1585–8.[3] The notes are of a theological kind but with a peculiarly Ramist flavour, since they consist of logical analyses of the Gospels and Epistles, taken at specific dates during these years. For example, in May, 1585, the author took notes from the logical analysis of the Acts of the Apostles 'ex domino Thoma Cartwright'. They were taken at weekly intervals throughout the year and were probably associated with a theological course. The notebook possibly belonged to Cartwright's associate, Arthur Hildersham, whose name occurs at least three times in it, or to someone who was closely associated with him. This notebook also contains Ramist outlines of dialectic, grammar, rhetoric, physics, medicine and ethics. In each case there was a reference to a particular textbook by Ramist authors, Scribonius, Freigius, Beurhusius, Timothy Bright and

---

[1] R. Bancroft, *Dangerous Positions and Proceedings* (London, 1593).
[2] A. Peel (ed.), *The Notebook of John Penry 1593*, Camden Society, third series, 67 (London, 1944), p. 96.
[3] B.M. Harleian MS 3230.

William Temple. In this one notebook, we are provided with a clear example of the links between theology and arts in Ramism, and of its connection with Cartwright. The names of the text-books also indicate the continental affiliations of the movement. In 1595, complaints were laid against the Cambridge Puritans that 'they suffered a conventicle of Mr. Cartwright and his complices to be gathered in our colledge [St. John's] anno 1589, Mr. Alvey keeping our master's lodging where they then met'. It is not improbable that this note-book provides a record of this and other occasions.[1]

This notebook clinches what might have been suspected, that Ramism was closely associated with the Presbyterian movement at Cambridge and the surrounding area during the 1570s and 1580s. The list of Cambridge Ramists reads like a list of the most radical Cambridge Puritans, Cartwright, Hildersham, Fenner, Alvey, Perkins, Ames, Downham, Richardson, Travers, Penry, Temple and Gouge.[2] It was a movement which was spread over several colleges, with Christ's, St. John's and King's as the most important. Emmanuel, newly founded by Sir Walter Mildmay, took its tone from Christ's, which provided its first Master and most of its early fellows. The most noticeable gap was at Trinity, where Whitgift was Master from 1567–77. Whitgift expelled Cartwright from his fellowship at Trinity in 1572 and turned the face of the college resolutely against Ramism. Whitgift's accounts for his pupils show that he did not ask them to buy Ramist text-books. The anti-Ramist tradition of Trinity college continued after Whitgift became Archbishop of Canterbury and it may well be from his years there that Francis Bacon derived his critical attitude towards Ramism.[3]

The connection of Ramism with radical Puritanism was both its strength and its weakness. It made headway in Cambridge more quickly than any mere intellectual vogue would have done. It cut across college allegiances to form a movement of university dimensions. It had the cachet of a European background. William Temple, for example, was a Ramist with a continental reputation.

[1] J. Heywood and T. Cartwright, *Cambridge University Transactions* (London, 1854), pp. 75–8.
[2] For most of these see Howell, *Logic and Rhetoric*, pp. 173–246.
[3] See below p. 99

Above all, it had roots in the urban Puritanism of John Field. On the other hand, Ramism shared in the discredit which the radicals experienced during the 1590s especially after the publication of the Marprelate Tracts (1588).

The battle of court and urban 'ideologies' was fought out in the interminable bickering of college politics. In 1600, then as now, the dominant colleges in Cambridge were Trinity and St. John's, and whichever party dominated them was in a position to control the university. In 1593, the tide decisively turned against the Ramists with the royal decision to appoint Thomas Neville as Master of Trinity.[1] Neville once had been a Fellow of Pembroke, where he clashed with the Ramist sympathizer Gabriel Harvey, and his anti-Puritan views commended him strongly to Bancroft. Neville was in a position in 1595 to influence the crucial election at St. John's, when Whitaker, its veteran Puritan head, died. The issue lay between the Ramist Henry Alvey, friend of Cartwright, and Neville's candidate, Lawrence Stanton. At first Stanton had the Queen's backing, and then when she changed her mind another anti-Puritan was elected, Richard Clayton, Neville's successor as Master of Magdalen.

Academic politics do not always revolve around points of intellectual principle, but there can be no doubt that this was a decisive election. From now on, Ramism at Cambridge was to be very much on the defensive. Under Neville's mastership, the tone of teaching at Trinity had an Aristotelian flavour. Robert Booth, for example, who took his M.A. there in 1610, dedicated to Neville his *Synopsis Totius Philosophiae*, a work which took its bearings from Aristotle, Aquinas and Zabarella and shows no signs at all of Ramist influence. At St. John's, the Ramist cause suffered a setback when Alvey left for Trinity College, Dublin, in 1600, presumably because the atmosphere was no longer congenial at Cambridge. At Christ's, hitherto a centre of Ramist teaching, events took a similar course. William Perkins died in 1602. George Downham left Christ's for Ireland in 1593. Ames found the atmosphere of Christ's intolerable and left for Holland in 1610. The appointment of Valentine Cary as Master in 1609 was a crucial turning-point in the history of Christ's. A former fellow of St. John's, he acted as the hammer of Ramism. It is small

[1] On Neville, see *D.N.B.*

wonder that Milton should not have been given a fellowship at Christ's during its post-Perkins era.[1]

At King's, Roger Goad enjoyed a long period as Provost, from 1570, when he was appointed by Grindal, until 1610. Under this man, sympathetic to Puritan views, the Ramist tradition of Temple survived. A notebook dated *c.* 1612 provides evidence of systematic study of Ramist textbooks, Beurhusius, for example, and Ramus's dialectic.[2] The student took notes from Piscator and Temple, and made particular use of a Ramist textbook by Pierre Grégoire, *Syntaxeum Artis Mirabilis*, published originally in 1580, and again in 1610. The Puritanism of King's derived in part from its close connection with Eton, whose Provosts during Elizabeth's reign had had religious views well to the left of their sovereign.

From the last decade of the sixteenth century, the main stronghold of Ramism was Emmanuel College. Its first Master, Lawrence Chaderton, who did not retire until 1622, presided over a period of calm, at a time when other colleges were being forced to change. Chaderton himself lectured on Ramus and influenced men such as Abraham Fraunce and Ames. Unfortunately, no Emmanuel notebooks for this early period have survived,

5.

A word now about Oxford. Here Ramism did not take root to anything like the extent it did at Cambridge. The likeliest explanation for this seems to lie on the fact that Oxford adopted a distinctive form of country Puritanism from the mid-century onwards. For thirty years from 1560 the figure of Lawrence Humphrey dominated Oxford life and with him the social ideal of the godly gentleman. For all their early radicalism, men of his generation were highly critical of the extremism, as they saw it, of younger men like Cartwright. The new-model Puritans seemed to be going too far and too fast. Humphrey was willing to work for godly reformation within the existing framework of the Church of England but the likelihood is that he threw his weight against any manifestation of unrest at Oxford.

In the Oxford student notebooks which are dateable to this

[1] *D.N.B.*   [2] Bodleian MSS Rawlinson D. 318 (6).

period, Ramism is mentioned several times but always disparagingly. In 1581, for example, John Rogers of Christ Church copied out an attack made by a fellow of the college upon Ramists and Romanists alike, one for loving Aristotelianism too little, the other for loving it too much.[1] At Oriel, teaching was also conducted on non-Ramist lines and included a reasonably heavy dose of metaphysics.[2] In 1582, John Case of St. John's wrote an attack upon Ramus which he dedicated to the Earl of Leicester, from which we may infer that Leicester, the university Chancellor, was hostile to the new movement.[3] At Corpus, the fact that Brian Twyne was put to reading Aristotle's *Physics* in the original Greek as well as in Latin with the support of a non-Ramist commentary, is sufficient indication that even in Rainolds's own college, Ramism did not carry all before it.[4] Twyne's only reference to Ramus is a brief paragraph with the heading 'why Ramus criticised Aristotle'. In 1606, the year before Rainolds died, Daniel Fayreclough, Fellow of Corpus, attacked Ramus in his oration in praise of Aristotle.[5] Perhaps most interesting of all are the letters of Robert Batt of Brasenose and University College. Writing in 1583 to his cousin at Cambridge, Batt made playful reference to the publication of Sir William Temple's Ramist treatise. Batt expressed the hope that it would soon be refuted by some Oxford champion, possibly Sir Henry Savile of Merton or William Fulbecke of Corpus.[6] At St. John's in 1601, there is no mention of Ramus in a student notebook which may have belonged to Richard Baylie or John English. (English was a year later than Baylie in matriculating and may have been glad of the loan of the latter's notes.)[7] The neo-scholastic commentators Javellus and Toletus are both mentioned and there are notes also from an analysis of Aristotle's *Physics*. On the evidence of a fair range of college material around 1600 we may conclude that Ramism had little direct influence at Oxford.

[1] Bodleian MSS Rawlinson D.273 f. 242.
[2] Bodleian MSS Rawlinson D.274.
[3] Howell, *Logic and Rhetoric*, p. 190.
[4] *Bodleian Library Quarterly*, vol. V, pp. 213–18, 240–6, 269–72. A notebook of Twyne's is in Jesus College, MS XXX.
[5] Bodleian MSS, Rawlinson D.47.
[6] Bodleian MSS Rawlinson D.985 f. 46.
[7] Bodleian MSS Rawlinson D.1423. On English, see W. C. Costin, 'The inventory of John English [1586–1613]' in *Oxoniensia*, 1946–7.

6.

This is an appropriate point to discuss the significance of a Ramist educational institution established in London during the 1590s— Gresham College. Sir Thomas Gresham, who may be described as Elizabeth's economic minister, died in 1579, leaving money by will to establish a college in London.[1] His own religious views are a matter for speculation. What seems certain is that by the time his wife died and the Gresham money became available for the college, decision-making about its future lay in Puritan hands. This is indicated by the appointment in 1595 of at least two Puritans among the first professors, Anthony Wotton and Henry Briggs.

Anthony Wotton was a scholar at Eton and then after graduating at King's, he became a fellow of the college. He took his M.A. in 1587 and his B.D. in 1594. He became Gresham Professor of theology in 1596 but his appointment lasted only two years. He then became a lecturer, namely a Puritan preacher, at All Hallows' Barking until his death in 1626. Wotton translated the *Logic* of Ramus. This suggests that his original appointment to Gresham was part of a Ramist pattern.

Henry Briggs came from a similar Puritan background. He entered St. John's, Cambridge, during the mastership of the Puritan, William Whitaker, and took his M.A. in 1585. Like Wotton, Briggs was interested in Ramism but in his case this led him towards practical mathematics. He was appointed Gresham Professor of Geometry in 1596 and remained so until 1621 when he moved to Oxford.

Two Ramists did not make a Grand Design but they formed part of an educational pattern at Gresham in which the curriculum was organized on more practical lines than those of the ancient universities. Lectures in Latin were given in the mornings, those in the vernacular in the afternoons. There were close links with the world of commerce and with the royal dockyards. Briggs was involved in practical surveying. The inference behind all this is that Ramism was a dominating influence behind the foundation of Gresham College.

But the history of the College, like that of Ramism itself, did

[1] W. K. Jordan, *Charities of London*, pp. 254-5.

not follow an unchequered course. The universities were hostile, or, to put it in more historical terms, anti-Ramists within the universities were powerful enough to exert influence upon the fortunes of Gresham. First signs of this came with the dismissal of Wotton in 1598. The close connection with the universities, maintained and kept up throughout the first four decades of the seventeenth century, ensured that safe appointments were made.

The tone of the college in the 1630s may be illustrated from the career of Richard Holdsworth, Gresham Professor of Theology from 1629. Holdsworth was a product of St. John's, Cambridge, during the post-Puritan phase of its history. The fact that he was appointed to Gresham College and later, to Emmanuel College, during Laud's period of control in the Church, suggests that he was no Puritan. This is borne out by his theological lectures at Gresham, by his behaviour in 1640 and by his correspondence. Holdsworth, in short, was no Ramist, and Gresham College itself seems to have lost most of its Ramist flavour after the departure of Briggs in 1621.

An adequate modern history of Gresham College has still to be written, though there is much to be gleaned from the work of F. R. Johnson and Christopher Hill.[1] From our point of view, the interest of Gresham lies in the substantial hints which its early history offers, of a link between Ramism and urban Puritan groups.

Another urban college, successfully established on Ramist lines, lay across the Irish Sea. Trinity College, Dublin, founded in 1591 by courtesy of Queen Elizabeth and Archbishop Adam Loftus (1533–1605), resembled Glasgow or Edinburgh far more than it did Oxford or Cambridge. The land for the college was donated by the Corporation of Dublin, and its students at this time were drawn from the Anglo-Irish, urban, commercial families, if we may take as typical the Usshers, who provided the college with its first, and perhaps greatest, scholar. There was as yet no ascendancy of Anglo-Irish gentry, whom the college was to attract later in the century. The gentry in 1600 were still by and large Catholic and this was to remain the case until after the

---

[1] F. R. Johnson, 'Gresham College, Precursor of the Royal Society' in *Journal of the History of Ideas*, vol. I; C. Hill, *Intellectual Origins of the English Revolution* (Oxford, 1965). The standard work is still John Ward, *Lives of the Professors of Gresham College* (London, 1740).

Cromwellian confiscations in the 1650s. Thus it is tempting to regard Trinity College as the equivalent of Gresham College, or the Scottish town colleges of the Melville era, an institution of higher education established in a metropolis.[1] Its role as a town college is also hinted at by the presence of two Scottish scholars, Fullerton and Hamilton, among the early fellows. Its second Provost was Walter Travers (1595–8), Master of the London Temple, who had been invited by Melville in 1591 to occupy a chair at St. Andrews. It may well be in fact that the fortunes of Gresham, Trinity and Melville's colleges were directly linked as part of a Ramist pattern. We may also note that Trinity was founded in the face of a great deal of opposition from the Lord Deputy Perrot, who seems to have had a gentry-orientated, more secular and less Puritan foundation in mind.[2]

During the first thirty years of its existence (1591–1620) Trinity College was a Ramist foundation. Its first three provosts included Henry Alvey and William Temple, both of them Cambridge Ramists who left, like Henry Briggs, during the decades of anti-Puritan pressure. Thomas Cartwright himself had been in Ireland in the 1560's and had been an associate of Adam Loftus, who had recommended him for the See of Armagh, and Adam Loftus was a prime mover in the foundation of Trinity College. Another Cambridge man closely associated with Trinity College in its early days was Luke Challenor. Trinity was in some ways the Irish Harvard, with the Roman Catholics taking the place of the Indians as the enemy without the walls.

In Dublin, the Ramists were presented with a unique opportunity of setting up a university curriculum *de novo*. The teaching statutes themselves do not survive but we are fortunate enough to have the student notebooks of several students including James Ussher, later Archbishop of Armagh.[3] Ussher's notebooks show an arts curriculum, almost completely dominated by Ramism. In one of them, he drew up, either for himself or a pupil, a time-

[1] J. P. Mahaffy, *An Epoch in Irish History* (London, 1903); T.C.D. MSS D.3.12; D.3–20; D.3.16; D.1.9.

[2] On this admittedly obscure episode, see R. Bagwell, *Ireland under the Tudors* (London, 1885–90), vol. III, pp. 131–5; *Cal. S. P. Ire, 1574–85* (London, 1867), pp. 519–564; ibid., *1588–92* (London, 1885), p. 437.

[3] I am very grateful to W. O'Sullivan, Keeper of Manuscripts, Trinity College, Dublin, for great help in connection with the Ussher MSS.

table for a course of reading over the academic year, in which specific references are given each month to Ramus's lectures on grammar, rhetoric and dialectic. Aristotle's *Topics* and *Ethics* were to be read in the light of these. Ussher listed Ramist authors and took notes on them, and when he had become a teacher, in his turn, he lent Ramus's books to his pupils. Along with this went a good deal of Puritan reading. He took notes on Travers's *Book of Discipline* and he lent to others writings by Cartwright, Perkins and Fulke. The authors listed in the Cambridge document of the 1580s, such as Beurhusius and Freigius, are also to be found in Ussher's lists, time and again.

If we take Ussher as an example of a mind trained on Ramist principles, we must first make the point that he himself was no revolutionary. He accepted first a bishopric and then an archbishopric, and if he was a Puritan, he was well to the 'right'. Nevertheless, even Ussher in his sermons made no use whatsoever of the notion of natural hierarchy. Continually, even when preaching before the King, he emphasized the contrast between the godly and the ungodly. This was, for him, the real division in the world:

> Civility be a good stock whereon the science of grace may be grafted, but if a man had nothing besides what nature and education can teach, what moral philosophy can store us with, we have nothing to do at this table of the Lord.

In 1627 when Ussher preached before Charles I, he explained the basis of peace in a Christian society in terms not of the Chain of Being, but of grace:

> God doth make men the children of peace by infusing certain heavenly graces into them whereby they are disposed to a heavenly temper . . . the neglect of this spiritual salt makes unquietness. . . .

It was in this sermon that Ussher criticized the use of nicknames such as 'puritan':

> We know who are esteemed by Christ and were it not a vile thing to term him a puritan?[1]

[1] C. R. Elrington (ed.), *Ussher's Works* (Dublin, 1847–64), vol. XIII, pp. 202, 339.

The Trinity arts course seems to have been drawn up almost exclusively with the Bible in mind. The liberal arts were to be the instrument of interpreting God's word. One notebook, that of John Travers, shows that Aristotle's *Topics* were studied both in Greek and Latin, with Ramus as a guide. Travers also read Euripides, in Greek and Latin.[1] But there is little trace in any of these notebooks of literary or philosophical interests. Trinity had a lecturership in mathematics, but the chief object of this appointment seems to have been to teach Biblical chronology. In history, Ussher read Raleigh's *History of the World* and a textbook of Roman history. He also took some notes on arithmetic and Virgil's *Georgics*, again with Ramus as a guide.[2]

Thus the arts curriculum was not an independent entity. Teaching in the humanities was left to the junior fellows and the decisive say depended upon the senior fellows, who, without exception, were divines. The fourth Provost, William Bedell, complained to his Cambridge friend, Samuel Ward, that 'we lack the faculties of Physics and Law wholly'.[3] What divinity there was, was of a Puritan character. It was too much so even for George Abbot, Archbishop of Canterbury, but no high churchman, who described it as 'flat puritanical'.[4] Joshua Hoyle, Professor of Divinity from 1623, was Puritan enough to be acceptable as master of an Oxford college during the Cromwellian régime. His method of teaching was to lecture upon a verse of the Bible each day, which he did for over fifteen years. He regarded the Jesuits as 'these croaking Egyptian frogs',[5] an attitude which Ussher conveyed more diplomatically when he advised his students to 'read no Jesuits at all, for they are nothing but ostentation and never understood the scriptures'.[6] In the attitude of Hoyle and Ussher, we may infer a distrust of the philosophical approach in religion, which the Jesuits represented *par excellence*.

In Ireland, more so than in England, the contrast was acute between the values of the urban elect and those of the gentry. The *élite* in Ireland in 1600 was still Catholic and by definition, in

[1] T.C.D. MSS D.2.10.   [2] T.C.D. MSS D.3.12.
[3] C. McNeill (ed.), *Tanner Letters* (Dublin, 1943), p. 77.
[4] Ussher to Chaloner, 9 April, 1613, *Ussher's Works*, vol. XV, p. 72.
[5] Joshua Hoyle, *A Rejoynder to Master Malone's Reply concerning Reall Presence* (Dublin, 1641), preface.
[6] Queen's College, Oxford MSS 217.

Ramist eyes, ungodly. In Ireland, a Ramist needed to feel no qualms about doubting the values of a natural hierarchy. Indeed, one argument for the presence of the Puritans in Ireland was the fact that they constituted an elect confronting the forces of anti-Christ. Here perhaps more than elsewhere, the Puritans were committed to the cause of social revolution,[1] in overthrowing the power of the Catholic gentry. Trinity College was to be the instrument of Ramism, righteousness and urbanization.

[1] C. Hill, *Intellectual origins of the English Revolution*, chap. 1.

CHAPTER IV

The Radicalism of the Sectaries

So far I have confined my attention to the educational activities of the English ruling *élite*. In doing so, I have perhaps over-emphasized the function of the universities as instruments of social mobility. It is now time to redress the balance and point out that such social mobility as there was took place at the top of the social scale and affected only a small proportion of the population. The net result of two generations of university education in England was to accentuate the differences between the gentry and the rest.

To those excluded from the universities, these institutions appeared to be civil seminaries, dedicated to producing worldly-wise clergymen, who claimed to monopolize the teaching of Christian truth. In the eyes of this critical minority, drawn from lower urban social groups, the universities fostered a false principle of hierarchy within the Church. The Bible had set all men free. The university men with their false learning were busy fixing the shackles in place once more. The renewal of scholasticism within the universities seemed to confirm the point.

The most violent attack on the ecclesiastical hierarchy came with the publication of the Marprelate Tracts in 1588-9. But though the author launched a violent attack on the bishops, he left the universities alone,[1] and there is no hint in the tracts that the author was opposed to the kind of education which was being given there. The implication is that given a change in Church government from bishop to presbyter, the Church of England would be well on the road to reformation. The author, whether he was John Penry or not, was no sectary but a man sympathetic to the ideas of Thomas Cartwright.

Well to the left of Marprelate, so far as the universities were

[1] The authorship of the Marprelate Tracts is still a matter for debate. Cf. P. Collinson, *The Elizabethan Puritan Movement* (London, 1967), p. 391.

71

concerned, were the 'Sectaries', led by Henry Barrow, Robert Harrison, Robert Browne and John Greenwood. All of them were Cambridge graduates, three from the same college, Corpus Christi. In due course, Barrow and Greenwood were executed, Harrison emigrated to Holland with his congregation, and Browne eventually conformed, first as a schoolmaster, then as a rector. All four of them had come to accept the belief that the true Church is the individual congregation. They rejected episcopacy and presbytery alike, on the grounds that ordination divided the minister from his congregation. They thought godliness more important than learning.

In contrast to the Marprelate Tracts, the pamphlets of Barrow, Harrison, Browne and Greenwood were violently critical of the content of university education. Henry Barrow thought that universities

> can by no meanes be made to accorde to the gospel and kingdome of Christ, whereof these university divines have ever bene professed and most bitter enemies.[1]

Like Thomas Becon earlier, he criticized the schools which taught 'the Latin tongue from the most heathenish and prophane authors, lascivious poets, etc.' He went on to criticize the way in which the universities relied upon Aristotle for logic, rhetoric and philosophy:

> Out of his ethickes, economickes and politickes they fetch the order and government of their maners private estate and commonwealth. He yet further instructed them of the soule and of the worlde in lardge and speciale bookes of the heavens, of natural and supernatural things of Nature, Fortune, the eternitie of the world and perpetuitie of all creatures in their kind in specie. . . .[2]

He criticized the way in which university divines used logic and rhetoric to expound the scriptures:

> As to rhetoric and logic they are so necessary, as without which to understand or divide one part of the scripture aright; as

[1] L. H. Carlson (ed.), *The Writings of Henry Barrow 1590–91* (London, 1966), p. 212.
[2] Ibid., p. 214.

without which they cannot understand or declare to the people by what trope or figure, by what form of argument or syllogism the Holy Ghost speaketh.[1]

Barrow saw no justification in the scriptures for the Oxford and Cambridge colleges, where ministers lived after a 'monastical manner' and 'where God's holie ordinance of honest marriage is by express law forbidden'. He was prepared to abolish the two universities and set up facilities

where the tongues and other godly artes were taught not in universities or in a few places only but in all places where an established church is *at the least in everie citie of the land*. . . . Then that the arts and sciences which are thus taught and studied be not vayne, curious or unlawful but necessarie and godlie.[2]

If these reforms were carried out Barrow thought that 'the seminaries of anti-Christ' would disappear to be replaced by 'scholes of all godlie learning to furnish the commonwealth with fit and virtuous men for every pale office and estate'.

Robert Browne went even further and attacked Ramism itself, with its obsession about logic:

Could Ezra give the meaning of the Scriptures, as in Nehem 8 or could the people understand his meaning without your syllogismes, without predictables and Predicaments and your arguments of invention. . . .[3]

It becomes clear that Ramism is the target when he writes:

Logike is reason or reasoning, nowe it is defined as the art of reasoning . . . so also ye must have one art of one virtue and another of an other and for seven liberal arts we shall have seven hundred.[4]

He told his reader to

look further into the method of logike and you shall find it so patched as is the cloak of a beggar and so filled with good order as is a tubb of kitchen sink draff.

[1] Ibid., p. 217.   [2] Ibid., p. 223.
[3] A. Peel and L. H. Carlson (eds.), *The Writings of Robert Harrison and Robert Browne* (London, 1953), p. 171.
[4] Ibid., pp. 197, 192.

He saw no need of logic in handling the scriptures,

> for except we seeke smoke to give us light instead of the sunn we must judge that so great a light as the scriptures give hath no need of such rush light.

The educational ideal of the 'sectaries' was centred more exclusively on the Bible than even the Ramists. Barrow believed that the Bible was the source of all knowledge:

> In Aristotle there learn they the causes of the rainbowe, the makings of the windes, cloudes and of the whole sky far otherwise than is set down in Genesis.[1]

For Browne, Paul, Job and Solomon were examples enough. Paul condemned all vain philosophy. 'Job disputed with his friends but did he urge them with syllogisms?'. Solomon had true knowledge without the need of logic and rhetoric:

> The countries marvelled at him (saith Ecclesiastes) not for his Logic and Rhetoricke but for his Songs, Proverbs, Similitudes and Interpretations.[2]

Browne refused to consider any appeal to the witness of the Early Fathers:

> How many foolish toys, prophane fables and vile errours be in Augustin, Ambrose, Chrysostom and others and what monstrous heresies and philosophical delusions are forged and maintained by others.[3]

Here was the classic statement of anti-intellectualism, which was to be re-formulated in the middle decades of the seventeenth century. It was a case argued with wit, eloquence, and logic, much more than their opponents were able to command. But for all their violence against secular learning, the sectaries denied the label of 'anabaptist' which the bishops were trying to attach round their neck. Barrow denounced anabaptistical errors. Greenwood in his reply to the bishop's spokesman, Gifford, repeatedly denied the charge of being an anabaptist.[4]

[1] Carlson, *Barrow*, p. 214.   [2] Peel and Carlson, op. cit.   [3] Ibid., p. 189.
[4] L. H. Carlson (ed.), *The Writings of John Greenwood 1587-90* (London, 1962), pp. 47, 79, 91.

Nevertheless, there were social implications behind these religious criticisms of the universities. To the orthodox the implications were clear enough. Barrow wanted to do away with the centralized system of Oxford and Cambridge in order that 'every Christian man' might be able to bring up his children in some such place 'where a Christian congregation is'. Browne objected to the insistence upon a university-trained ministry because 'by that aim the people which have not learned logicke are shut out and discouraged from talking, pleading and mutual edifying in the church meeting'. All this points to the fact that the so-called sectaries were speaking for the educationally deprived sections of the population. The demand for local colleges was to be heard again in the Puritan revolution, some fifty years later. It was an appeal for educational facilities close at hand, easily available, and free from the centralized and social control to which Oxford and Cambridge were exposed. The 'sectaries' saw independence in education as a necessary concomitant of independence in religion. The 'gathered church' of the locality would have a 'gathered college' at its side. The demand for local colleges was the opposite position from that of the government's, namely that a centralized system of education was a necessary part of the foundations of the state, in which the Elizabethan position was no different from that of Catholic, Lutheran and Calvinist states on the continent.

The attack of the 'sectaries' on the universities brought out the crucial point that the interpretation of the Bible was at stake. In the wrong hands, wrong that is from the episcopal point of view, the Bible could be a revolutionary document. Conservative obsession with the threat of the anabaptists shows that the lessons session with the threat of the anabaptists shows that the lessons of Münster were still thought relevant.[1] It was essential to set a fence round the Bible, not merely from the religious and political viewpoint, but from the social viewpoint as well. Catholic countries solved the problem by denying the laity access to the Bible. Protestant countries could no longer take this way out even if they wished to. It was all the more important, therefore, to ensure that explication of the sacred text was in authorized hands. It was here that the significance of the universities lay, and in attacking the universities and the university curriculum, the 'sec-

[1] *H.M.C. (Salisbury)* vol. I, p. 253.

taries' were not making merely academic points. Logic, rhetoric and the rest were seen as part of an establishment pattern, a barrier against religious and social change.

The universities' insistence upon Latin and the Latin classics, at a time when the Bible was available in English, seemed to many a sinister piece of popery. But it was also part of a social situation in which Latin, the language of the law courts and of medicine as well as the universities, was the language of the ruling *élite*. The religious radical even if he did not realize it himself was protesting against a social organization in which all the dice were loaded against him. Hence anti-intellectualism was a form in which bitter social discontent was expressed. The sect itself was the basis of a new status system, in which godliness and not gentlemanly style of life was the criterion.[1]

[1] For interesting parallels in modern America, see L. Pope, *Millhands and Preachers* (Newhaven, 1942).

CHAPTER V

The Revival of Scholasticism

Scholasticism in the first generation of the sixteenth century, humanism in the second, Ramism in the third; such had been the pattern. A further twist was given to intellectual change in the last decade of the century, with a revival of scholasticism. The names of the medieval schoolmen began to reappear in academic circles, and along with them the neo-scholastics, including Suarez and Bellarmine. If we seek an explanation for this revival, we may find it in part in the turn of the wheel of intellectual fashion. A taste for scholastic modes of thought and turns of phrase is to be found in John Donne, a poet of the 1590s, as part of a reaction against what seemed to be the excessive sweetness and lack of intellectual content of the lyrical poetry of the day. From this point of view, scholasticism was the philosophy of the young men, the reaction of the younger generation against their fathers.[1]

From another point of view, the revival of scholasticism at Oxford and Cambridge was part of a wider European movement. A reaction against Ramism had already taken place on the continent in some of the Dutch universities, in the German Lutheran universities and in some Calvinist academies, not least in Geneva itself. In these circles, there was a general willingness to return to a fuller version of Aristotelianism than Ramus was willing to allow. The role and scope of reason was expanded to take in metaphysics and truths which were not explicitly outlined or mentioned in the Bible. Hooker's outlook was certainly sympathetic towards this development though he himself cast his arguments in a non-technical, non-scholastic mode.

But the most familiar names in the movement were European. Scheibler, professor at the Calvinist university of Giessen (1589–

---

[1] There were, of course, several scholasticisms as there were several humanisms. More research is needed on seventeenth-century scholasticism before the main currents become clear.

1653) and known as 'the Protestant Suarez', was the most famous Protestant metaphysician of the day, but he merely headed a list which included Timplerus and Combachius.[1] In the 1650s Thomas Barlow, an influential Oxford don, wrote a guide to students advising them to read John Combachius—

> his Metaphysicks (which is an obscure but a rational Epitome) and after him Scheibler (who is more full and perspicuous) and lastly Suarez (who is incomparably the fullest and acutest author that ever writt of that subject). . . .[2]

Barlow himself made Scheibler available to Oxford M.A. students and the Oxford Press edition of Combachius was dedicated to John Prideaux, Rector of Exeter College (1612–41) and Regius Professor of Divinity (1615–41).

We have spoken of 'court humanism' and perhaps we should also speak of 'court philosophy' represented in this case by the new scholasticism. In Counter-Reformation countries the scholastic revival was associated with the spread of Jesuit colleges and universities. And everywhere the Jesuits made themselves the allies of the court. Jesuit scholastic treatises from the university of Coimbra were particularly popular. Perhaps in this case, logic gained an added lustre in the Protestant world by reflecting the political power of the Hapsburgs. Scholasticism made headway in those states in which the court was strongest politically and socially—the Lutheran states of Germany and those Calvinist states which were nearest to the Lutheran position. In Holland the most Aristotelian of the universities was Utrecht, the most traditional of the northern provinces and nearest in its social structure to the aristocratic provinces of the southern Netherlands. Even Leyden moved nearer to scholasticism during the professorship of Franz Burgersdijk from 1620 to 1635.[3]

In England, also, it is tempting to see the revival of scholasti-

---

[1] On Scheibler and protestant scholasticism, see M. Wundt, *Die deutsche Schulmetaphysik des 17. Jarhunderts* (Tübingen, 1939); W. T. Costello, S.J., *The Scholastic Curriculum in Early Seventeenth-century Cambridge* (Cambridge, 1958); P. Dibon, *La philosophie neerlandaise au siècle d'or* (Amsterdam, 1954).

[2] A. de Jordy and H. F. Fletcher (eds.), *A Guide for Younger Schollers* (Illinois, 1961): cf. critical review by Eric Jacobsen in *Journal of English and Germanic Philology*, vol. LXIII (July, 1964), pp. 506–16.

[3] See Dibon, op. cit., pp. 90–2, for details of Burgersdijk's life (1590–1635) and career.

cism as part of a general trend towards authority and the court. The 1590s were a decade of repression and reaction. They saw the execution of Penry, Barrow and Greenwood for holding Protestant opinion, which were thought to be seditious. The 'classical movements' within the Church of England was broken up and its leaders scattered. John Whitgift had become the Torquemada of the Church in Cecil's eyes and Elizabeth seemed content with the role of Isabella. A new emphasis on the role of political authority appeared. In this difficult decade when anarchy seemed very near, the attractions of absolutism grew. In many of his plays, Shakespeare took as his theme the dangers of rebellion. Perhaps we should look to these years for origins of Stuart absolutism.

Against this background, intellectual trends within the universities cannot be treated in isolation from the general religious, political and social pressures of the day. Whitgift's elevation to the see of Canterbury in 1583 meant that a former Master of Trinity and Vice-chancellor was now in the Privy Council. The government was well placed to take a closer interest in university affairs. Increasingly, in the state papers, we find government action within the universities, including nomination to fellowships and pressure upon elections for heads of houses. The election at St. John's, Cambridge, in 1596, when a Crown nominee replaced a prominent Puritan, was one of the most spectacular of these.[1] But it was possible for the Crown to change the character of a college over the years by regularly nominating fellows of a suitable persuasion.

It is illuminating to watch the regular way in which Elizabeth, or her ministers speaking in her name, bespoke fellowships in Oxford and Cambridge colleges for her nominees. Between January and May, 1597, the Queen intervened four times at least in recommending individuals to particular colleges for fellowships.[2] The impression given by the state papers is that this form of influence became very obvious from the 1590s onwards, when Crown pressure was being exerted on the Puritans in every direction. The fellows of New College protested in 1596 against government attempts to create Henry Cotton Warden of Winchester, a key appointment in the running of New College.[3] Another prac-

[1] Curtis, *Oxford and Cambridge in Transition*, p. 219.
[2] *Cal. S.P. Dom. 1593–97* (London, 1867), pp. 109, 111, 351, 415, 496, 504, 558.
[3] Ibid., pp. 226, 230.

tice which seemed common during these years was the provision of a certificate for students to show that they were 'well affected in religion', as well as 'diligent in study'.[1]

The conservatives in the 1590s used a 'smear technique' in dealing with their opponents by accusing them of advocating anabaptist doctrines.[2] What this meant was not very clear, but it could imply the charge that government itself was being rejected, by those who believed that the Gospel freed believers from any other than the divine law. It might also imply rejection of private property on much the same grounds. Anabaptists were also thought to believe that the true believer could not sin. The conservatives, like Whitgift, Bancroft, or their followers, argued that their opponents, by favouring anabaptists, threatened all the established institutions of society. In this way divergences from episcopal orthodoxy were made out to be doctrines implying social disturbance.

How real such a threat was is a matter for conjecture. The Puritans had no notion of following the anabaptists and destroying hierarchy altogether. They attacked the notion of a natural hierarchy only in order to establish a godly order in society, to 'live as it were in a seminary'. As Perkins put it with some force:

> Let no man thinke I here give the least allowance to Anabaptistical fancies and revelations; which are nothing but either dreams of their own or illusions of the Devil; for they condemne both humane learning and the study of the Scripture and trust wholly to the revelations of the Spirit.

He bitterly attacked 'the anabaptistical fancy' of bringing in anarchy, by taking away Christian magistrates and distinction between master and servant. In its social and political attitudes in fact, Ramism was less radical than its exponents claimed, or its critics feared. Like many English movements, it concerned itself with changing the *élite*, while using language which might seem revolutionary on a wider social basis.

---

[1] Ibid., p. 335.
[2] Richard Cosin thought that the Presbyterians held views on civil authority which resembled those of 'the Anabaptists of the Citie of Munster'. Oliver Ormerod in his *Picture of a Puritane* (1605) specifically referred to John of Leyden. Quoted C. H. George, 'Puritanism in History and Historiography', in *Past and Present*, vol. XLI (Dec., 1968), p. 79.

One of the great bogies was the notion that the Puritans were democrats. James I, in warning his son against the Puritans, described how

> some fierie spirited men in the ministerie gote suc a guyding of the people at that time of confusion as finding the guste of government sweete, they begouth to fantasie to themselves a democratick form of government. . . .[1]

Hutton, Archbishop of York, wrote to Whitgift in 1603 that 'Presbytery is more popular, Bishops more aristocratical'. To Hooker who is very much the precursor of the movement towards scholasticism, it seemed obvious that the Puritans' great dependence on the Bible would lead them to some form of anabaptism.

> When they and their Bibles were alone together what strange fantastical opinion soever at any time entered their heads, their use was to think that the Spirit taught them.[2]

And with this belief went revolution in both Church and state:

> The pretended end of their civil reformation was that Christ might have dominion over all. For this cause they laboured with all their might in overthrowing the seats of magistracy . . . in abolishing the execution of justice . . . in bringing in community of goods.[3]

Hooker and those of the same mind exaggerated the danger for the simple reason that they looked upon Puritans as anabaptists in disguise, in much the same way as the Puritans a generation later saw a Papist behind every Laudian. The scholastic revival was thus the reaction of conservatives who needed solid defences against attacks based on the word of God. This obsession with natural law, which we see in the neo-scholastics, may be explained as a method of supplying a God-given world of rational truth, in which property, government and learning had a right to exist independent of Biblical warrant.

It was in its emphasis on religious and social authority that

---

[1] J. Craigie (ed.), *Basilicon Doron* (Edinburgh, 1944), p. 75.
[2] R. Hooker, *Laws of Ecclesiastical Polity* (Oxford, 1850), preface, VIII, 7.
[3] Ibid., VIII, 8.

the great power of scholasticism lay. Superficially these great—to us, unreadable—tomes are amongst the most monstrous intellectual productions ever perpetrated by academics. What they stood for, however, was the defence of the *status quo*. They sketched the world as a rationally ordered cosmos in which law prevailed and in which monarchy and the social hierarchy were part of the rational order of things. It was a synthesis without loose ends, based upon Aristotle's concept of nature, metaphysics, ethics and politics. The scholastics brought this philosophy into conjunction with Christian doctrine. To the conservative mind, faced with the real or imagined threat of anabaptism, the scholastic synthesis possessed an overwhelming imaginative appeal.

In 1589, John Day, son of the printer of Foxe's *Book of Martyrs*, was an M.A. student at Oriel.[1] In his notebook he wrote down topics for over a hundred disputations on Aristotle's physics, metaphysics and ethics. It is obvious from the notebook that Day took his philosophical studies seriously; they were not literary exercises of a rhetorical character, as is often supposed. But the most interesting fact about the notebook is that Day paid a great deal of attention to scholastic and neo-scholastic commentators, such as Javellus and Fonseca. Scholasticism may have been banned from Oxford under Thomas Cromwell and Edward VI, but it had certainly returned during the closing years of Elizabeth's reign.

Like other revivals, the scholastic revival left its monuments behind, in this case on the bookshelves of college libraries at Oxford and Cambridge. The fellows of Magdalen College, Oxford, bought rows of scholastic folios in the 1590s, a few years after Lawrence Humphrey's death.[2] The buying continued up to the Civil War with 1637 as a vintage year, when a whole array of scholastics were acquired, thanks to the generous gift of £60 by a former fellow. In 1628, a fellow presented the college with a copy of Suarez's *Disputationes Metaphysicae*. At New College, Warden Pinke left a number of scholastic works to the college when he died in 1647, including the works of John Major, Gregory of

[1] Bodleian MSS Rawlinson D.274.
[2] Magdalen College MS. I am grateful to Dr. Neil Ker for drawing my attention to this manuscript.

Rimini and Suarez.[1] At St. John's, where Sir William Paddy left money for the library, some of the bequest was spent in 1633 upon books which included a high proportion of scholastic theology, but some sixteen years later when the rest of the money was spent, most of it went on Protestant theology and some on the works of Descartes, Gassendi, Mersenne, Digby and Torricelli. Clearly by 1649 the atmosphere was beginning to change.[2]

The revival of scholasticism may be dated from the 1590s and its progress traced within several colleges. It was most clearly marked at Oxford at Queen's, then the largest college. In 1619, Richard Crackanthorp, Fellow of Queen's and a well-known theologian, published his *Introduction to Metaphysics*, which, we may assume, was based upon his notes as a tutor written some years before. Crackanthorp, who had been a Fellow of Queen's since 1598, died in 1624.[3] The tradition of metaphysics at Queen's was carried on by Thomas Barlow who edited Scheibler's *Metaphysics* for the university press in 1637.[4] The scholastic tradition may also be traced in the notebooks of several Queen's students between 1613 and 1625. The influence of scholasticism within the college also helps to explain an undergraduate's remark about his contemporaries at Queen's in 1628, that 'some think it more piety to read Tully, Seneca or Aristotle upon the Sabbath then the bold and vaine speculations of scholemen'.[5] Certainly Crackanthorp's and Barlow's views did not seem to coincide with those of their Provost, Christopher Potter, who recommended 'Bishop Bilson for the soundest judgment, Rainolds for the greatest learning, Morton for the quickest apprehension, Field for the best schoolman'.[6] None of these he mentioned were sympathetic to the scholastic tradition.

There were similar examples at some of the other colleges. At Oriel, a group of notebooks indicates that John Day's interest in scholasticism was not an isolated example. John Gandy was a student at Oriel in about 1620, and his notebook shows that scholastic metaphysics formed an important part of his studies.[7]

[1] New College MSS. Library Purchase Book.
[2] St. John's College. The Library Benefactors' Book.
[3] *D.N.B.* [4] Ibid.
[5] F. S. Boas (ed.), *The Diary of Thomas Crosfield* (London, 1935), p. 18.
[6] Ibid., p. 16.
[7] T.C.D. MS D.4.27, 33 Bodleian MSS Rawlinson D.947 (Gandy).

At Exeter, John Prideaux wrote a handbook for disputations in scholastic metaphysics.[1] He was a Fellow of Exeter for many years and the likelihood is that this small volume was based upon his college teaching. At Balliol, a notebook belonging to Francis Boughey indicates that teaching on scholastic lines took place there in the late 1630s.[2]

At Cambridge, the same scholastic revival may be noted. At Trinity College under Neville's mastership, Robert Boothe wrote a synopsis of philosophy on scholastic lines and dedicated it to Neville himself.[3] At Queen's, Lawrence Bretton left notes in which he declared that 'vera et sana philosophia est vera Aristotelica'.[4] Professor Costello has drawn our attention to other examples.[5]

One of the best-known tutors using scholastic textbooks was Joseph Mede, Fellow of Christ's and tutor in the college for thirty years.[6] To judge from his work on the Apocalypse, *Clavis Apocalyptica*, Mede had no sympathy for the scholastics and one might have been tempted to write him down as a Ramist since his early education at Christ's was in the heyday of Perkins, and hence presumably under Ramist auspices. Indeed, his own works show little interest in philosophy. Like Ussher, he was greatly absorbed in matters of chronology and scriptural interpretation, not least the nature of the millennium. A letter in which he praised a book which identified Rome as anti-Christ is revealing in this regard:

> That discourse or Tract of the number of the Beast is the happiest that ever yet came into the world. . . . I read the book at first with as much prejudice against such numerical speculations as might be . . . but by the time I had done, it left me as much possessed with admiration as I came to it with prejudice.[7]

Despite these interests Mede was no Puritan. He wondered why one Puritan writer 'escaped so long' from the hands of High Commission:

> For in every company he came, he took an intolerable liberty

---

[1] *Fasciculus Controversiarum Theologicarum* (described in F. Madan, *Oxford Books*, vol. II, pp. 483–4).
[2] B.M. Harleian MS 1779.   [3] B.M. Harleian MS 5356.
[4] Queen's Cambridge MS. Unclassified.   [5] Costello, op. cit.
[6] On Mede, see E. L. Tuveson, *Millennium and Utopia* (Berkeley, 1949), pp. 76–85.
[7] *The Works of Joseph Mede* (London, 1672), p. 1067.

of invectives and contumelies against the Ecclesiastical State, when no occasion was offered him . . . I dare almost affirm that the alienation which appears in our Church of late from the rest of the Reformed hath grown from such intemperancy and indiscretion as this.[1]

Mede, in fact, was a middle-of-the-road Protestant, who may be grouped with Barlow and Crackanthorp. His general teaching was clearly on non-Ramist lines, in which metaphysics had a place. His favourite metaphysics textbook in the 1620s was that of the anti-Ramist Martinus.[2] The list of recommended books also included Crackanthorp's *Introduction to Metaphysics*, Scheibler's *Compendium* and Timpler's *Metaphysicae Systema*.[3] Clearly Oxford and Cambridge both looked to Protestant Europe for their metaphysics, and to Lutheran Germany in particular.

Another court academic was Richard Holdsworth, Master of Emmanuel from 1637, a prominent university figure who has attracted some attention in recent years.[4] Originally a Fellow of St. John's and tutor to Simond d'Ewes among others, he became Professor of Theology at Gresham College, London, from 1629. He was strongly supported as a candidate for the mastership of his old college in 1634, but Laud put forward a candidate of his own. In 1637, he was appointed Master of Emmanuel, where he remained until he was ejected during the early years of the Civil War and imprisoned in the Tower. He died in 1649.

Holdsworth's court-oriented views were revealed explicitly in a sermon which he preached before Charles I in March, 1642.[5] He told the King 'there is no nation in the world which hath had the condition of religion so pure and prosperous as we for almost three hundred years'. He saw the English as a happy people, although 'amidst the very throng of all these blessings there are some murmurings and complainings in our streets'. He did not see this as surprising, for since the beginning of the world, men

[1] Ibid., p. 1067.
[2] H. F. Fletcher, *The Intellectual Development of John Milton* (Urbana, 1956–), vol. II, p. 184.
[3] On these and other Protestant scholastics, see Wundt, *Die deutsche Schulmetaphysik*, passim.
[4] Curtis, op. cit.; Hill, *Intellectual Origins*, pp. 307–9.
[5] R. Holdsworth, *Sermon*, 27 March, 1642.

complained that the times were bad even when they were at their best. 'Winter and summer are both alike distasteful to impatient men'. Holdsworth's words recall the opening paragraph of Hooker's *Laws of Ecclesiastical Polity*—'He that goeth about to persuade a multitude that they are not so well governed as they ought to be, shall never want favourable hearers'. In his conclusion, Holdsworth stated his opinion that

> the state of religion has never been worse since the first reformation than this present year: in respect first of the greatness of our distractions, which have divided us all from one from another; then of the multitude of sects and sectaries . . . lastly in respect of the many dishonours done to the service of God.

Holdsworth's sermons, given at Gresham between 1630 and 1638, have fortunately survived in sufficient quantity to form a folio volume of over seven hundred pages.[1] They are of great interest because they show Holdsworth returning again and again to the scholastic tradition of natural law. Where Hooker was content with a friendly wave in the direction of Aquinas, Holdsworth goes out of his way to quote the scholastics. Holdsworth's argument was that 'moral law was founded in nature'. He turned to the classical authors to prove that the pagans knew what the natural law was and he quoted from Homer, Euripides, Aeschylus, Theocritus, Plato, Hesiod, Menander and Pythagoras. Holdsworth's intellectual position therefore was an interesting mixture of classical humanism and scholasticism. This is enough to suggest that his sympathies at this date were not Puritan. But he also alluded to the Puritans, in saying that he did not respect the opinion of anyone who went to recent commentators without looking at the Fathers first.

The scholastic revival extended widely in English university circles and it is difficult to find a common denominator for its adherents. But if we look for a feature shared by Richard Crackanthorp and Thomas Barlow at Queen's, John Prideaux at Exeter, Joseph Mede at Christ's and Richard Holdsworth at Emmanuel, it seems to lie in their common acceptance of the pre-Laudian Church of England. They were middle-of-the-road Protestants

[1] Holdsworth, *Praelectiones Theologicae habitae in collegio Greshamensi*, ed. R. Pearson (London, 1661).

poised between the excesses, as it seemed to them, of Puritanism on the one hand, and of Arminianism on the other. Tempting though it may be to link up the coming of scholasticism with the coming to power of William Laud, the simple facts are against it. Scholasticism in England was part of a broadly European Protestant movement. By comparison, Laudianism was a narrowly-based English phenomenon.

We may see the distinguishing characteristic of the Anglo-Protestant scholastics in English universities as social and political. They were not cut off absolutely from Puritan divines like Preston and Sibbes. They were willing to sign the manifesto which the Puritan John Dury produced, urging the reunion of the Protestant Churches.[1] They had no strong belief, if any, in the divine origin of episcopacy. But their political outlook was different from that of more radical colleagues. Scholasticism provided them with a social and political prop as well as a theological crutch.

If we now turn to the affairs of Scotland we find the same alliance between scholasticism and the forces supporting the social hierarchy. Melville's fall from power in 1606 was a victory less for the Crown than for the aristocracy. The pendulum swung once more against the towns and in favour of the great lords, especially those of the North-east. The Archbishop of St. Andrews came back into his own.

Melville's disgrace left the universities open to government influence. Old Ramists like John Johnston, who had been described by James Melville in glowing terms, were winkled out. to be replaced by more acceptable men. George Gladstanes, Archbishop of St. Andrew's, appointed his son-in-law as Professor of Canon Law at St. Andrew's. He wrote to James I that this was

> one ready way to bring out the Presbiterian discipline from the hearts of the young ones and to acquaint even the oldest with the ancient Church Government.[2]

In 1610, at St. Salvator's College, Ramism was being attacked as 'maimed and useless' and in 1612, at St. Leonard's, an equally

[1] Hill, *Intellectual Origins*, p. 308.
[2] D. Laing (ed.), *Original Letters relating to the Ecclesiastical Affairs of Scotland* (Edinburgh, 1851), vol. I, 269.

anti-Ramist note was sounded. Along with this, went the highest praise for Aristotle, whose *Organon* was compared in 1613 to 'Ariadne's thread'.[1]

Edinburgh, as a town college, was able to put up some kind of resistance to the new orthodoxy. There was no bishop in Edinburgh and no obvious way in which the college could be brought to heel. As a result, the teaching at Edinburgh, while no longer Ramist, did not show the full-blooded Aristotelianism which was to be found at St. Andrew's and Aberdeen. It was to the urban refuge of Edinburgh that students came from other colleges, as fugitives, after Melville's downfall. But in 1617, James VI paid the college the dubious honour of thinking it worthy of 'oure name' and hence more open to royal control. Robert Boyd, who had been critical of royal ecclesiastical policy at Perth, was invited to become Principal in 1622. He found it impossible to hold out against royal hostility and soon resigned. The next step in royal pressure upon Edinburgh came with Charles I's decision in 1633 to create the see of Edinburgh which was filled by the Arminian, William Forbes. Under this kind of pressure, the town college found it prudent to conform to the general type of university teaching throughout Scotland, at least until the covenant crisis of 1638.[2]

A similar course of events occurred at Glasgow, where Gabriel Maxwell[3] was appointed Regent in 1605, at the moment of Melville's decline. Maxwell[4] bought neo-scholastics like Zabarella's *Logic*, Fonseca's *Commentary* on Aristotle's *Metaphysics*, and the *Metaphysics* of Timplerus, clearly following the pattern of Aberdeen and the English universities. Unfortunately, no students' notebooks have survived for Glasgow[4] during this period, which makes it impossible to say how far Maxwell's outlook was typical of the regents as a whole. It is unlikely, however, that the Glasgow Regent, Robert Baillie, who flowered into such a stern Presbyterian after 1638, should have conformed to the letter, during his years as Regent from 1626. Even Aristotle was not above sus-

[1] Worcester College, Oxford MS 4. 30 (7).
[2] A. Grant, *The University of Edinburgh during its First Three Hundred Years* (Edinburgh, 1884), pp. 176, 204.
[3] *D.N.B.*
[4] C. Innes and J. Robertson (eds.), *Munimenta Almae Universitatis Glasguensis*, vol. III, pp. 410–11.

picion. The authorities felt that commentaries on Aristotle's *Politics* could be made to serve seditious uses, and seized Robert Blair's lecture notes on Aristotle, after dismissing him from his regentship.[1] This was in 1623, just after an official order had been issued, demanding that all holders of university posts should take the oath of supremacy.[2]

At Aberdeen, the influence of Bishop Patrick Forbes was paramount from his appointment in 1618. He appointed his son Professor of Divinity at King's, a post which he held for twenty years. At Marischal, the town college and former Ramist stronghold, Robert Baron, formerly Regent at St. Andrew's in the post-Melville period, became Professor of Divinity, and destroyed whatever remnants there were of the Ramist tradition in this college. Baron became well known as a metaphysician, and wrote a textbook on scholastic philosophy which was still used at Oxford and Trinity College, Dublin, in the late seventeenth century.[3] His lectures on metaphysics were collected for publication by Gabriel Maxwell.[4] In the lecture notes taken by his students the familiar names of Timplerus, Keckermann and Zabarella all appeared, clear proof of the scholastic flavour of the teaching.[5] In 1635, David Leech, one of the Regents and Sub-principal, referred favourably to Suarez, and in the next year, to the contemporary Jesuit philosopher Arriaga.[6] Aberdeen, the seat of episcopalianism, seems to have been the most Aristotelian of the Scottish universities.

These years marked the victory of the conservative North-east, from which James VI drew a good deal of his support. James Melville had noted that the General Assembly at Perth in 1597, at which the King held the initiative, was attended by an unwonted number of 'the ministers of the Northe'. James VI successfully employed the same gambit some years later at the Perth General Assembly of 1618. The presbyterian system was not destroyed, but the bishops backed by the Crown and a proportion of the aristocracy held the initiative. Episcopalians from the

[1] W. Row (ed.), *The Life of Mr. Robert Blair* (Edinburgh, 1848), p. 45.
[2] Innes and Robertson, *Munimenta*, vol. II, p. 300.
[3] On Baron, cf. *D.N.B.* For references to his textbook, see below p. 164.
[4] Trinity College, Cambridge MS 894.
[5] Edinburgh University Library, MS Small Bequest, Theses (1).
[6] Aberdeen University Library MS Λ² the M 631 (6)

North-east could now be sure of patronage. William Forbes from Aberdeen was appointed Bishop of Edinburgh, a position which aroused hostility on grounds of local patriotism as well as 'odium theologicum'. Alexander Ross, former graduate of Aberdeen, became a chaplain of William Laud.

Few, if any, of these scholastics were distinguished from the presbyterians by wide theological differences. They were all Calvinist in sympathy, with exceptions like William Forbes, Bishop of Edinburgh, who was near to the Laudian position. Robert Baron, one of the six Aberdeen theologians who took the title 'doctor' was certainly Calvinist in his opinions. What seems to have marked their position off was a conservative view of politics and society. Bishop Mathew has pointed out that 'the Jacobean bishops in Scotland were closely connected with the lay peerage. Bishop Patrick Forbes had once held a castle and an estate'.[1] Archbishop Spottiswood bought a lairdship in 1616. If we add to this the ubiquitous influence of the Gordons in the North-east, together with the backing of James VI's government, the social alliance of episcopacy, aristocracy and scholasticism takes on an understandable consistency. Reaction, when it came, developed in the urban centres of Edinburgh and Glasgow.

[1] D. Mathew, *Scotland under Charles I* (London, 1955), p. 85.

CHAPTER VI

Clerical Offensive and Country Reaction

I.

The coming to power of William Laud as Bishop of London, in 1628, as Chancellor of the university of Oxford in 1629 and then as Archbishop of Canterbury in 1633, marked a new departure in the history of the universities.[1] Laud, a former don, certainly had university reform in mind from the beginning, and during his decade of power he made his influence felt in Oxford, Cambridge and Dublin. The larger implications of his policies seem to have brought a change in the social function of the universities, with a renewed emphasis upon them in the role of clerical seminaries. This had political implications, in that it looked ahead to a clergy dependent more on the court than the country.[2] It was a policy aimed at reducing the power over the Church enjoyed by aristocracy and gentry. As a crucial element in his reforms, Laud proposed to free the universities from undesirable influences and place them firmly under the control of the court. He saw both Church and universities enjoying their true freedom under the aegis of divine-right monarchy. Under Laud, the concept of a court academic changed. The support of the court was given to a narrower group, men who looked to a combination of absolute monarchy and Arminian theology for the salvation of England. For these men scholasticism was not enough. The scholastic tradition as represented by Bellarmine and Suarez stood for a concept of limited monarchy which they found unacceptable. The Laudians looked beyond the scholastics, not to the Bible alone, as many Puritans did, but to the more amenable of the early Fathers, who wrote under a Christian emperor.

There was a social dimension to all this, indicated by the fact

---

[1] On Laud generally, see H. R. Trevor-Roper, *Archbishop Laud 1573–1645* (London, 1940).
[2] Laud's social outlook is discussed by H. R. Trevor-Roper in *Religion, Reformation and Social Change* (London, 1967), p. 71.

that the Laudian bishops, almost to a man, were drawn from well outside the ranks of the gentry. Harsnet, Archbishop of York was the son of a baker, Corbet of Oxford was a gardener's son, and Laud himself was the son of a clothier.[1] The Puritan peer Robert Greville, Lord Brooke, was to state the social objections to the episcopate in his *Discourse touching the nature of episcopacy* (1641). He complained that the bishops were drawn from the excrement of the people, 'ex faece plebis':

> Now for such a lowborne man to be exalted high, so high and that not *gradatim*, step by step, but *per saltum*, all at once, as oft it is . . . must needs make as great a chasme in politiques, as such leapes use to do in naturals.

He believed that 'high place causes a swimming in the braine'. 'Those horses which are designed to a lofty ayre and generous manage must be of a noble race'. He objected to intellectuals in politics, since 'long, active, costly and dangerous observations are the onely way to make a wise stateman', [whereas the Laudians]

> spend their time in Criticall, Cabalisticall, Scepticall, Scholasticall learning; which fills the head with empty, aerial notions, but gives no sound food to the reasonable part of man.[2]

Similar complaints were made against the bishops in the Root and Branch petition, presented to the Commons in 1641, namely:

> the encouragement of ministers to despise the temporal magistracy, the nobles and the gentry of the land . . . knowing that they, being the bishops' creatures, shall be supported.'[3]

Thus in the eyes of many gentry, Laud appeared as a dangerous social radical, whose emphasis upon divine right, monarchy and episcopacy was a concealed and sinister form of social mobility of intellectuals at their expense. Clarendon himself took pains to point out in his *History* that Laud's college, St. John's, was the poorest in Oxford.[4]

---

[1] Kenyon, *The Stuart Constitution* (1966), p. 151.
[2] Haller, *Tracts on Liberty in the Puritan Revolution* (New York), 1934), vol. II, pp. 47–53.
[3] Kenyon, op. cit., p. 172.
[4] W. D. Macray, *Clarendon's History* (Oxford, 1888), vol. I, p. 120.

As an ex-don Laud saw the reform of the universities as a matter of the highest importance. He wrote in 1634 about his plans for new statutes at Oxford:

This work I hope God will soe blesse as that it may much improve the honour and good government of that place, a thing very necessary in this life both for Church and Commonwealth; since soe many young gentlemen and others of all ranks and conditions have their breeding for the publike in that seminary.[1]

Laud's 'reformation' of Oxford seems to be directly related to the criticisms made of court views by Oxford dons, including John Prideaux and Daniel Featley. Richard Montague, spokesman for divine right and friend of Laud and John Cosin, felt that his most bitter enemies were to be found among the crypto-Puritans, as he saw them, in Oxford. Montague told Cosin in 1625 that 'at Oxford they are all on fire'. 'Dr. Prideaux if he had him there, would teach him better divinity. In Bocardo, you must imagine'. He referred to that 'hobby horse', Featley. Almost every letter to Cosin shows an obsession with 'whole or half Puritans'. 'Let Puritans run on. . . . Let [Prideaux] pass for a Puritan. . . . For these Oxford braggarts I fear them not.' Montague saw himself as sailing through the gap between Puritanism and Popery, the Scylla and Charybdis of ancient piety. Of the doctrine of Grace he wrote:

I shall not Calvinise it, nor yet Arminianise it, but with the Church of England, Augustin and Prosper go the middle way.[2]

Within a short time of these letters being written to Cosin, the high-church party was in power and the universities were under great pressure.

In 1629, the reform of the Oxford statutes was brought forward as a Laudian measure. Real power lay with the independent colleges, each of which had its own statutes. The university constitution as a whole was republican in character, without any centralized authority, though the Crown could and did intervene

[1] Strickland Gibson (ed.), *Statnta Antiqua Universitatis Oxoniensis* (Oxford, 1931), p. LXIV.

[2] G. Ormsby (ed.), *The Correspondence of John Cosin* (Surtees Society, 1869), vol. I, pp. 23, 50, 125.

on a day-to-day basis. Laud's aim was to reduce this happy and effective anarchy to some sort of order. By 1635, the Laudian version of the university statutes was ready, in theory merely a compilation of existing legislation.[1] But there was one important change. The new statutes placed the government of the university in the hands of the heads of the colleges. The Hebdomadal Council at the head of the university structure which had been hitherto an elected body, was transformed into a committee consisting of the college heads. This was decisive. Laud had succeeded in creating an effective instrument for centralized government within the university. It remained to ensure that when headships of colleges fell vacant, they should be filled up with suitable nominees.

By the time that the Oxford statutes had received the royal assent, in 1636, this process had already gone some way. Brian Duppa, whom Laud was to appoint Bishop of Chichester in 1638, had been appointed to the key position of Dean of Christ Church in 1629. William Juxon, a close associate of Laud's was President of St. John's until 1633, when he made way for another Laudian, Richard Baylie. Gilbert Sheldon, later to be Archbishop of Canterbury under Charles II, was made Warden of All Souls'. Robert Pinke, the amiable and ineffectual Warden of New College, gave no trouble and backed the government of the day without demur. Of the headships of the bigger colleges, by 1638 only Queen's and Exeter remained to fall to Laud.

Laud attempted the same policy at Cambridge, where he was convinced that Puritanism was rampant. From a report which he received in 1635, it appeared that many of the colleges were in a very unsatisfactory condition—by Laudian standards. The colleges which seemed most open to criticism were Trinity, Emmanuel, Caius, Trinity Hall and Benet Hall. Laud's informant accused the fellows of Emmanuel of ignoring the *Book of Common Prayer* in their services, of leaving off their surplices in chapel, and of receiving the sacrament 'sitting upon forms about the communion table'.[2] They were said to pull the loaf one from the other after the minister had begun, and to drink the cup 'as it were to one another, like good fellows, without any application of the

---

[1] Strickland Gibson, op. cit., p. lxviii.
[2] B.M. Harleian MS 7033 (Baker Collection).

said words more than once for all'. At Caius, the fellows were said to receive communion each sitting in his seat. At Benet Hall, it was reported that the fellows sang long psalms of their own choosing, while at Trinity certain tutors with large numbers of pupils held private services of their own in their rooms. Sidney Sussex was linked with Emmanuel as being thoroughly unsatisfactory. The colleges which were found most pleasing were St. John's, Queen's, Peterhouse, Pembroke, and Jesus, while Clare and Magdalene were regarded as tolerable.

This report may well have come from John Cosin, who was appointed Master of Peterhouse in 1635. William Beale, later to die in Spain as a royalist exile, was appointed to Jesus and then in 1634 to St. John's as Master '*per mandatum regis*'. Other Laudians were elected to Queen's and to Pembroke. These colleges were soon to lose their Laudian masters and fellows, when they were ejected after the outbreak of the Civil War.

In Ireland, the pattern which Laud followed at Oxford may be discerned during the deputyship (1633–41) of Thomas Wentworth, later Earl of Strafford.[1] The Puritan tradition at Trinity College had continued during the decade after Provost Temple's death. William Bedell, who succeeded him in 1627, soon resigned after finding it difficult to control the senior fellows, with whom effective power lay. His successor, Robert Ussher, brother of the Primate, was unsatisfactory from the Laudian point of view. The appointment of Strafford's own nominee, William Chappell, former Fellow of Christ's, led to the suppression of opposition in the college in 1634–5. (Strafford actually went down to the college to order the fellows to elect Chappell.) Laud wrote to Bishop Bramhall in 1635 asking him to

> get some of the factious senior fellows . . . some way preferred out of the college. And when they are out, I thinks that some towardly Englishmen might be sent out of our universities to begin a good example and settlement in that college for the Irish to follow.[2]

Strafford successfully imposed a few young and more controllable scholars from Cambridge upon the college. But the time

---

[1] H. F. Kearney, *Strafford in Ireland 1633–41* (Manchester, 1959), pp. 114–15.
[2] *H.M.C.* (*Hastings*), vol. IV, p. 64.

available was too short. The discontented at Trinity could always look to Archbishop Ussher for sympathy, if not active support. Strafford's fall from power in 1640 made the lot of his nominees in the college most unattractive and nothing more was heard of them. The tide was running in the Puritan direction once more.

Though no notebooks have survived from this period of Trinity's history, it seems that Laud, as the new Chancellor of the university, planned to undermine the dominant position of Ramism within the college. The new college statutes, drawn up at his behest, not only gave the Crown a more direct say in the government of the college, they also laid down that the text of Aristotle's *Organon* should be studied without commentary and that Aristotle's *Metaphysics* should be read. Earlier in January 1633–4, Laud had ordered the teaching of arts to be suspended.[1] The leader of the opposition was Anthony Martin, one of the fellows appointed earlier in the century, who outlasted Laud, to become Provost in 1644.

So far as the curriculum is concerned during the period immediately before the Civil War, scholasticism remained dominant in the great majority of the colleges. The typical curriculum offered a blend of humanism and scholastic elements. The rival traditions of Ramism and Arminianism were very much those of a minority. Ramism barely survived in Dublin, and among the Puritan remnants at Oxford and Cambridge. Arminianism could rely upon the backing of the court and had successfully infiltrated among the heads of houses, but was still weak at teaching level.[2]

This was the position within the universities. It takes no account of the hostility which was building up against them outside the walls. The universities were unpopular, partially because they still catered for the needs of a social *élite*, drawn, though more and more were going up to universities, from the same privileged social groups. This restrictive approach was to come under criticism during the next decade. The universities were also criticized for teaching scholasticism. The exponents of the scholastics

[1] R. B. McDowell and D. A. Webb, 'Courses and Teaching at T.C.D. during the first 200 years', *Hermathena*, vol. LXIX (May, 1947), pp. 9–30; W. Knowler, *Strafford's Letters* (London, 1739), vol. I, p. 188.

[2] Unfortunately there are few notebooks for this period. In general, too much reliance has been placed on 'Holdsworth's Guide to Students' [*sic*] which may well belong to the late 1640s or 1650s and not be by Holdsworth at all. (See below, p. 103.)

were able to offer a defence of their methods when called upon during the revolutionary period, but to their critics they seemed to be perpetuating a highly technical approach to Christian truth, which had the added disadvantage of Popish associations.

Professor Stone has drawn attention to an 'educational revolution' during the period 1540–1640, when he estimates that a higher proportion of the relevant age-group went to university than was to be the case again until the twentieth century. He sees this as a part, and perhaps a cause, of the extraordinary cultural renaissance of those years. But there was also a counter-revolution in the making, a 'backlash' in our own terms, which was a protest against the domination of the gentry in church, state and higher education. The full bitterness of this movement was not to be seen until after the civil war. It can only be sensed in such incidents as the refusal of the Newington sectaries in 1632 to show a proper respect for their superiors by taking the oath as required. Laud knew their attitude when he told them:

> You call us abominable men, to be hated of all, that we carry the mark of the Beast, that we are his members.[1]

2.

The summoning of the Long Parliament in December, 1640, brought to an end the short-lived régime of Laud and Strafford. Strafford was executed in May, 1641, and a series of reforming statutes were passed through Parliament. This was the beginning of the great ferment which many historians have seen as a period of revolution, analogous to the French Revolution of 1789 and the Russian Revolution of 1917. Within the decade, the monarchy and the House of Lords were done away with, and the whole relationship between Church and State changed radically. Ireland and Scotland were soon to be organized into a single political unit, ruled from Westminster. In religion, clerical authority was called into question, and a wide religious tolerance became a practical possibility. When all this is taken into consideration it is difficult to withhold the description 'revolution' from these years.

Some historians would also make a case for an educational

[1] J. P. Kenyon, *The Stuart Constitution* (Cambridge, 1966), p. 186.

revolution during this period, and given a little goodwill on the part of the reader, the evidence appears persuasive.[1] There was certainly a good deal of criticism of the universities. There was also the feeling in certain quarters that the time was ripe for a radical change in the content of the curriculum.

Francis Bacon was the best known advocate of educational reform and his ideas had grown in influence since his death in 1626. In his *Advancement of Learning* (1605), and *New Organon* (1620), Bacon argued that root and branch reform was necessary in the field of education. He thought that the authority of the ancients was being accepted too uncritically, especially where the study of nature was concerned. Dependence upon logic and syllogism was leading men into dubious speculation, when the most fruitful approach was by means of experiment. Social prejudice also played its part.

It is esteemed a kind of dishonour unto learning to descend to enquiry of meditation upon matters mechanical.[2]

The time had come to sell books and build furnaces, to look again at long-established practices in education and to change the excessively professional character of the universities which had hindered research at large in the arts and sciences.

Had Bacon's plans for education been carried out, they would certainly have brought revolutionary changes in the field of university education. One of the most important would have been the separation of secular from sacred learning. Bacon saw the association of the arts curriculum with divinity as one of the prime causes of conservatism in the academic world. It meant, he pointed out, that those who advocated change could be accused of being turbulent spirits. What Bacon had in mind was a situation in which new discoveries within the arts and sciences would not be thought to have theological implications. He looked forward to a situation in which Aristotelian metaphysics, now a supposed link between the world of nature and the sphere of the

[1] Christopher Hill tells us that Baconian ideas entered Oxford in the wake of the Parliamentary armies (C. Hill, *The Century of Revolution* (Edinburgh, 1961), p. 180). Hugh Trevor-Roper makes out an eloquent case for Baconian enthusiasm among the 'country' gentry in *Religion, the Reformation and Social Change*, p. 244.

[2] Bacon, 'Of the Advancement of Learning', Book II: J. Spedding, R. L. Ellis and D. D. Heath (eds.), *Works of Francis Bacon* (London, 1857–74), vol. III, p. 332.

divine, would simply disappear. As he wrote in 1622 to a Catholic professor in Savoy:

> Be not troubled about metaphysics. When true physics have been discovered there will be no metaphysics. Beyond the true physics is divinity only.[1]

Another decisive change would have been the abolition of the disputation and the syllogism as a means of education. The supporters of these saw them as an occasion which brought together in fruitful conjunction the twin arts of rhetoric and logic, to be used in both the arts and the divinity courses. Bacon could see little virtue in them, since they led to a situation in which a debating victory counted for more than discovery of truth. He thought that from his method of inductive reasoning real benefits to mankind would result.[2]

Perhaps most important of all, Bacon rejected traditional ideals of education in the English universities. He saw little value in the ideal of eloquence which had been brought into prominence by the English Ciceronians in the mid-sixteenth century. He attacked the neo-scholasticism of the late sixteenth century, which sought to reconcile reason and revelation. Bacon also rejected Ramism for its excessive reliance upon logical dichotomizing. In place of all these he proposed to substitute an ideal of progress in arts and sciences, of power and of utility. Significantly, poetry came low down on Bacon's list of priorities.

The obstacles in the way of change were enormous, as Bacon himself found during his own lifetime. The universities in England in the early seventeenth century were dedicated by and large to the training of ministers and to a lesser extent to the intellectual formation of gentlemen. Bacon described them, in effect, as professional institutions. The arts curriculum was arranged by divines with a view to the further study of divinity.

Even more to the point was the fact that in 1640–41 universities were not fully discredited in the eyes of the Puritan majority of the House of Commons. Laud's innovations had tarnished the image of Oxford and Cambridge, but he had not had the time to change

---

[1] Ibid., J. Spedding (ed.), *Letters and Life of Francis Bacon* (London, 1874), vol. VIII, p. 377.
[2] Bacon, *Works*, vol. IV, p. 24

the whole character of the universities. Nothing indeed is more surprising than the absence of a radical policy towards the universities in 1641 within the Houses of Parliament. No changes in the curriculum were contemplated. Action was taken against isolated individuals like John Cosin or particular colleges like Emmanuel, but in the main little was done by the sub-committee set up by the House of Commons.[1]

At this date, 1640–41, the only real enthusiasm for Bacon's ideas was shown by a small group headed by Samuel Hartlib, who looked to the Czech reformer, Comenius, for leadership.[2] Hartlib had friends, or more strictly perhaps, acquaintances, in high places, John Pym among them. A refugee himself, he was associated during the thirties with plans for Protestant reunion, along with the Scot, John Dury. The group took over some of Bacon's ideas, but placed them in an intellectual context which he himself would hardly have recognized. Comenius looked upon education as a practical means of ironing out the differences between the various Protestant Churches. He dreamed of a universal wisdom which would bring all Christians eventually into a true harmony, but this was associated with a scheme of textbooks designed to make the paths of learning accessible to all. In a sense, Comenius was a seventeenth-century Jeremy Bentham.[3]

The Baconian element in the Comenian dream was minimal. He drew up a list of textbooks in 1641 in which the main emphasis was upon learning to read and write, to be followed by Latin, Biblical history and ethics. Indeed it soon became clear that one of Comenius's main objectives was social reform, in the sense that he hoped to make it possible for poor children to develop their talents. But this note of social reform was not to be found in Francis Bacon himself. Bacon, unlike the 'Baconians' of the 1640s, was a conservative, in both social and religious matters. To regard him as a Puritan, as some historians have done, is to fly in the face of the evidence. His ideas certainly appealed to those Puritans who needed a stick to attack the orthodoxy of scholasticism, or the

[1] A bill for the 'better regulating' of the universities came to nothing, *Commons' Journal*, vol. II, p. 233 (3 August, 1641).

[2] G. H. Turnbull, *Hartlib, Dury and Comenius* (Liverpool, 1947).

[3] See Trevor-Roper's brilliant analysis of this group in *Religion, the Reformation and Social Change*, chap. 5.

social conventions of a gentleman's education, but none of this radicalism was to be found in Bacon himself. In this, the Royal Society, the arch enemy of religious enthusiasm and the defender of social conservatism, read Bacon more truly than did Comenius.

Perhaps Comenius's own links with the Puritans have been exaggerated. In fact, the suggestion that Comenius should be invited to England was made first by John Gauden, later the presumed author of *Eikon Basilike*, in a sermon to the Long Parliament on 19 November, 1640. The trend of the sermon suggests that what Gauden had in mind, and the group of divines for whom he was speaking, was advice about Protestants living together in peace and unity. There was not a word in the sermon about social or educational reform. There was, however, a great deal about the need to avoid religious strife.[1]

Comenius arrived in England in the autumn of 1641 under the impression that he was being asked to initiate a vast scheme of reform, which would put his ideas into practice, with a top-dressing of Baconianism. Perhaps Hartlib was most to blame for exaggerating the extent of his own influence upon the English government. In any event, Comenius's advice about religious unity would have been useless. By 1642, any moderate position was out of the question.

The Comenian episode, in my view, shows how unlikely educational reforms on Baconian lines were in 1641–2. It is, of course, possible to argue that but for the Civil War, such reforms would have taken place, but this view has to reckon with the fact that Comenius was invited for purposes of religious unity. When he arrived, his own ideas, naturally enough, seemed more important to him than Bacon's, and, in any event, so little was done that he left the country in the spring of 1642. Curiously enough, one of those who were most sympathetic towards him was the royalist gentleman, Justinian Isham, which points to the fact that Comenius was dealing in the main with a middle range of opinion, not merely the Puritans. If there was a leader of a pro-Comenian group in England at this date, it was John Williams, Archbishop of Lincoln, and the sad fact is that Williams was imprisoned in the Tower by the Puritan leaders during most of the period that Comenius was in England.[2]

[1] For a different view, see Trevor-Roper, op. cit., p. 300.   [2] *D.N.B.*

Another advocate of educational reform was John Milton, whose pamphlet *Of Education* was published in 1644, though possibly written in 1641. Milton addressed the pamphlet to Samuel Hartlib and he agreed with Hartlib about the need for 'the reforming of education for the want whereof this nation perishes'. The pamphlet, however, was not an answer to the Baconians but a reply to their arguments. Milton was not a 'Modern'. He gave pride of place to the Ancients and he took as his model

> those ancient and famous schools of Pythagoras, Plato, Isocrates, Aristotle and such others, out of which were bred up such a number of renowned philosophers, orators, historians, poets and princes.[1]

Milton did not mention Bacon, and though he criticized the educational system, it was in terms of means rather than ends. Milton's ideal was a gentlemanly Puritan education from the age of twelve to twenty in which all the arts and sciences could be acquired in a leisured manner. In this he looked back beyond Bacon to Lawrence Humphrey. Hartlib's views may appeal more to the twentieth-century historian, but Milton's outlook was more characteristic of the Puritan ruling *élite* during and after the Civil War.

3.

The first decisive change in the universities occurred first in Cambridge, as a consequence of the signing of the Solemn League and Covenant. At this time, late in 1643 and early in 1644, the Presbyterians were in the ascendant, and with the backing of Edward Montagu, second Earl of Manchester, radical changes took place. The remnants of the Laudian fellows were finally ejected for refusing to take the covenant. New heads were appointed to colleges and new fellows were elected with the approval of the Westminster Assembly. At the same time, William Dowsing went round the colleges religiously destroying statues and stained glass.

To what extent did this represent a social or an intellectual revolution? Of the dozen new heads of houses who were appointed, nine were members of the Westminster Assembly and

[1] Milton, *Of Education* in F. A. Patterson (ed.), *The Student's Milton* (New York, 1930), pp. 725–31.

seven were former members of Emmanuel College. They all came from within the university community. Almost all had Presbyterian sympathies. They were all divines. They all needed the support of Manchester, the parliamentary commander in the area and a man of socially conservative and Presbyterian opinions. And what was true of the heads of colleges was true also of the newly-created fellows. The years 1644–50 were a period of mainly Presbyterian dominance in which two of the five 'Smectymnuans' (Presbyterian divines who wrote a pamphlet in 1641 attacking episcopacy) were appointed heads of colleges, Thomas Young at Jesus, and William Spurstowe at St. Catherine's.

The prominence of fellows of Emmanuel in the Presbyterian reorganization of Cambridge might well suggest intellectual radicalism of some kind. But the evidence which remains does not indicate that Cambridge at this date offered anything over and above the accepted scholastic curriculum.

A crucial piece of evidence for this period is provided by an educational document, *Directions for a Student*, which has attracted a good deal of attention in recent years.[1] Hitherto the *Directions* have been dated to the period before 1640 on the basis of an un-supported ascription to Richard Holdsworth, Master of Emmanuel from 1637. In fact, however, the *Directions* recommend several books which were published long after Holdsworth had severed any active connection with Cambridge and this makes his authorship unlikely.[2] These books, published in 1646 and 1647 suggest that we should push the writing of the *Directions* into the late 1640s at least.

This dating which places the *Directions* to *c*. 1648–50 is supported by a Cambridge notebook of the 1640s. Its owner took notes, along with the date they were read, over the time range from 1648–50, from twenty-three books, nine of which are recommended in the *Directions*.[3] Philosophical books recommended in

---

[1] Emmanuel MS 1.2.27, Curtis discusses it at length in *Oxford and Cambridge in Transition, passim*, but wholly in connection with the pre-1640 period.

[2] The books are Thomas Fuller, *The Historie of the Holy Warre* (1639); Edward Reynolds, *A Treatise of the Passions* (1640); Fuller, *The Holy State* (1642); James Howell, *Epistolae Hoelianae* (1645); Sir Thomas Browne, *Pseudodoxia Epidemica* (1646); Alexander Ross, *Mystagogus Poeticus* (1647).

[3] Camb. Univ. Add. MS 6160. The books included Edward Brerewood, *Enquiries Touching the Diversity of Languages and Religions* (1614); More's *Utopia* (1551); John

the *Directions*, notably Burgersdicius and Eustachius, were also reprinted by the university press between 1647 and 1654.

The new dating also fits the ascription found on the only contemporary copy of the *Directions*, which is entitled 'Short directions for a student by John Merryweather B.A. late of M.C. in Cambridge 1651-2'.[1] Merryweather had been admitted sizar at St. John's in 1634 and had taken his B.A. in 1637-8 and his M.A. in 1641. He became a fellow of Magdalene and B.D. in 1652. Such a career suggests a middle-of-the-road Puritanism, which the *Directions* imply in recommending Sibbs, Preston, Bolton, Downham and Perkins.

The new dating is important because it implies that the *Directions* throw as much light upon Puritan Cambridge of the late 1640s as the Cambridge of the 1630s. We may perhaps go further and look upon the *Directions* as the Cambridge equivalent of Barlow's Oxford *Guide to Students*, drawn up with the same purpose in view, to defend the academic syllabus against the onslaughts of the sectaries. Against this background, the *Directions* take on a new interest. The existence of such a document suggests that it was drawn up to defend a particular academic standpoint against attack.

What then are the assumptions which lie behind the *Directions*? The first is that universities are institutions which provide a 'liberal' education for ministers and gentlemen. In view of the political pressure which was to be exerted in favour of a more utilitarian emphasis, this was no theoretical assumption. The author stood squarely on the side of social conservatism against those radicals who attacked the notion of a clerical monopoly of learning and the concept of a gentleman's education. The author also showed no signs of being influenced by Baconianism or the new philosophy, though he went so far as to recommend Bacon's *Essays*. The weight of the document is thrown against intellectual change.

Broadly speaking, the author of the *Directions* recommended the study of scholasticism in the mornings and of the classics in the

---

Earle's *Characters* [sc. *Micro-cosmographia*] (1628); Howell's *Epistolae* (1645); Bacon's *Natural History* [sc. *Sylva Sylvarum*] (1626), *Henry VII* (1622) and *Essays* (1625); Fuller, *Holy Warre* (1639); Dr. Browne's *Errors* [sc. *Pseudodoxia Epidemica*] (1646).
[1] Bodleian MSS Rawlinson D.200.

afternoons. Logic and ethics were to be studied in the first year, physics and metaphysics in the second year, more logic, ethics and physics in the third year, and in the fourth years Seneca and Lucretius and Aristotle's *De Coelo* and *Meteorology*. All this was the clearest possible statement of the old philosophy, and the familiar names of Burgersdicius, Eustachius, Crackanthorp, Scheibler, Zabarella, Fonseca and Suarez come up again and again. The figure of Aristotle dominated, and the document, by implication, indicates the interlocking strength and emotional attraction of the old synthesis, though it was now necessary to say 'he can hardly deserve the name of scholar that is not in some measure acquainted with his [Aristotle's] works'.

The *Directions* is not the only piece of evidence to illustrate the intellectual conservatism of Cambridge during this period. A *Guide* to students drawn up by Nathaniel Sterry, graduate of Emmanuel in 1648–9 and Fellow of Merton from 1649, runs on similar lines:

> First read over Ramus and Burgersdicius his logick. Then read Aristotle's *Organon* with Pacius his Comment which will both further your philosophy and the Greek tongue. . . . In ethics read Eustachius . . . and when you have done him read Aristotle with Magirus his comment. . . . For Physics read Zabarella and after him Magirus but lightly . . . for metaphysics read with any painetaking but Suarez. . . .

Apart from the reference to Ramus at the beginning, the world picture assumed by Sterry was that of the academic world before the Civil War.[1]

A student's notebook which has survived for this period also bears out a generally traditional emphasis in the curriculum at Trinity. Daniel Foote, who was admitted as a sizar to Trinity College in 1645, took notes, beginning in March, 1646, from the *Logic* of Burgersdicius, the *Ethics* of Eustachius, the *Physics* of Magirus and the *Meteorology* of Fromondus, all of them contemporary exponents of scholasticism. He also disputed over cer-

---

[1] Bodleian Tanner MS 88 f. 5. I have used Sterry's Guide with reference to Cambridge. It could be used to equal effect for Oxford since he was a fellow of Merton. Part of its interest lies in the points raised about the effect, of the influx of Cambridge men to Oxford in 1649. (See below, p. 108.)

tain metaphysical questions.[1] Fifteen years later, the young Isaac
Newton, newly arrived at the university, was also to take notes
from Magirus and Eustachius.[2]

An alternative viewpoint to that put forward by the *Directions*
was to be found among the group known as the Cambridge
Platonists. The centre of the group was Christ's, where Henry
More and Ralph Cudworth were Fellows, and Cudworth Master
from 1654. Benjamin Whichcote, Provost of King's from 1645
until the Restoration and William Dillingham, Master of Emmanuel, 1653–62, were sympathetic to this point of view, and so
also were Simon Patrick and John Tillotson, Fellows of Queens.
Other Cambridge Platonists included John Smith (1652 +) and
Nathaniel Culverwell. The amount of unanimity in this group
seems to have been exaggerated by historians, and hence it is
difficult to pin down their precise influence on the curriculum.
But it seems safe to say that some of them welcomed at first the
alternative to Aristotelianism, which Descartes offered first in his
Discourse on Method (1637) and then in his *Principia* (1644). Henry
More, for example, in 1658 recommended a student who he said
had read Descartes's *Principia* over and over.

But precisely because these men for their religious tolerance and
literary interest are so attractive to many twentieth-century minds,
we may very well exaggerate their contemporary significance at
Cambridge in the 1640s and 1650s. Influential though they were,
they were still in a minority within the university. Unfortunately,
there are very few surviving notebooks for this period, but it
seems likely that the attacks made by the sectaries between 1649–
53 strengthened the hands of the conservatives. In any case, Henry
More himself who had welcomed Cartesianism in the late 1640s,
had second thoughts a few years later.

All this scarcely amounted to an intellectual revolution. Rather,
Cambridge Platonism apart, it reflected the conservatism of the
Westminster Assembly, which was desperately trying to set up a
theological orthodoxy, as circumscribed and as traditional as
Laudianism had been. The chief fear of the conservative leaders in
the Westminster Assembly was lest anabaptism and sectarianism
should spread, a subject on which they were well, perhaps too

[1] B.M. Sloane MSS 586, 600.
[2] Cambridge University Library Add. MS 3996.

well, briefed by their Scottish guest, Robert Baillie.[1] They set their face in the main against the type of compromise which Comenius and Samuel Hartlib represented and they resisted the arguments of the few Independents in the Assembly, who favoured toleration. Men of this type were disturbed by the possibility that traditional doctrines of the Church were now being called into question, even the divinity of Christ. The safest course to them seemed to be to trust in the methods of the past.

Royalist Oxford was as conservative as parliamentarian Cambridge. A notebook belonging to Thomas Braithwait, Fellow of Queen's, shows that he lent to his pupils the *Logic* of Burgersdicius, the *Physics* of Magirus, the *Metaphysics* of Scheibler, the *Physics* of the Jesuits at Coimbra and the *Meteorology* of Fromondus.[2] In the choice of classics and neo-scholastics, royalist Oxford and Puritan Cambridge coincide. If we seek a reason for this it may be suggested that the same fears affected both. The traditional shape of society, of nature and of the Church, were all being exposed to change, and the forces of conservatism within the universities rallied to the old ways.

In 1647, one year after the end of the Civil War, a Parliamentary Commission was despatched to Oxford by the Long Parliament. Its membership and its outlook were Presbyterian, and for a time it was able to proceed unchecked in making mainly Presbyterian appointments to headships of colleges and to fellowships. The membership of the commission consisted of Nathaniel Brent, John and Henry Wilkinson, Francis Cheynell, Edward Corbett, Edward and John Reynolds. Four of these were Merton men, a revenge for the pressure which Laud had brought on the college in the 1630s.[3]

Within a short time, the commission removed all heads of houses who had had royalist loyalties. The Covenant was used as a test. In April, 1648, the Visitors ordered the Presbyterian form of service to be followed in all the chapels of the university, and in May and for several months later, each fellow was asked the simple question: 'Do you submit to the authority of Parliament

---

[1] Robert Baillie, *Letters and Journals 1637–62* (Edinburgh, 1841).

[2] Queen's College, Oxford MS 423 f. 1.

[3] M. Burrows (ed.), *The Register of the Visitors of the University of Oxford 1647–58* (Oxford, 1881).

in this visitation?' About half the academic body refused, but their places were not long left vacant. Two hundred fellowships were filled up in 1648–9, a quarter of them with newly-imported Cambridge men. Some of the new fellows came from the poorer Oxford halls, where Puritans had sought refuge under Laud. The Visitors appointed four of their number to college headships—Edward Reynolds to Corpus, John Wilkinson to Magdalen, Francis Cheynell to Christ Church, and Nathaniel Brent to Merton (this, in fact, was a reappointment since he had been Warden since 1622). Other appointments included John Wilkins to Wadham, John Conant to Exeter, and Henry Stringer to New College. Gerard Langbaine who had been elected Provost of Queen's was allowed to remain.

The rule of the Visitors came to an end with Pride's Purge and the execution of Charles I. Francis Cheynell, who had the reputation of being the most bitter of the Visitors and the most intolerant, refused to take the engagement, in effect a simple oath of loyalty to the new régime, and gave up the headship of St. John's. He was followed by Nathaniel Brent and Edward Reynolds at Merton and Magdalen respectively. John Wilkinson died and was saved from having to make a decision, but there is no reason to think that he would have acted differently from the rest.[1]

The social changes introduced by the Presbyterian visitors at Oxford during these years do not seem to have been remarkable. The college with the highest proportion of gentlemen's sons among its fellows before the Visitors was Christ Church, with a percentage of somewhere between 30 per cent and 60 per cent. Of the 41 gentlemen's sons who were fellows before 1648, only 17 were left after the purges,[2] but much of the new blood in the university came from Cambridge, where it is difficult to see that the influence of the Earl of Manchester had acted in the direction of wider social entry. In the absence of definite evidence, however, we must leave a question mark. The likelihood is, that under the Presbyterians, the social composition of the universities remained

---

[1] Ibid. By a decision of the House of Commons, 11 October, 1649, all office-holders, including university teachers, were required to accept the Engagement. *Commons Journal*, vol. VI, pp. 306–7.

[2] Burrows, op. cit.

unchanged, and it was this conservatism which increased the social bitterness among the radical sectaries and the soldiers of the New Model Army.

Such changes as took place in the universities, between the summoning of the Long Parliament in 1640 and the execution of the King in 1649, were made under the auspices of the Westminster Assembly. There is no evidence at all to suggest that they resulted in any important changes in the curriculum. The Presbyterians who had been Ramists in the days of Melville and Cartwright had moved round by the 1640s to a curriculum in which Aristotelianism was accepted as the basis for the education of a divine. The breezes of the new philosophy were beginning to blow but they seem to have had the effect of making the Presbyterians more conscious of the virtues of the old philosophy. Their conservatism can also be explained by the fact that the very notion of a learned ministry was being denounced in quarters that could no longer be ignored—the regiments of the New Model Army.

Perhaps the most remarkable fact about the universities during the Civil War was the similarity of the curriculum at Oxford and Cambridge. Historians may assume that new ideas followed in the wake of the Parliamentary armies, but to do so means losing sight of the fact that the Civil War was fought between two sections of the gentry, who, as the war dragged on, became ever more conscious of the dangers of social radicalism. There seemed little point in leaving the safe harbours of the old philosophy for the sake of an intellectual adventure, which might end in shipwreck. If this seems surprising, we need think no further ahead than the intellectual reaction in England, during the years following 1789.

CHAPTER VII

The Cromwellian Decade

I.

At the end of 1647, when the debates took place at Putney between the army officers and the agitators of the New Model Army, and in 1648, the year of the Second Civil War and Colonel Pride's Purge, social and religious tensions became far more marked. A period began in which revolutionary hopes were aroused and encouraged, by the execution of the King, and the abolition of the House of Lords. The notion of religious orthodoxy on Presbyterian lines had now been rejected, and to some it seemed that the notion of an established Church would go with it.

The next stage, it appeared, would be the abolition of tithes, of the system of Church patronage controlled by the gentry and the universities, and of the parish as a social and religious unit to which all belonged, irrespective of whether they were godly or not. The alternative to the parish was to be the 'gathered' congregation, supporting its pastor by voluntary contributions, choosing its own pastor and running its own affairs without control by the state. These hopes were to be diappointed in the long run, but there is no doubt that they were strongly held among the new groups which came to power after Pride's Purge.[1] The scene of execution at Whitehall in January, 1649, was to be the prelude to a true reformation of England.

The universities, as pillars of the *ancien régime*, might well have been affected by decisions as drastic as that which removed the House of Lords. Certainly, during the course of the year 1649 there appeared two movements which showed themselves highly critical of the universities. One of them, the Levellers, enjoyed some support in the New Model Army and among the artisans and apprentices of London.[2] The other, the Diggers, was less significant

[1] J. E. Farnell, 'The usurpation of Honest London Householders: Barebone's Parliament', *E.H.R.* (Jan., 1967), pp. 24–46. See also Leo Solt's illuminating article, 'Anti-intellectualism in the Puritan Revolution', *Church History* (1956).

[2] The social origins of the Levellers still needs examination.

numerically, but it illustrates the depth of feeling against the universities among the socially under-privileged groups in society.

The Leveller attitude was expounded in the pamphlets of William Walwyn. Walwyn was the son of a London merchant, and, though not himself a university graduate, was a man of wide reading and culture.[1] Walwyn attacked the universities for holding on to the study of Hebrew, Greek and Latin at a time when the scriptures were in English. He was unconvinced by arguments in defence of a learned ministry and saw them as little more than 'the learned . . . defending their copyhold'. In another pamphlet he wrote:

> They have made it a difficult thing to be a minister and so have engrossed the trade to themselves and left other men by reason of their other professions in an incapacity of being such in their sense.

Like many another, he pointed out that Christ's Apostles were unlearned men and he saw both Episcopalian and Presbyterian alike as aiming at oppression and tyranny by monopolizing learning.

> When they commend learning it is not for learning's sake but for their own; her esteeme gets them their livings and preferments and therefore she is to be kept up or their trade will go down.[2]

Another social radical, the Digger leader, Gerrard Winstanley, also denounced the universities as the sources of false learning. His objection to them was basically a religious one. First as a Baptist and then as a Seeker, he felt that the true path to God did not lie through book-learning. As he put it in his pamphlet *The New Law of Righteousness* (1649),

> the Universities are the standing ponds of stinking waters, that make those trees grow, the curse of ignorance, confusion and *bondage* spreads from hence all the nations over.[3]

[1] W. Haller (ed.), *Tracts on Liberty in the Puritan Revolution* (New York, 1934), vol. I, p. 40.
[2] 'The Compassionate Samaritane', ibid., vol. II, p. 83.
[3] G. H. Sabine (ed.), *The Works of Gerrard Winstanley* (New York, 1941), p. 238.

In his reference to bondage, clearly there were social overtones to his criticisms. Winstanley felt that the right to teach had been taken from the fishermen, the shepherds and the husbandmen who were the rightful successors of Christ, and taken over by the scholars who made laws to keep 'the inferior men of the world so-called' in bondage. The result was that

lay people, tradesmen and such as are not bred in schools, may have no liberty to speak or write of the Spirit.[1]

What Winstanley had in mind was a system of education in which all children should be trained in practical matters, agriculture, gardening, mining, cattle-breeding, carpentry and astronomy. 'He that is an actor in any or all (of these) is a profitable son of mankind'. Some historians may see a hint of Baconianism in Winstanley's emphasis upon using the strength and power of the earth for 'the use and profit of mankind'. But the most prominent note in Winstanley's writings was one of social protest, and this is absent in Bacon. What Winstanley objected to was traditional knowledge, as opposed to true practical and laborious knowledge. Those who followed traditional learning did not set their hands to work and from their ranks arose the clergy and lawyers,

who by their cunning insinuations live merely upon the labour of other men. . . .

The same note may be detected in William Dell, the controversial minister who became Master of Caius in 1649.[2] In his pamphlet 'The Right Reformation of Learning, Schools and Universities according to the State of the Gospel', Dell argued in favour of doing away with the traditional curricula:

This is the sin also that is like to undo and ruin the university and to raze it to the ground . . . shall then your master Plato, Aristotle, Pythagoras and wretched heathens who with all their wisdom knew not Christ, but are dead and damned many hundred years ago, be able to deliver you? Or shall Thomas

[1] Ibid., p. 239.

[2] The account of Dell given in the *D.N.B.* conflates two different individuals. Our William Dell was apparently a graduate of Emmanuel, who became a preacher in the army of Fairfax and a prominent independent. See H. R. Trevor-Roper's note in *E.H.R.*, vol. LXII (1947), pp. 377–9.

and Scotus and the other schoolmen with their cold vain and anti-Christian divinity help you?[1]

Dell also restated the idea of breaking down the privileged central position of Oxford and Cambridge. With him, as with the Elizabethan sectaries, the reasons for this were religious. The objection to the existing universities was that they imposed a central direction upon the religious life of the country. Universities in the larger towns would be less amenable to central control in this way. Dell and others were not speaking for the country gentry; their purpose was to ensure greater freedom of religion and religious teaching. Dell considered that 'the unction of the spirit' was enough to make a man a true minister 'without any regard to a man's outward calling or condition in the world'. In his view Christ did not care whether a man was a scholar, a clergyman or a gentleman.[2]

2.

This evidence suggests that among some social groups, there was a rising sense of expectancy in England during these years, which resembled a similar feeling in New England during the previous decade. The 1630s in New England, in fact, had placed the early Puritan settlers in the same difficult situation as the Puritan victors of the Civil War. Both faced the challenge and the problems of creating a new society out of the materials and prejudices of the old.

In the new colony of Massachusetts, problems of social control were raised during the first decade, in 'the business of Mistress Anne Hutchinson'. Anne Hutchinson emigrated to New England in 1634. She was a woman of formidable energy, who had experienced at least two religious conversions. She held strongly antinomian opinions which she clearly hoped to propagate in the freer atmosphere of the New World. To be antinomian was radical enough, to be a female antinomian was a revolution in itself.

Mrs. Hutchinson taught that the mystical experience of divine grace was decisive for a true Christian. Orthodox doctrine and good works came a poor second. Inevitably, there was a strongly

---

[1] W. Dell, *The Stumbling Stone* (London, 1653), p. 30.   [2] Ibid., p. 23.

anti-intellectual current among her disciples, one of whom was reported as saying:

> I'le bring you to a woman that preaches better Gospell than any of your black coates that have been at the Ninniversity. . . . I had rather heare such a one that speakes from the meere motion of the spirit without any study at all, then any of your learned scollers, although they may be fuller of scripture.[1]

From 1635–7 there was a crisis of conscience throughout the colony, in which the political and religious future of the original leaders was at stake. A trial of strength took place in 1637 and Mrs. Hutchinson's supporters, who included Sir Henry Vane the younger, lost their places as magistrates. Later in the same year, Mrs. Hutchinson and her friends were tried and condemned to banishment. From the religious point of view, 'the business of Mistress Anne Hutchinson' was a struggle between orthodoxy on the one hand and antinomianism on the other. But, as in England later, the religious tone of the conflict with the authorities concealed a social side to it all. Mistress Anne drew a good deal of her support from Boston—the traders, the artisans, the servants, and last but also least, the women. The only gentleman in her following was the enigmatic and unstable young man, Harry Vane. In the eyes of her critics, her support came from those of 'meane condition and weake parts', some of them illiterate. But as Professor Battis has shown, this was a propaganda view. Mistress Anne's entourage may not have included gentlemen, but it was made up in part of successful citizens who had made their fortunes in trade. What Mistress Anne represented, in short, was basic criticism of the social ideal of the gentleman and the ecclesiastical order which supported it.

Against this threat to the social order, the gentry, the learned clergy and the Emmanuel graduates, of whom Professor Morison makes so much, rallied behind the founding father of Massachusetts, that great social conservative, John Winthrop. His former rival, Thomas Dudley, who was even more conservative in his views than Winthrop, joined him as a hammer of heresy. The conflict was not one solely between the haves and have-nots,

[1] E. Battis, *Saints and Sectaries* (Chapel Hill, 1962), p. 116.

it was also between the gentry and the *nouveaux riches*. Winthrop believed in a social order, divinely established, in which

> in all times some must be rich, some poor, some highe and eminent in power and dignity: others meane and in subjection.[1]

Mistress Anne appealed to those with a more fluid concept of society. In fact she was tried for sedition, not heresy. The result could have been foreseen. The social radicals were driven out of the colony and a period of sterner social measures was inaugurated, in which the more lenient Winthrop took his cue from Thomas Dudley.[2]

The most lasting monument of this unsettled period was Harvard College, founded in 1638 and taking its name from John Harvard, 'a godly gentleman and a lover of learning'.[3] Higher education in other colonies was a matter of pious aspiration, but in Massachusetts it was of great social urgency. Historians of Harvard have ascribed the speed of its foundation to the Puritans' zeal for learning.[4] In fact, the object of the new foundation was to establish a supply of learned ministers, without which the ruling *élite* felt itself dangerously exposed.

The social function of Harvard was made clear in the first statutes of 1646:

> When any Scholar is able to read Tully or such like classical author extempore and speake true Latin in verse and prose *suo* (*ut aiunt*) *Marte* and decline perfectly the paradigms of Nounes and verbs in the Greek tongue, let him then and not before be capable of admission into the Colledge.[5]

This insistence upon Latin and Greek played its part as a social hurdle in the New World as successfully as in the Old. It implicitly excluded lower social groups from the possibility of entering the ministry and effectively curtained off the mechanick preacher or the enthusiast from key offices. As if to hammer this point home, the statutes also declared that the students

[1] John Winthrop, 'A Model of Christian Charity', from *Winthrop Papers, 1623–30* (Boston, 1931), reprinted in E. S. Morgan (ed.), *The Founding of Massachusetts* (New York, 1964), p. 190.

[2] Battis, op. cit.   [3] Morison, *Founding of Harvard*, p. 433.

[4] S. E. Morison, *The Founding of Harvard College* (Cambridge, Mass., 1935); *Harvard College in the Seventeenth Century* (Cambridge, Mass., 1936), 2 vols.

[5] Ibid.

shall honor as their parents, Magistrates, Elders, tutors and aged persons, by being silent in their presence (except they be called upon to answer) not gainsaying showing all those laudable expressions of honor and reverence in their presence that are in use, as bowing before them, standing uncovered or the like.

It so happened that these precautions proved insufficient to exclude dangerous heresy at the very top. In 1654, a year in which the echoes of Barebones were still reverberating in England, Henry Dunster, President of the College since 1640, began to show unorthodox views on the question of infant baptism. This was as much as to raise the spectre of anabaptism in one of the centres of social control within the colony. Dunster was dismissed and replaced by a safer nominee. The law of 1644 under which he was charged specifically mentioned that for a hundred years past, anabaptists had been 'the Incendiaries of Commonwealths'.[1] Appropriately enough, Ramism seems to have made an appearance in the Harvard curriculum during his presidency. We know this from a letter of Leonard Hoar who graduated at Harvard under Dunster, and wrote some years later to his nephew, Josiah Flynt. He recommended Ramist notes on logic, physick and theology, and, failing this, suggested Ramus himself, or William Ames's *Medulla Theologiae*.[2]

Gentlemen at the frontiers of civilization needed the protection of the Church even more than their old-world counterparts. The college drew upon the upper reaches of society for its clergy, though it allowed members of the lower social groups to join the Church as part of the congregation. The lesson of Mistress Anne Hutchinson was taken well to heart. A generation later at Harvard one of the students expressed the official myth concerning the dangers of the 1630s:

> The ruling class would have been subjected to mechanical cobblers and tailors: the gentry would have been overwhelmed by lewd fellows of the baser sort, the sewage of Rome, the dregs of the illiterate plebs, which judges much from emotion, little from truth.[3]

[1] Morison, *Harvard College*, p. 306. [2] Morison, *Harvard College*, p. 640.
[3] P. Miller, *The New England Mind* (New York, 1939), p. 84.

The episode was not a remote happening in a far-away colony. Many of the people involved were in England during and after the Civil War. Sir Harry Vane was now in a position of power. Mrs. Hutchinson's husband, whom it does not seem appropriate to refer to as Mr. Hutchinson, was Commissioner of the Navy after 1651. Hugh Peter, who had been on the conservative side in New England and Roger Williams, the arch-radical, also made their voices heard during the post-war period.[1]

3.

If we turn now to the English universities during the period after the Civil War, we will be tempted to see a similar pattern of events. Among the non-gentle social groups in England, there was a similar rising of expectation, though this time the emigration was internal. There was no need to cross the Atlantic to experience a new sense of hope, and a belief that England was rousing itself like a strong man after sleep. In contrast with New England, however, the radicals were in a position of strength. They were entrenched in the New Model Army and in Major-General Harrison they had a determined leader. Above all they were strong among the rising anti-monopolists of London, a parallel to Mrs. Hutchinson's strength in Boston, though of much greater significance.

The criticisms which they made of the universities were basically social criticisms. The universities appeared as part of a gigantic system of social monopoly by which the prizes of the professions including law and medicine, as well as divinity, were reserved for the few. The criticisms made of the universities by Walwyn and Winstanley were echoed in the field of medicine by the apothecaries, who complained that the physicians made a gentleman's monopoly of medicine. Nicholas Culpeper, who translated the *Pharmacopea* into English, wrote that

> the liberty of our commonwealth is most infringed by three sorts of men, Priests, Physicians and Lawyers.[2]

[1] P. Miller, *Roger Williams* (New York, 1953). R. P. Stearns, *The Strenuous Puritan* (Urbana, 1954).
[2] Quoted by C. Webster, 'English medical reformers of the Puritan Revolution', *Ambix*, vol. XIV (Feb., 1967), p. 17.

The Inns of Court, third university of the realm, were another bulwark of the establishment to come under attack and the reasons were the same, namely that they were a gentleman's institution, designed to protect the property of gentlemen, in an arcane language which the people did not understand. To critical eyes, the court of chancery seemed 'a mystery of wickedness and a standing cheat'. Vavasour Powell, the religious radical, looked forward to the day when

Law should stream downe like a river freely, as for twenty shillings what formerly cost twenty pounds, impartially as the saints please, and it should run as rivers do close to doors.[1]

The educational changes which the radicals proposed would have had important social consequences. For example, the establishment of local universities on the lines suggested by William Dell, and earlier by the Elizabethan sectaries, would have had the effect of changing the social image of the universities. A local university meant cheaper education. The cost of university education was one of the barriers keeping out 'the meaner sort...' since 'the expencefulness of such a breeding sets it beyond their reach'.[2] Local universities also meant urban universities, which the local artisan might attend or send his sons to. There was a world of difference between this social ideal and that of an Oxford college, catering for the sons of gentry.

The radical emphasis on a practical curriculum also had social implications. Classical learning such as formed part of a university curriculum, implied that there were liberal arts suitable for a gentleman, as opposed to mechanical arts, which were totally unsuitable. A classical education also served to mark off the ruling *élite* from those below it. The classical tag was a class shibboleth of unerring simplicity. In contrast, the radicals envisaged a society in which godliness would come before gentility. As Petty saw it, a practical education implied social and political change:

---

[1] Farnell, op. cit., p. 43.

[2] [Anon.], *The Gentleman's Calling*. Richard Schlatter's article 'The higher learning in Puritan England' is very useful: *Historical Magazine of the Protestant Episcopal Church*, vol. XXIII (1954), pp. 167–87.

Many are now holding the plough [he wrote] which might have been made fit to steer the state.[1]

For this reason, Bacon's teaching that the furnace should replace the library appealed to the radicals as a stick with which to beat the establishment. A practical education involved doing away with Aristotelianism, that intellectual structure on which so much of the justification of the *ancien régime* depended.

The highwater mark of the agitation to reform the universities was reached in 1653 after Cromwell's dismissal of the Rump. In radical eyes, the Rump had been moving too slowly in many areas, especially in legal reform, where the propertied group were sensitive to the effects of change. Cromwell's decision to summon a nominated assembly was an attempt to deal with the frustrations and disappointed hopes of the sectaries and the New Model Army.

When the nominated Parliament met, it soon became clear that political differences existed even in the most godly assembly. Two parties soon formed. The radicals, drawn from the London Baptists, and the Fifth Monarchy men, demanded a religious settlement which left no place for a learned clergy. The supporters of Major-General John Lambert accepted the social conservatism of Henry Ireton. The gulf between the two was as much social as religious. The radical sectaries had as little love for the gentlemen of England as for the established ministry.

The final battle was won and lost in the Barebone[2] Parliament. This was not the completely lower-class assembly described by Clarendon in his history, but there was in it a solid core of anti-gentry radicalism. Barebone himself was a prosperous leather-seller who had formed his own religious congregation in 1640. The other opposition leaders were successful businessmen, and there was more than a hint of support for them from critics of the monopoly of trade exercised by the chartered companies. Support also came from John Goodwin's congregation. This was a group or assemblage of groups, which attacked the clerical profession and the universities as bitterly as they attacked the abuse

[1] 'The advice of W. P. to Mr. Samuel Hartlib,' *Harleian Miscellany* (1810), vol. VI, p. 3.
[2] On Barebone's Parliament, see also A. Woolrych, 'The Calling of Barebone's Parliament', in *E.H.R.* 80 (1965), pp. 492 ff.

of law and lawyers, as they saw them. As with Mistress Anne Hutchinson's followers, there was not a gentleman among them.[1]

The radicals were nearer to victory than is often supposed. An anonymous pamphlet lists sixty members of the Parliament opposed to a learned ministry and universities, as compared to eighty-odd in favour.[2] But God—as he so often is—was on the side of the big battalions. The dissolution of the Parliament left the initiative in the hands of Lambert and the conservatives, who were even then moving towards an understanding with the 'Presbyterians' (if we may so term their former opponents).

Yet in a sense, the crucial decisions so far as the universities were concerned had already been taken, in 1650, when the Presbyterian heads of colleges had been replaced by Independents. Cromwell's influence was apparent in the appointment of his chaplain, John Owen, as Dean of Christ Church, and his physician, Jonathan Goddard, as Warden of Merton.[3] Similar appointments were made to other colleges in Oxford and Cambridge. The victor of Ireland was already beginning to flex his muscles.

The influence of John Owen increased during the next few years, and it was to be thrown against the radical side. In 1652, he preached an attack upon the apparent religious anarchy which had emerged:

> What now by the lusts of men is the state of things? Say some there is no gospel at all—say others, if there be, you have nothing to do with it. . . .[4]

There was clearly distress in high quarters at the possibility of anarchy. Now that presbyterianism was ruled out, a new emphasis was placed upon indirect control by means of the universities. Oxford and Cambridge were the only channels by which the Independents could hope to influence the supply of ministers into the Church and ensure some kind of orthodoxy.

The conservative role which the universities were expected to play is revealed by the connection between them and the system of Triers and Ejectors, set up under the auspices of Owen and

---

[1] Farnell, op. cit.   [2] Madan, *Oxford Books*, vol. III, p. 36.
[3] Burrow, *Register*.
[4] W. H. Goold (ed.), *The Works of John Owen* (London, 1851), vol. VIII, p. 381. Owen urged the heads of Oxford colleges to support sound doctrine in the preface to his *Doctrine of Saint's Perseverance* (1854). *Works*, vol. XI, pp. 7–17.

Lambert after the failure of the Barebone Parliament. The list of Triers was headed by six heads of colleges at Oxford and Cambridge with John Owen as leader. The plan was conservative in the sense that it had its origins in proposals made in the 1640s under Presbyterian auspices.[1]

The linking up of the 'Triers' with the universities placed Oxford and Cambridge at the centre of the independent scheme for a guided orthodoxy. No more was to be heard of the sectaries' plans for decentralized colleges, since the two ancient universities filled so efficiently the role of centralizing and controlling higher studies. The only exception was the establishment, or attempted establishment, of a college at Durham. It seems not unlikely that this was to play the same role in the royalist north as Trinity College, Dublin, had in Elizabethan Ireland. It was to be at once a safety-valve for getting rid of enthusiastic nuisances and a means of evangelizing missionary areas.[2]

Lambert headed the committee which vetted this proposal, and two of the moving spirits, Dickenson and Lascelles had sat in the Barebone Parliament on the conservative side. This was no starry-eyed attempt to bring sweetness and light to the conservative north. On the contrary, the initiative seems to have come from the gentry and persons of quality worried at the spread of sectaries in those parts, and the success of George Fox. Fox himself saw the colleges as a deplorable instrument of orthodoxy in which knowledge of the liberal arts was to be the substitute for godliness.[3]

As he wrote in his journal in 1657:

And soe from thence wee came to Durham & there was a man come doune from London to sett upp a Colledge there to make ministers of Christ as they saide.

And soe I & some others went to ye man & reasoned with him & lett him see yt [was not ye way] to make ym Christs ministers by Hebrew greeke & latine & ye 7 arts which all was

---

[1] Lomas (ed.), *Carlyle's Letters and Speeches of Oliver Cromwell*, vol. II, pp. 324–5.
[2] Lomas, ibid., vol. II, pp. 186–7. There is no satisfactory account of the Durham College episode but see M. James, *Social Problems and Policy during the Puritan Revolution, 1140–60* (London, 1930), pp. 324–6.
[3] N. Penney (ed.), *The Journal of George Fox* (Cambridge, 1911), vol. I, p. 311.

but ye teachinges of ye naturall man: for ye many languages begann att Babell & ye greekes yt spoake ye naturall greeke ye preachinge of ye crosse of Christ was foolishnesse to ym & to ye Jews yt spoake naturall Hebrew Christ was a stumbleinge block to ym & as for ye romans yt had Ittalion & latine they persecuted ye Christians: & Pilate (one of ye Roman Magistrates) coulde sett Hebrew greek & latine atoppe of Christ when hee crucifyed him.

Fox restated here the intellectual position of the Elizabethan sectaries.

The shift to conservatism during the years after 1653 was accelerated by setting up 'Ejectors' on a country basis. Committees of fifteen to thirty members from each country were empowered to eject 'scandalous, ignorant and insufficient' ministers. This could be interpreted as a move against royalist clergy, but in the aftermath of the Barebone Parliament, it could also be used to remove the godly ignorant. The judges, after all, included conservative gentry like Sir Thomas Fairfax. It was small wonder that a sectary like John Goodwin should raise his voice against this system of social control. The rule of the saints was over, the lordship of the safe and secure had begun. The hysteria aroused in Parliament by the case of James Naylor shows how much social sensitivity was involved with what appears at first sight to be a purely religious affair.

Naylor had been a quarter-master in Lambert's regiment and, after leaving the New Model Army in 1651, he had been converted from independency by George Fox. He was imprisoned in 1656 on religious grounds, and on his release he entered Bristol, amid scenes of popular tumult which recalled Christ's entry into Jerusalem. Crucifixion, of a kind, duly followed. His case came before Parliament later in the year and after a debate which revealed fears that Naylor's views struck at the foundations of society it was resolved to make an example of him. It was ordered that he should be set in the pillory, whipped, his tongue to be bored with a hot iron and his forehead branded. The sentence was duly carried out.[1]

---

[1] C. H. Firth, *The Last Years of the Protectorate* (Oxford, 1909), pp. 84–101; see also J. T. Rutt (ed.), *Diary of Thomas Burton* (London, 1828), vol. I, pp. 24 ff.

4.

At the back of all this, lay the enigmatic figure of Oliver Cromwell. In religion Cromwell was torn between his desire for order and his sympathy for the sectaries. But socially speaking, he threw his weight on the conservative side. As he said of the Levellers in 1654:

> A nobleman, a gentleman, a yeoman; the distinction of these: that is a good interest of the nation and a great one. The natural magistracy of the nation, was it not trampled under foot, under despite and contempt by men of Levelling principle? I beseech you for the orders and ranks of men, did not that Levelling principle tend to the reducing all to an equality?[1]

Cromwell's social conservatism was here expressed eloquently. In itself, it is almost enough to explain why the universities retained their social position throughout the so-called English Revolution.

If the universities changed so little, this is enough to explain why evidence of intellectual and social change within the universities is hard to come by. The students' notebooks of the 1650s are indistinguishable from those of the 1640s. A notebook of Edward Turner, who was an undergraduate at either Wadham or Merton in the 1650s shows that he spent a great deal of time with Scheibler's *Metaphysics* as well as the similar works of Burgersdicius and Jachaeus.[2] At Christ Church, under John Owen, the notebooks of Benjamin Gostlette and Henry Parker show a clearly Aristotelian bent.[3] Robert South of Christ Church defended the proposition that the heavens influenced inferior beings.[4] At Exeter, which was as Puritan a college as one could hope for, John Hearne, who matriculated in 1653, used Scheibler's *Metaphysics* and referred to the neo-scholastics Fonseca and Suarez.[5] In his physics and astronomy, he was obviously Aristotelian. In 1655, Thomas Duncombe, a student at Corpus, discussed the motion of the sun in pre-Copernican terms as well as considering the scholastic concepts of act and potency, with specific references to Aristotle and Scheibler. This is a very interesting

---

[1] Cromwell in 1654. Lomas, *Letters and Speeches*, vol. II, p. 342.
[2] Bodleian MSS Rawlinson D.1452.   [3] Bodleian MSS Rawlinson D.233.
[4] Bodleian MSS Rawlinson D.258.   [5] B.M. Sloane, MS 1472.

notebook, which provides the actual dates on which Duncombe met his tutor, Master Ford.[1]

But perhaps most surprising of all is the notebook which belonged to Nicholas Floyd, an undergraduate of Wadham and later a fellow of the college.[2] The so-called 'Wadham group' of scientists, including Seth Ward and Christopher Wren, have taken the eye of intellectual historians, and the conclusion has been drawn, perhaps unconsciously, that the teaching at Wadham was more progressive under its Warden, John Wilkins, than elsewhere. But Floyd's notebooks show us that the presence of several great men in a college need not lead to any changes in the undergraduate curriculum. Floyd refers constantly to Aquinas, Fonseca and Suarez and he shows a thoroughly traditional reliance upon the old cosmology.

If we seek an explanation for the generally conservative tone of undergraduate teaching at Oxford in the 1650s, we may find it, I believe, in the influence of Thomas Barlow. Barlow, a former tutor of John Owen, became Bodley's librarian during the period of royalist control in 1642–6, and he survived the Presbyterian Visitors in 1648. In 1657 he was elected Provost of Queen's, Owen's old college. The kind of curriculum which Barlow envisaged may be seen in the guide 'A library for younger scholars' (see above p. 83) which, in its intellectual tone, pushes us back at once to the Oxford of the 1630s.[3]

In this guide, Barlow put forward the familiar notion that the liberal arts were the handmaid of divinity, but he takes a broader view of them than many of his Puritan fellows would have done. He included rhetoric and poetry, Homer, Virgil, Plautus and Martial, in the editions issued by Farnaby. In logic and ethics he took a broadly Aristotelian view. He did not recommend Ramus or any of his followers, and in metaphysics, he praised Suarez 'who is incomparably the fullest and acutest author that even writt of that subject'. Among the books he recommends for physics, we find Aristotle mentioned first, and various other scholastic authors, and then almost as an afterthought, he tells his reader 'you may add to these Gassendus, Descartes, Digby, White, Bacon's Natural History or Centuries of Experiments'.

[1] Bodleian MS Savile 89.   [2] Bodleian MSS Rawlinson D.254.
[3] Jordy and Fletcher, *Guide for Younger Schollers.*

Thus Bacon and Descartes appear, but only in the margin of a guide which is almost exclusively theologically orientated in the old style. Barlow went so far as to say that, in ethics, the best writers were Aquinas and his neo-scholastic commentators. Barlow was still breathing the air of scholasticism, not the new philosophy, and the books which he recommended were read by the students at Wadham as well as Christ Church.

We may look upon Barlow's treatise as part of the defence which the universities put up against the attacks which were made by the Levellers and the Sectaries. Barlow's companions in the firing-line included Edward Waterhouse, whose *Apology for Learning* appeared in 1653, George Kendall who also wrote an *Apology for Humane Learning* in 1653, and Edward Leigh whose *A Treatise of Religion and Learning* was published in 1656. It was their views which gained the day in high places and not the practical suggestions of Samuel Hartlib, William Walwyn and John Webster.

Barlow's outlook was echoed to some extent even by men more acquainted with intellectual novelty than he, notably John Wilkins, Warden of Wadham and Seth Ward of the same college, Professor of Geometry. Wilkins, who had been appointed under the Presbyterian Visitors in 1648, associated himself with Ward in defending the teaching of theology in the universities on the grounds of its utility and thus cut the ground from under the feet of the sectarian critics. Ward in *Vindiciae Academiarum* (1654) wrote:

> I am sure that the preparatory studies required to the profession of Physic or Civil Law are no more than for this theology nor is it less copious for its extent or of less importance and usefulness for its end than either of the other faculties.[1]

He also defended the study of logic on the ground that it was 'universally subservient to all truths'. He even argued in favour of the use of Aristotle:

> The chief reason as I conceive why Aristotle hath been universally received as Magister Legitimus in Schooles hath been; the universality of his Enquiries; the brevity and method of

[1] *Vindiciae Academiarum* (Oxford, 1654), p. 4.

them fitting them for institutions and not the truth or infalli-
bility of his works.[1]

In other words, Ward argued that the study of Aristotle was of
considerable educational value.

Though Seth Ward was a member of the group which met at
Oxford to discuss problems of natural philosophy, he did not
think that Baconianism was the answer to the study of perfect
natural philosophy and medicine. Even less was it suitable for
undergraduate teaching.

> Which of the Nobility or Gentry desire when they send their
> sons hither that they should be set to Chymistry or Agriculture
> or Mechanicks? Their removall is from hence commonly in
> two or three years, to the Inns of Court and the desire of their
> friends is not, that they be engaged in those experimentall
> things, but that their reason; and fancy, and carriage be im-
> proved by lighter institutions and exercises that they may be-
> come rationall and graceful speakers and be of an acceptable
> behaviour in their countries.[2]

These comments of Ward's are illuminating because they show
that he accepted, presumably along with Wilkins, a socially conservative view of the universities. Ward's radicalism was confined
to his reading of Descartes, mathematics and philosophy. In social
as well as in religious matters, his views were poles apart from
those of the sectaries.

There is more than a hint here that the influence of Baconian
ideas was less than it might have been, because of an association
with the sects and the lower social groups of seventeenth-century
England. Bacon himself had been aware of the difficulty of over-
coming gentlemanly prejudices against things 'mechanick', but
the events of the English Revolution had done nothing to diminish
upper-class distrust of their social inferiors. When the ideas of the
new philosophy began to influence the gentry, it was almost as if
there was a social criterion involved, with the views of Descartes
having a greater social cachet than those of Bacon.

In fact, the Wadham group of scientists, which has received a
good deal of attention from historians, was by and large a group

[1] Ibid., p. 39.   [2] Ibid., p. 50.

of gentlemen. Lawrence Rooke, one of its most prominent members, went to Eton and King's. Both he and Christopher Wren were fellow commoners, and two other members both married into the gentry. The medical men among the group took their stand with the socially acceptable College of Physicians, not the plebeian Apothecaries. Its most noble member was Robert Boyle, son of the Earl of Cork; the least noble was William Petty, who set himself up as an Irish landlord. In a word, the Wadham Group, like its successor, the Royal Society, was an intellectual club for the social *élite*.

The Wadham Group showed little of the religious radicalism with which historians have sought on occasion to connect it. The secretary was Gerard Langbaine, Provost of Queen's, who can in no sense be described as radical. He was a classical scholar cast in the Erasmian mould, who complained to Selden in 1653 about the way in which men of peaceable views were being displaced by religious zealots. He also wrote a history of both Oxford and Cambridge in 1650 as his contribution to their defence and spoke at a public doctoral disputation at Oxford in 1651 in defence of the thesis that good letters were necessary for the theologian. John Wilkins was associated with him, along with several others in the symbolic act of accepting a doctorate at a moment when academic learning was under violent attack.[1] It is doubtful whether any member of the group can be described as radical in religious matters, even John Owen. The Wadham Group, in fact, seems to have stood out against the enthusiasm of the sectaries and practical reforms in the curriculum, both derived from the same socially suspect 'mechanical' sources.

But social prejudice was not the only factor involved, nor perhaps the most important. There was also a sharp intellectual difference. The dominant scientific outlook among the Wadham Group was mechanistic, deriving from Galileo, Mersenne and Torricelli. The Torricellian experiment with a tube of mercury was performed several times at Oxford, with the object of demonstrating a vacuum. In contrast, the critics of the medical teaching in universities drew much of their inspiration from the sixteenth-century German alchemist, Paracelsus, whose ideas

[1] MS Smith 21; Bodleian, Quaestiones fol. θ659.

were an appealing amalgam of mysticism, medical insight and social criticism. He himself had worked among the mining communities of South Germany and he criticized the academic and upper-class tone of orthodox Galenic medicine with its doctrine of 'humours' and 'bleeding'. He looked to the three 'principles' of mercury, salt and sulphur for the basis of a new medicine. Among the apothecaries and the socially deprived groups of mid-seventeenth-century England, Paracelsan ideas made considerable headway. Thus in resisting the attacks of the sectaries the medical profession acted on intellectual as well as social grounds. Seth Ward for his part scoffed at Webster for accepting Paracelsan principles.

> How they should come to ravish the soul of M. Webster [he wrote] I cannot tell, unless it should be in contemplation of the benefits he hath received from them viz. of salt at dinner, of sulphur in the Mange, and of Mercury in salivation.[1]

[1] *Vindiciae Academiarum*, p. 36. For a fuller discussion of the various intellectual strands within the Scientific Revolution see H. Kearney, *Science and Change* (London 1970).

CHAPTER VIII

Scotland

1.

In Scotland since 1606 the conservative policy of the Stuarts made steady progress inside and outside the universities, but by 1637 the Episcopalians in Scotland had exposed themselves to the charge of taking their cue from England. Opposition which had been building up piecemeal was given a cause. The result was a fervour of popular feeling in the Lowlands, which led to the meeting of the first Melvillian General Assembly since 1606. Royal influence was minimal, the precedents of the government-dominated assemblies were countermanded, and the power and influence of the bishops was destroyed. By 1640 a revolution had taken place in which the universities were immediately involved.

The revolution was, more than is generally realized, a social one. Its leaders, Alexander Henderson, Samuel Rutherford and Robert Baillie, came from middling social groups. Henderson was the son of a tenant farmer, Baillie was the son of a Glasgow tradesman, Rutherford's brother was a schoolmaster. Their hostility was reserved for the socially conservative North-east, with its gentry and sub-gentry background, though on basic theology they had much in common with men like Patrick Forbes. They wished to do away with the system of hierarchy within the Church, in which social standing or influence at court could be all-important, and to substitute a more broadly based hierarchy of their own, in which the approval of the general assembly would be the decisive factor. They had a horror of sectaries, with all the social overtones which that implied, and they had no sympathy for a policy of toleration. Theirs was a middle-class movement, which was only joined by nobles like Argyll, when it had shown itself successful. But its aristocratic fringe was never happy in moments of crisis and when the movement split, as it did towards the end of the decade, it was upon social lines.

Dislike of England and the anglicization of the past three

decades was a powerful factor. Robert Baillie did not distinguish clearly between the three dangers of having 'our religion lost, our throats cutted, our poor country made an English province'. He referred to the English as 'our slippery neighbour' and this distrust of things English was a constant theme of his correspondence. He criticized Dr. Panter, Professor at St. Andrew's during the 1630s, for the reason that

> he had no sooner settled himself into his chair while he began to recommend the *English method of studie*, to begin with the Popish schoolmen and Fathers and to close with the Protestant neoterics, a most unhappy and dangerous order.[1]

The reaction against things English penetrated into the field of education as well as Church government. Neo-scholasticism in theology was objectionable because it was associated with the twin horrors of Episcopalianism and England. Thus, within the universities changes were made almost immediately, with the General Assembly taking the initiative in the field of university appointments. At Edinburgh, Alexander Henderson, moving spirit of the revolution, became the Rector of the university. At St. Andrews, Samuel Rutherford became the chief agent of the revolution, though the aged Robert Howie succeeded in maintaining a fictional authority as principal. Rutherford was a graduate of Edinburgh who had been 'exiled' to Aberdeen from his ministry in Galloway. At Aberdeen in 1636-7 he had disputed with the 'Aberdeen Doctors'.

At the other two universities, the situation was more complex. Aberdeen remained aloof from the covenanting movement until military pressure finally forced the Aberdeen Doctors to give way and to seek refuge in exile. But the whole area of the North-east remained unstable throughout the decade, and it was by no means clear at any particular moment whether the writ of the General Assembly was effective. Even in Glasgow, the General Assembly found it difficult to deal with Principal Strang, under whom the university maintained a precarious independence. The only two members of the Glasgow faculty on whom the Assembly could rely were the Professors of Theology, David Dickson, and (from 1642) Robert Baillie. In September, 1643 Baillie complained that

[1] Robert Baillie, *Letters and Journals* (Edinburgh, 1841-2), vol. I, p. 148.

Strang filled vacancies on the faculty and elsewhere with 'men who notoriously were not onlie at his own devotion . . . such as Vice-Chancellor and Dean of Facultie, but also otherwise minded in the public affairs than we did wish, such as the Marquesse of Hamilton . . .'. Baillie considered that three of the regents were Strang's creatures 'to be employed for anie thing he pleased'.[1] Strang, for his part, objected to the way in which Dickson and Baillie regarded themselves as ministers liable to be called by the Glasgow Presbytery to represent it at the General Assembly. Despite these difficulties, Strang survived until 1650, when the Presbyterians achieved a short-lived victory.

In this confused situation, it was not until the King surrendered in 1646 and negotiations began for a final settlement that outlines of Presbyterian educational policy became clear. Alexander Henderson died in 1646 and from then on the moving figure was Robert Baillie. Baillie's experience at Westminster Assembly had not made him any more sympathetic to the English ideal of university education and he looked to the continent for inspiration.

It is some indication of the changes which had taken place since Melville's day that Baillie should turn to Holland. The prestige of French Protestantism and of Ramism had declined. The Palatinate was occupied by Spanish troops and the Palatine library had been shipped off to the Vatican. Geneva, no longer led by Calvin or Beza, had lost its influence over the Calvinist community. Holland became the example for Calvinist intellectuals. But there were several Hollands, and the one with which Baillie made contact was the intellectually conservative landward province, represented by Gisbert Voetius and the newly-founded university of Utrecht.[2]

Voetius was a champion of the old philosophy in a country which had given shelter to Descartes and toleration for Cartesian ideas. To Voetius, as to Baillie, Cartesianism was synonomous with atheism and, Baillie would add, with ignorance. In such desperate circumstances, the attractions of Aristotelianism seemed greater than ever before. The old philosophy provided a picture of a universe in which purposive action was part of the law of nature. It was a cosmology which harmonized, or could

[1] Ibid.
[2] On Voetius and Utrecht, see Dibon, op. cit., especially chap. 5.

be made to harmonize in most important respects, with Biblical truth. The prospect of this being thrown over for the mechanical, infinite, purposeless universe of Descartes was appalling to contemplate and Baillie, like Voetius, proceeded to nail Aristotle to the Presbyterian mast.

Baillie's educational ideal may be seen in the proposed curriculum which was drawn up in 1648 by a committee set up by the General Assembly.[1] The most striking feature of the curriculum is the emphasis which it lays upon uniform teaching throughout the Scottish universities. In itself this was perhaps no more than a restatement of the ideal of Andrew Melville in the new circumstances of the 1640s. But it took on an added force from Baillie's obsession with sectarianism ('that democratic anarchy and independence of particular congregations') and with atheism (sc. Cartesianism), neither of which had been regarded as a serious menace in Melville's day. This obsession led Baillie to see virtues in Jesuit-style uniformity, a model which he hoped the university philosophers might follow in constructing an agreed textbook. From another point of view, Baillie's curriculum was also an attempt to bring Aberdeen under the intellectual control of the lowland universities. It was the answer of Glasgow and Edinburgh to the earlier domination of the Aberdeen Doctors.

Baillie's proposed arts course did not exclude the student from all contact with pagan literature, but such contact as there was, was kept to a minimum. The object was to learn enough Latin and Greek for the purposes of Biblical exegesis. The student read carefully-selected extracts from Homer, Isocrates and Hesiod, but the New Testament was the larger end. In Latin authors, the choice was even more confined. A notebook of William Sharp, student at St. Leonard's in 1643, shows that he read Buchanan, Terence, and an oration of Cicero, along with extracts from Sallust and a little classical history based on Justin's *Epitome*. Rhetorical illustrations were taken from the Bible. There was no hint of Ovid, Horace, or even Virgil. On the other hand defenders of the curriculum could argue that in his last two years the student acquired a thorough grounding in Aristotelian philosophy.

Baillie made some ritual gestures in the direction of Ramism in the curriculum, but, in the main, the philosophy teaching was

[1] Baillie, *Letters*, vol. II, p. 464.

nearer to English neo-scholasticism than his earlier strictures would have led one to expect. For example, he wrote to Voetius that the Scots were using the textbooks of Keckermann, Burgersdicius and Scheibler, all of which had been common at Oxford and Cambridge during the previous decades.[1] It seems fair to conclude that conservatives in all religious camps were being forced to adopt similar intellectual positions.

Baillie's educational policy was shortlived. Within three years, the Presbyterians were swept from power, and though Baillie himself kept his chair at Glasgow, he was never again to be in a position where he could decisively influence events. Yet his curriculum is of some interest since this same concept of uniformity was to reappear in the 1690s when the General Assembly was once more a force in the land.

There was a certain paradox in the contrast between the social radicalism of the Presbyterians in the 1640s, and their intellectual conservatism. The same people who were backing Baillie's reorganization of the universities passed the Act of Classes in 1649, which in effect was a social revolution in the name of religion. This Act excluded from political power all those who had favoured agreements with Charles I, in effect the whole of the traditional ruling *élite*. It was clearly possible, if not very logical, to overthrow hierarchy in the political world while holding on to it in the intellectual world at the same time. The problems which this might have posed were postponed in 1651 with the coming of the New Model Army.[2]

2.

In a recent article, Professor Trevor-Roper has seen the Cromwellian period in Scotland as an anticipation of the Golden Age of the eighteenth century, in which the Scottish universities were granted a temporary respite from the dictatorial, priestly and theocratic rule of the Calvinists.[3] Their saviour, if only for a short time, was Cromwell, who brought the values of the English

[1] Ibid., vol. II, p. 115. Baillie described Descartes as an 'ignorant atheist', vol. III, p. 31.

[2] Ibid., vol. III, p. 269.

[3] 'Scotland and the Puritan Revolution' in *Religion, Reformation and Social Change* (London, 1967).

country gentry into Scottish intellectual life. He gave the universities money to build, he chose 'moderate' men as principals, he encouraged the study of medicine and of law within the university structure. He became the patron of men like Patrick Gillespie, Robert Leighton and John Row. A chair of mathematics was set up at Glasgow. For a decade the Scottish universities were able to thrive.

This is an interesting thesis argued with great skill and force. There is little doubt that previous accounts of the Scottish universities during this period have accepted too readily the hostile judgments expressed by Baillie in his letters. On the other hand, we may doubt whether the contrast between Cromwell's England and Baillies's Scotland was quite such an affair of darkness and light as is suggested: it attributes a consistency and harmony of ideas to Cromwell's policy in Scotland which it did not possess in England and assumes too readily that 'anglicization' and 'civilization' are readily interchangeable terms. One of the chief objects of this criticism is Scottish clericalism. Yet one may argue that in seventeenth-century Scotland the minister played the same role as the priest did in nineteenth-century Ireland, as the spokesman for a rural population which had been dominated for centuries by great landlords.[1] To assume that lay ideas were superior to clerical ideas[2] is, in terms of the seventeenth century, perhaps to draw too sharp a contrast.

The Cromwellian Golden Age, it is argued, was the short period when the Protector had most freedom of action, from December, 1653 to September 1654 and the months of the Major-Generals, from the summer of 1655 to the end of 1656. It appears that Cromwell chose as his advisers a small group of 'enlightened' Scots, Sir William Lockhart, Sir James Hope, Sir John Swinton and Alexander Jaffray, who agreed with his policy of reducing the 'oppressive patronage' of the great lords and the 'intolerant kirk'. Positive 'reforms' were to include decentralization and simplification of law and the training of 'liberal' ministers. A favourable view is taken of the implications of these changes, but this interpretation need not be accepted without

[1] Broghill described the ministers as having 'a papal power' over the people. Thurloe, *State Papers*, vol. IV, p. 41.
[2] Ibid.

qualification. To press ahead with legal and ecclesiastical changes, as Cromwell did, might well imply an attempt to create a gentry-dominated society in Church and state. To introduce the English Justice of the Peace and decentralized law meant handing over local power to the gentry, and to set up a clergy acceptable to the 'laity' meant the establishment of a gentry-dominated Church. From this point of view, Baillie's description of Cromwell's Scottish advisers as 'our three complying gentlemen' is illuminating.

One of the major points in Cromwell's Scottish reform policy, on this view, was his reorganization of the universities. The key Scottish instruments here were Patrick Gillespie in Glasgow, John Menzies in Aberdeen and Robert Leighton in Edinburgh, whom Trevor Roper sees as apostles of toleration and intellectual change. In Scotland, as in England, however, the universities were linked with the system of Triers and Ejectors and only men who received their approval received 'a kirk and a stipend'. The Scottish universities received new endowments from the Protector, symbolized by the building of Cromwell's Tower at Aberdeen, but the price was high, in the sense that the colleges were expected to become seminaries for a complaisant clergy. Even Cromwell's encouragement of medical studies cannot be seen as intellectual adventure, innocent of social implications.

If we look for evidence of intellectual change within the Scottish universities during the Cromwellian period, there is, unfortunately, little evidence in the way of student notebooks and regents' dictates, but what does remain does not suggest any radical improvement or innovation in the curriculum. At Glasgow, for example, James Veitch was appointed as Regent by Patrick Gillespie against the wishes of Robert Baillie. His theological views may have been open to criticism by Baillie, but his notebooks show his teaching to have been on traditional Aristotelian lines.[1] In 1653-4, he taught Aristotelian logic, ethics, metaphysics and physics. In June, 1654, he began by stating that metaphysics was the most eminent and perfect of all the sciences. In his commentary on Aristotle's *Physics* he discussed questions of 'materia prima' and substantial form. There is no sign here of Baconian ideas, and we may take it that the same was true of St. Andrew's,

[1] Glasgow University MSS, Murray Collection.

which held out against change longer than the other universities.

There are two pieces of evidence which suggest some measure of intellectual change, but neither of them fits neatly into a pattern. The first of them is a 120-page thesis written by Andrew Cant, son of the Presbyterian leader, at Marischal College, Aberdeen.[1] This is full of references to neo-scholastics like Scheibler, Suarez and Arriaga, but there is also a good deal of material relating to the science of the day. Cant discussed the views of Harvey and Descartes on the circulation of the blood, though he regarded the septum theory as 'more probable'. He also discussed Descartes's *Dioptric*. On theological points, it is noticeable that he referred to English divines like Downham, Hooker and Ames. Cant came down heavily on the side of Galen against the 'fanatical delirium', as he saw it, of Paracelsus and his contemporary disciple Van Helmont. He was undoubtedly acquainted with the 'moderns' and he mentioned Galileo, Harvey, Descartes and Heerebord, among others, but his sympathies and his conclusions were the scholastics and his intellectual approach was the traditional one of balancing one authority against another. Cant devoted a good deal of space to 'scientific' questions, such as the existence of the vacuum, but on this, as on so much else, he came down on the side of Aristotle. He adhered to the Aristotelian doctrine of substantial forms and the four qualities of hot, cold, moist and dry. The general framework of the thesis was theological, beginning, as it did, with God and the angels, and ending with free will and predestination. Like his English counterparts, Cant was very much exercised by the threat of the anabaptists and it was presumably with them in mind that he quoted, approvingly, the arguments of Aquinas and Bellarmine to the effect that laws bound in conscience. There was no hint of Baconianism in this treatise.

Shortly before his father's death Cant became involved in a controversy with Principal Menzies about which Robert Baillie relates that Menzies was on the conservative side against the 'Arminian', Cant. This suggests that the Cromwellian nominee, Menzies, was defending traditional doctrine against the radical young man.

Another notebook belonged to a student who studied at Edinburgh under George Sinclair, one of Patrick Gillespie's ap-

[1] Cant, *Theses Philosophicae* (Aberdeen, 1658).

pointments, and a man criticized by Robert Baillie.[1] Sinclair gave his notes under the heading of 'disputations on the eight books of Aristotle's physics', but his outlook was by no means that of a simple Aristotelian. He referred, for example, to 'doctissimus Galileo', and the problem of acceleration. The only cosmology which he discussed was that of Tycho, in marked contrast to almost every other regent. With George Sinclair, mathematics was coming into its own, and it is certainly significant that this should occur during the Cromwellian régime.

On the other hand, if we press this further and try to see it as evidence for the introduction of Baconian subjects into Scottish universities, we run into difficulties. Sinclair published a brief introduction to arithmetic, astronomy, geography and geometry in 1661.[2] In the astronomy section, which is the largest part of the book, he relied heavily upon the Jesuit Christopher Clavius's commentary on John of Holywood and he actually used some of Clavius's classical quotations in order to illustrate a point. To describe this procedure as Baconian is obviously reading too much into the evidence. The most that one can say is that Sinclair was more responsive than other regents to the importance of mathematics. He carried on experiments of his own which, though not original, show that he had heard of contemporary interest in these matters on the continent. His views seemed unoriginal to the Royal Society and later absurd to James Gregory.

Another piece of evidence for this period is the notes for lectures which George Meldrum gave at Aberdeen in the second half of the 1650s, but they cast no Baconian light on our problem.[3] Meldrum, who was Regent during the Cromwellian period (1655–9), showed no trace of Bacon's influence. If he had a master it was William Strang whom he mentioned on more than one occasion, and this would take us no further than the Aristotelianism of Glasgow. Meldrum mentioned Descartes only to dismiss him, on the grounds that the principle of methodic doubt was too hazardous a starting-point for philosophy. He was also more sympathetic to the views of Tycho and Copernicus than Ptolemy, though he thought that the stars influenced human beings and

---

[1] National Library of Scotland MSS Acc. 3020 (2), Uncatalogued.
[2] Sinclair, *Tyrocinia Mathematica* (Glasgow, 1661).
[3] Meldrum, *Theses Philosophicae* (Aberdeen, 1659).

that hence 'astronomy was necessary to doctors'. He dealt with magnetism without referring to Gilbert, preferring instead Cardanus, Scaliger and Keckermann. It is true that Meldrum attacked many of the philosophical views of the Jesuits in the course of his lectures, but this was on theological grounds. He tended to lump them with the Remonstrants and Arminians, but there is no doubt that he spoke the same language as they did. Meldrum's lectures show clearly that in Cromwellian Aberdeen the old philosophy was still very much in the ascendant.

In attempting a general conclusion about the nature of the Cromwellian régime in Scotland there is no need to take absolute sides for or against Baillie, Gillespie or Broghill. But even if it be allowed that Cromwellian reforms were enlightened, the fact remains that these plans were not carried out in an atmosphere of rational calm. Scotland had been as near anarchy during these years as it had ever been. The English army had brought control, but hardly peace. Against the background of social turbulence, it seems unreasonable to expect a radical Cromwellian policy in Scotland and a conservative pattern in England. The reasonable assumption must surely be that universities were expected to carry out the same conservative social function in Scotland as they were in England. To this extent, a division of the Scots into 'lay' and 'clerically-minded' tends to cloud the issue. These are not social but emotive terms.

Much depends on the significance attributed to Cromwell's representative, Roger Boyle, Lord Broghill. We are invited to see him as a man who encouraged lay 'Baconian' ideas. In social terms, however, we must surely see him as an Anglo-Irish landlord, a second-generation aristocrat of conservative views. In the light of this, we are not surprised to find Broghill turning for support to the Presbyterians and the conservative North-east. This was precisely the pattern which followed in England during the 1650s, when the threat of radicalism drove the conservatives together. Common fears of anarchy made bedfellows of Patrick Gillespie and Robert Baillie. Broghill's later decisions bear this interpretation out. He resigned his post in Scotland when he smelt the first whiff of the Restoration and he was back in Ireland at the crucial moment to ensure the safe return of monarchy.

The picture in Scotland is by no means clear-cut. The history

of Scotland during these years has still to be written—Trevor-
Roper's article was the first piece of serious analysis ever to be
made. But, so far as the universities were concerned, the trend
seems similar to that in England. The conservative North-east
was willing to throw in its lot with Cromwell because he promised
security. Some ex-royalist gentry were willing to accept Cromwell,
especially when his government began to swing to the right after
1655. Finally, even the Resolutioners (i.e. those among the
covenanting party who, in 1650 supported resolutions to compromise with Charles II against Cromwell) began to come round,
when it became clear that Cromwell was the enemy of religious
radicalism, not its instrument. Conservatism won the day in Scotland as in England. And the Scottish universities played the same
role as their English counterparts.

3.

Ireland

The history of Trinity College, Dublin, during the Cromwellian
period is enveloped in obscurity and seems likely to remain so.
In Ireland, the main pre-occupation of the English government
was to carry through successfully the wholesale transfer of land
from Catholic landlords to those who had lent money for the conquest of Ireland and to soldiers willing to accept land in lieu of
payment. But the letters of Henry Cromwell, Oliver's son, who
was in Ireland from 1653 (as Deputy from 1665) and reported
regularly back to Thurloe, show him to have been very concerned
about the social threat within the army from anabaptists and
Quakers. Of the Quakers he wrote to Thurloe, 'I think their
principles and practices are not very consistent to civil government, much less with the discipline of an army'. Henry Cromwell
himself maintained close touch with 'the good ministers' of Dublin, so much so that he was accused of being 'priest ridden' by the
anabaptists. The role of Trinity College, under its safe Provost,
Samuel Winter, seemed to be all the more important as a means of
social insurance against dangerous novelties.[1]

[1] Thurloe, *State Papers*, vol. IV, pp. 327, 348, 508, 672. Winter defended infant
baptism and criticized the anabaptists. See *The summe of diverse sermons preached in*

The same may also be said of the decision to introduce medical studies into the college for the first time.[1] The moving spirit here was John Stearne, a scholar and Fellow of the college in the 1640s, and, later, a student of medicine at Cambridge. Stearne also may have been associated with Seth Ward's group in Oxford, and with William Petty in Ireland. Stearne's decision to establish medicine on a formal basis took place in 1654, which places it as part of the conservative reaction after the Barebone Parliament. Henry Cromwell's arrival in Ireland as Lord Deputy fits into the same picture. The final point to be mentioned is that Stearne's medical faculty was transformed after the Restoration into the Royal College of Physicians of Ireland, a restrictive body on English lines. There was thus some social continuity in Ireland after 1660, the clue to understanding which depends on seeing clearly the social function of Trinity College, and the medical faculty associated with it. It was symbolized by the fact that Stearne became first President of the Royal College of Physicians. Against the confused social background of the period of the Cromwellian confiscation and the rise of the sectaries, the College, we may suggest, was the rallying point of the learned professions against the dubious avocations of lay preacher and apothecary.

If we attempt a general conclusion about the social role of the universities in all three kingdoms during the English Revolution, it must surely be that they reflected the conservative posture of the gentry against the dangers of social and religious radicalism. Latin remained as the medium of instruction, a phenomenon which we may take as a useful social index. During two decades when the universities were attacked as citadels of privilege and ungodliness, their social value to the *élite* became even more clear. University education, like the law of property, a learned clergy and a restricted franchise was seen to be one of the pillars upon which the 'Gentry Society' rested.

Dublin before the Lord Deputie Fleetwood and the Commissioners of Parliament for the Affairs of Ireland wherein the doctrine of infant baptism is asserted and the main objections of Mr. Tombs, Mr. Fisher, Mr. Blackwood and others answered, Dublin, 1656.

[1] J. P. Mahaffy, *An Epoch in Irish History* (London, 1903), p. 320. On Stearne, see *D.N.B.* and St. J. D. Seymour, *The Puritans in Ireland 1647–61* (Oxford, 1921).

CHAPTER IX

Social and Intellectual Trends after the Restoration

I.

Twenty years of conflict and turmoil between 1640 and 1660 inevitably left their mark upon English society, and though social historians have yet to work out the precise impact of these events, some of their effects seem clear enough. The financial burden of these years upon the Royalist gentry led to the decline of a section of English landed society. The number of middling-sized estates dwindled, a change from which the larger landed proprietors benefited. The great landlords were sufficiently small in number to profit from royal grace and favour, whereas the vast majority of gentry could never hope to catch His Majesty's eye, and painlessly recoup their fortunes.[1]

Comparison of the rudimentary statistics provided by Thomas Wilson in 1601 and Gregory King in 1688 seems to bear out the conclusion that the prosperity of the gentry declined in the second half of the seventeenth century.[2] The 16,000 gentry of 1601 had a larger total income than the 17,000 gentry of 1688. Allowing for the fall in the value of money, this was a more substantial change than appears at first sight. The occupation of landed gentleman became financially more difficult to follow, and John Locke, for example, found it more profitable to turn to medicine than to run his small estate in Somerset, as his father had done before him.

In contrast, the great landlords represented by the peerage and

---

[1] Restoration England is still relatively unexplored by social historians. On the landowners, see H. J. Habakkuk, 'English Landownership 1680–1740' in *Econ. Hist. Rev.* (1940). On trade, see especially D. C. Coleman's biography of Sir John Banks (Oxford, 1963). The economic background is well described by C. Wilson, *England's Apprenticeship* (London, 1965).

[2] 'Wilson's State of England', ed. F. J. Fisher, *Camden Miscellany* (London, 1936), vol. XV; King's statistics are readily available in A. Browning (ed.), *English Historical Documents 1660–1714* (London, 1953), pp. 515–17.

the upper gentry doubled their share of landed wealth. The tendency was for control of the land to be concentrated in few hands. England, by 1700, was moving towards an aristocratic polity which was to have its hey-day in the eighteenth century. By then, Whig government had come to mean rule by a handful of peers, while Tory opposition was a spasmodic affair carried on by economically hard-hit gentry. All this had its roots in the late seventeenth century when the expansion of the greater landlords like the Finches took place at the expense of the lesser gentry.

There was also another side to all this. Trade and the trading interest had been important since the days of Edward III, but it was only from the seventeenth century that the commercial interest began to rival the landed interest in wealth and influence. By the reign of Charles I, the fifty-odd great merchants of London could command more financial power than the House of Lords. For these the Civil War proved to be a blessing in disguise. As in the Great War of 1914–18, the gentlemen died happily in battle, while in London hard-faced businessmen did well out of the needs of the army. Sir Josiah Child and Sir John Banks were not alone in taking advantage of this stroke of good fortune. The Navigation Act and the Anglo-Dutch War may serve as evidence of the political influence of the merchants, while the antagonism aroused among the merchants by Cromwell's anti-Spanish policy helps to explain the collapse of the régime after his death.

After the Restoration, the significance of the merchant community continued to grow. The proportion of trading peers in the aristocracy rose, mercantile wealth was the basis of many a noble pile, and the City, based on the ever-expanding re-export trade, became the centre of a number of new professions, of which banking was the most important. In some ways indeed this was the Gilded Age of English history with Charles II playing the role of Edward VII.

These social changes must be borne in mind if we are to explain the central phenomenon of the educational scene during this period, namely the catastrophic decline in the number of undergraduates at Oxford and Cambridge, a falling curve which continued until well into the second half of the eighteenth century. The universities now began to count for much less as a social factor than they had ever done. It is true that they did not dwindle into the total obscurity to which some historians have consigned them, but nevertheless their social role clearly changed. At a time when the population remained static or increased, the total numbers of undergraduates dropped. There was an absolute and a relative decline from the peak which had been reached in the years before the Civil War.

The reason must be sought in part in the effects of the Clarendon Code, which effectively cut off Dissenters from normal entry into the clerical and teaching professions. A high proportion of the Presbyterians and the Independents, though not the Baptists, had accepted the necessity of a university qualification; from 1662 this source of potential students dried up. Some colleges at Oxford and Cambridge were more affected than others. Exeter, for example, which had possessed a strong Puritan tradition, declined from being third largest college into one of the smallest. The few remaining halls, such as Hart Hall, New Inn Hall and Gloucester Hall, also began to feel the pinch for the same reasons. At Wadham from 1660 to the Hanoverian period, numbers entering the college steadily declined. (1661–70, *313*; 1691–1700, *241*; 1710–19, *175*.) At Cambridge, the numbers at St. John's College remained fairly steady, but those of other colleges declined.[1]

The two elements in English society—the clergy and the gentry —for whom university education was intended, declined in both numbers and importance during this period. The Church had undoubtedly suffered materially as a consequence of the Civil War, and the losses were not made up in succeeding years. By 1700 many clergymen were unable to make ends meet and while the establishment of Queen Anne's bounty removed some clerical distress, many clergymen together with their families were forced to wait for reward until the next world. As a consequence the status and the appeal of the clerical profession seem to have dropped. Eachard noted this but so also did other contemporary observers.[2] At the higher ecclesiastical level, there were still fat livings and well-endowed bishoprics, but of the 11,000 livings in the Church of England the majority were badly off. 'It is not un-

---

[1] R. B. Gardiner, *The Registers of Wadham College, Oxford, 1613–1719* (London, 1889); J. A. Venn, *Oxford and Cambridge Matriculations* (Cambridge, 1908).
[2] J. Eachard, *The Grounds and Occasions of the Contempt of the Clergy* (1670), reprinted in E. Arber, *An English Garner*, vol. VII (1883).

common' one clergyman noted plaintively, 'for a person of considerable birth, and extraordinary merit in all respects to be trampled on and abused, together with his wife and children, by illiterate, purse-proud peasants, purely because he is poor and a clergyman'.[1]

If this picture is correct, the universities could hardly fail to be affected. The number of clerical graduates dropped, as did the number of those seeking a clerical career. Whereas in 1640 too many would-be parsons were chasing too few livings, by 1700 pluralism was almost of necessity the order of the day. Moreover, in time of commercial expansion, the safe career offered by teaching or the Church lost much of its attraction. A pittance looked smaller amid plenty than it did when times were hard. In contrast, Ireland and Scotland were poor countries, in which a clerical living was literally the best living to be had. This was no longer true of Restoration England.

But equally important was the decline in the numbers of gentlemen and would-be gentlemen. Save in a political career, the social distinctions and privileges attached to gentility seemed less important in a more commercial age. The rise of commerce brought banking into a central position. Medicine, which had been low in the social scale in the first half of the seventeenth century began to rise rapidly. Insurance became prominent. The great trading companies, especially the East India Company, offered a safe and profitable career to young men whose fathers were able to pay the handsome apprenticeship fee. The army and navy from the 1690s offered possibilities. The lawyers continued to thrive. Only the clergy and gentry found themselves in a falling market.

Changes of this kind inevitably affected the fortunes of the universities. Medicine, like law, was a profession which thrived upon the needs and ills of the population of London. The capital offered the attraction of a large community, a well-to-do and expanding middle class and very soon a number of large hospitals. All Oxford and Cambridge could offer in return was a stable quota of hypochondriac dons.

The expansion of the medical profession took place outside the frontiers imposed by the Royal College of Physicians.[2] The

[1] Quoted in G. Best, *Temporal Pillars* (Cambridge, 1964), p. 14.
[2] P. M. Rattansi, 'The Helmontian-Galenist Controversy in Restoration England',

academic physicians succeeded in maintaining their monopoly in physic, but the bulk of medical practice soon came to be carried out by the apothecary and the surgeon. In 1745 there were only 52 fellows, 3 candidates and 23 licentiates in the Royal College of Physicians, which was almost too successful in restricting numbers. The accepted method of entry for the career of surgeon or apothecary was by apprenticeship, with the fees for the former trebling those for the latter. The universities, never strong in medical studies, did not catch the tide which could have led to a growth in the medical faculty.

Part of the reason for this lay in the unsuitable character of the university arts curriculum as a preparatory course for medicine. As we have seen, in the sixteenth century the faculty of theology called the tune in arts in both Oxford and Cambridge. Classical and philosophical studies held their place in Oxford as a propaedeutic towards divinity, even though only a minority eventually went forward to the full theological course. In the sixteenth century, it could be argued that this arts course was equally well adapted for a course in medicine. So long as the ancients were considered to be masters in medicine as in everything else, Latin and Greek were essential qualifications for serious medical studies. Astronomy was also understandably important when the stars were considered to influence the balance of humours within the individual. Francis Glisson, the seventeenth-century physician who has his assured place in the history of medicine, also wrote on metaphysics.

In the mid-seventeenth century, however, medicine became more Baconian in character. General principles seemed to be less important than close empirical observation. The hospital replaced the tutor's study as the most profitable place for a medical student to spend his time.

What was true of medicine was equally true of the other new professions. The normal road of entry was through apprenticeship of some kind, not through a formal course at the universities. Over the social scene generally, these new professions grew in importance, as English society changed into first a commercial, then an industrial society.

Ambix (1964), pp. 1–23; E. Hughes, 'Rise of the Professions', *Durham University Journal*, vol. I.

Yet so far as the universities were concerned, signs of intellectual change, one way or the other, are again difficult to come by. At Oxford, the Wadham Group dispersed. The Cromwellian heads of colleges were replaced by more acceptable nominees, and many of the fellows who had been installed after 1648 were ejected. But at the teaching level there was a remarkable degree of continuity between the 1650s and the 1660s. John Locke, product of Cromwellian Christ Church, remained after 1660 to teach under Dr. Fell. Narcissus Marsh, later Archbishop of Dublin, combined the benefits of life under Chancellor Cromwell and his successor, the Earl of Ormonde. Robert South and Thomas Barlow did the same, and so also did lesser lights such as Thomas Duncombe of Corpus, Nicholas Floyd of Wadham and John Hearne of Exeter. There was no doubt a large exodus, but so far as many college tutors were concerned, the Vicar of Bray rather than the Royal Martyr remained the pattern to be followed.

The dominant influence upon the curriculum remained that of Thomas Barlow, whose *Directions for Younger Schollers*, however uninspired, provided an acceptable blend of traditional framework with detailed recommendation of more or less up-to-date reading. It seems likely that John Locke, during his years as a tutor at Christ Church followed Barlow when advising his pupils what books to buy. The accounts of his pupils in 1661–2 show that at least half of the thirty-eight books they bought overlap with titles recommended by Barlow.[1] These included neo-scholastic works such as Scheibler, Zabarella and Magirus, and editions of the classics and the Early Fathers. A student at St. John's in or about 1675, John Abbott, refers specifically to using Barlow as a guide for his own reading.[2]

The combination of scholastic philosophy (logic, ethics, physics and metaphysics) and classical studies (oratory, poetry, history, grammar) outlined by Barlow, seems to have remained the pattern for all Oxford. At Christ Church, William Coker, at one time a pupil of John Locke, wrote classical proses which in his first year took the form of letters to the college fellows, and later, poems on philosophical subjects which he was presumably studying in a more technical form at the same time. Thus he wrote Latin poems

[1] Bodleian Locke MS f. 11.
[2] Bodleian MSS Rawlinson D.954 f. 49v.

on the themes 'An coelum sit corruptible? Neg', and 'An detur Vacuum? Neg'.[1] In 1658 Robert South had written similar kinds of poetry on such themes as 'An anima confletur ex atomis' and 'An coeli moveantur ab intelligentiis?'[2] This similarity of theme indicates direct continuity with the Commonwealth period.

Thomas Croft at New College was considering 'An detur vacuum' in the light of Scheibler's *Metaphysics* at the same time that Coker was writing his Latin verses.[3] At Wadham in 1677, Humphrey Hody took notes on logic and metaphysics, but we may presume from his later appointment as Regius Professor of Greek that his classical studies were not neglected.[4] Hody studied metaphysics on traditional lines, with references among others to Aristotle, Scotus and Smiglecius.

Other colleges in the 1660s and 1670s gave a similar impression. At St. Edmund Hall in the 1670s, Daniel Oughton took notes from Burgersdicius's *Ethics* and Eustachius's *Ethics*.[5] Thomas Tully, the most prominent teaching fellow in the college and yet another link with the Commonwealth, provided a college text-book in logic and ethics, which ran on accepted lines.[6] At Queen's, in 1675, Nehemiah Rogers studied logic, ethics and physics on traditional principles while at the same time writing Latin proses.[7] A contemporary of his, Henry Fleming, followed a similar pattern of studies.[8]

It seems likely that the attacks upon liberal studies during the Commonwealth had led to a reaction against change, at least at Oxford. The combination of classical and philosophical studies such as had existed in the 1630s survived into the 1670s almost unchanged. In the person of Thomas Barlow, Oxford resisted the pressure towards more 'modern' or more useful studies. Barlow's

---

[1] Bodleian MSS Rawlinson D.286.   [2] Bodleian MSS Rawlinson D.258
[3] B.M. Sloane MS 3779. The vacuum was a topic of immense interest in the mid-seventeenth century. Aristotle, in reply to the atomists, had denied the logical possibility of a vacuum. But the Torricellian experiment performed in Italy, France and England during the years 1640–70 raised the problem in acute form. The choice seemed to lie between atomism with its Lucretian implications of a universe governed by chance and the teleological outlook of the Aristotelians, with the vacuum as the touchstone between them.
[4] Bodleian Add. MSS A.65.   [5] Worcester College MS 4.17.
[6] Ibid.   [7] B.M. Harleian MS 5043.
[8] J. R. McGrath, *The Flemings at Oxford* (Oxford, 1904), vol. I, pp. 250, 262, 267, 289, 295, 304, 321.

standard of utility was that understood by a conservative divine nurtured in the college of Crackanthorp during the 1630s, but he was not alone in his devotion to traditional modes of thought. Dr. Fell at Christ Church was equally so. William Wake, who studied under Fell in the 1670s spoke later of Fell's enthusiastic support for the old philosophy.[1]

But Barlow was as much a symptom as a cause. His intellectual conservatism may be said to reflect the social anxieties of a gentry which was in decline. In standing by hallowed intellectual landmarks, Barlow, like Fell and many others, was the academic equivalent of those gentry who turned under Charles II to strong monarchy as a guarantee of traditional values in a changing world. This mood of social anxiety may be seen in the relentless attitudes of the Clarendon Code. It was expressed also by the author of *The Gentleman's Calling* (1660) when he wrote before the Restoration:

> Alas, Gentlemen, are not your estates wasted, your privileges violated, your splendours eclipsed, your persons restrained, your Families broken and shattered, your Dynasties trampled upon by the meanest of the vulgar, and finally yourselves quite transposed in your station, now made the Tail who were once the Head.

Twenty years later Dryden put this mood of social disgust into *Religio Laici* (1682) when he wrote about the sects:

> Study and Pains were now no more their Care
> Texts were explained by Fasting, and by Prayer:
> This was the Fruit the private Spirit brought
> Occasioned by great Zeal and little Thought.
> While Crouds unlearn'd with rude Devotion warm
> About the Sacred Viands buz and swarm. . . .[2]

These Tory attitudes came to include hostility towards the rising monied interest, which grew in political power and influence during the Restoration period.

Perhaps the most striking example of Oxford Toryism was seen in July 1683, when Convocation condemned 'certain pernicious

[1] N. Sykes, *William Wake* (Cambridge, 1957), vol. I, p. 10.
[2] J. Kinsley (ed.), *The Poems and Fables of John Dryden* (London, 1962), p. 292.

books'. Among the unhappy authors were Buchanan, Milton, Goodwin, Baxter, Owen and, in strange conjunction, Hobbes and Bellarmine, all condemned for their common belief that civil authority derived from the people. The loyal university forbade its members to read these books, which it ordered 'to be publicly burnt, by the hand of our marshal, in our school', on the grounds that they were liable

> to deprive good manners, corrupt the minds of unwary men, stir up seditions and tumults, overthrow states and kingdoms, and lead to rebellion, murder of princes, and atheism itself.

This passage alone tells a good deal of how the Oxford dons saw the function of their university.[1]

During the decades after the Restoration, the universities became the educational organs of a declining gentry and a declining Church. In these circumstances, academic conservatism seemed to be a test of loyalty to a way of life which was under attack. Barlow rejected the challenge of the new philosophy with the hysterical accusation that it was a Jesuitical attempt to undermine the Protestant cause. Scholasticism, which modern commentators identify with the counter-Reformation, was for Barlow, the editor of Scheibler's *Metaphysics*, a bulwark of Protestant soundness. The Aristotelian doctrine of matter and form was a sure defence against the atomism and Epicureanism which seemed to be infecting the new generation.

'I am troubled', Barlow wrote in 1674 in answer to Sir William Petty's lecture to the Royal Society, 'to see the scepticism (to say no worse) which now securely reigns in our miserable nation, while some dare profess and publish irrational and wild notions in philosophy and divinity too'. In a second letter, he pointed out that the Jesuits kept rigidly to the old philosophy in their own colleges:

> For they well know, that all their Schoolmen, Casuists and Controversy writers have so mix't Aristotle's philosophy with their Divinity that he who hath not a comprehension of Aristotle's Principles and the use of them in all Scholastick Disputes and Controversies of Religion will never be able rationally to defend

[1] Kenyon, *Stuart Constitution*, pp. 472–4.

or confute any controverted position in the Roman or Reformed Religion.

He regarded the uncertainties of the new philosophy, particularly the threat of atomism, as 'novel whimsies' by adopting which the Anglican Church would neglect to its cost the severer studies of the old philosophy and scholastical divinity. Without the older weapons, Barlow argued, the Church would be defenceless against attack.[1]

The same phenomenon was to be seen at Cambridge, where the Cambridge Platonists came under attack for selling the pass. Ralph Widdrington, a Fellow of Christ's since the 1640s, and Public Orator in the university under the commonwealth, attacked the college for being a nest of heretics. Henry More reported that 'they' (Widdrington and company)

'push hard at the Lattitude men as they call them, some in their pulpits call them sons of Belial, others make the Devil a Latitudinarian, which things are as pleasing to me as the raillery of a jaik pudding at the end of a dancing rope.'

Joseph Beaumont, Master of Peterhouse, was another outspoken critic of the Cambridge Platonists.[2]

Thus, in both universities the general trend was against change. Nevertheless, there were pockets of opinion which attempted to come to terms with the new philosophy. In Oxford, the foundation of the Oxford Philosophical Society in 1683 brought together a small number of fellows to perform experiments and discuss papers given in the Royal Society.[3]

At Cambridge during the period 1660–80, thanks to the influence of the Cambridge Platonists, Cartesianism made limited headway into the undergraduate curriculum, though without entirely displacing the old philosophy. Isaac Newton's notebooks, dated about 1661, show him to have studied Aristotle's *Organon* and *Ethics*, the commentary of Eustachius, and the natural philosophy, on scholastic lines, of Magirus.[4] But he also went on to consider the Cartesian proofs for the existence of God and, in

[1] Barlow's *Remains* (London, 1693), pp. 153–5.
[2] M. Nicolson, 'Christ's College and the Latitude-men' in *Modern Philology*, vol. XXVII, pp. 51–2 (1929–30).
[3] R. T. Gunther, *Early Science in Oxford* (Oxford, 1925), vol. IV.
[4] Cambridge University Add. MS 3996.

addition, he was clearly acquainted with More's work on the immortality of the soul. By 1664 he was subjecting Descartes's *Principia* to the closest scrutiny. He was also greatly indebted to Descartes's works on mathematics.[1]

What Newton was doing at one level, some undergraduates were soon to be considering in a less elevated manner. In 1668 Jonathan Comer, who had been admitted to Christ's the year before, took copious and clear notes about Cartesian Physics, from a textbook intended for novices.[2] The same introduction 'Physica incipientium sive Principia Cartesii tyronum captui accomodata' was used by other students at Cambridge—John Harrison (possibly of Trinity) and John Smith of Caius. Smith followed his notes on logic and ethics with a similar version of Cartesian physics. Other Cartesian notebooks of a similar date belonged to James Monson and Thomas Thomkinson.[3]

The existence of undergraduate teaching in Cartesianism is confirmed by Henry More's letters to Lady Conway. In 1674, Edward and John Rawdon were under More's guidance at Christ's. By September, 1674, More had taken one of them through the first three parts of Descartes's *Principia*. By December they had proceeded through the *Dioptrick* and were shortly to turn to the *Meteors*. On 31 December, 1674, More wrote:

> Mr Rawdon is now shortly for London, but we shall make an end of Descartes's Meteors before he goes. And for his De Methodo, he may read that himself as easily as an ordinarie Gazette.[4]

The publication at Cambridge of John Schuler's *Exercitationes ad principarum philosophiae Renati Descartes* (1686) confirms the fact that Cartesianism was well established at Cambridge.[5]

But modern interest in Cambridge Platonism and in the rise of science may easily lead us to overemphasize the significance of these groups within the universities. Isaac Newton, for example,

[1] D. T. Whiteside (ed.), *The Mathematical Papers of Isaac Newton* (Cambridge, 1967), p. 11.
[2] Cambridge University MS Dd.6.46.
[3] Cambridge University Add. MS Dd.12.33; 2640; Bodleian MSS Top. Oxon. e. 344; B.M. MS Sloane 2613. For another copy of this obviously popular treatise see Cambridge University Add. MS 3307.
[4] M. Nicolson (ed.), *The Conway Letters* (London, 1930), p. 399.
[5] *A List of Books Printed in Cambridge at the University Press* (Cambridge, 1935).

was an isolated figure in his university and it would be quite misleading to judge the intellectual atmosphere of Cambridge by reference to him.

2.

We may now turn to a brief consideration of matters Irish and Scottish. In Ireland, student numbers rose at Trinity College during the second part of the century, thus offering an interesting contrast with England. The explanation for this lies in the fact that the Cromwellian Plantation created a new ruling class of parvenu gentry, drawn from the ranks of Cromwell's army. An Irish equivalent of the 'Rise of the Gentry' occurred, in the sense that considerable numbers of landowners felt the need to seek gentlemanly culture and education. Thus Trinity College changed in character from being an essentially urban college catering for clergy and the Dublin Protestant *bourgeoisie* into a college which increasingly attracted the new Anglo-Irish landowner. In this way, the college became an essential social instrument in creating the Protestant ascendancy. Clergymen of the Church of Ireland were educated along with the gentlemen of the accepted political establishment. The great majority of Catholics and Dissenters were 'outside the pale'.

This offered a great contrast with the social function of the college in the first half of the century. It was accompanied by equally remarkable changes in the curriculum. The intellectual emphasis at Trinity resembled that at post-Restoration Oxford, and was symbolized by the appointment of Narcissus Marsh, Fellow of Exeter, as Provost in 1678.[1] Scholasticism, which had been condemned in Ussher's day, made an appearance in the curriculum, presumably under Oxford auspices. The familiar Oxford scholastic textbooks, Scheibler and Suarez were regularly taken out on loan from the library by junior fellows.[2] In view of this, the favour which Swift showed to the 'old philosophy' in his *Battle of the Books* and other writings seems less surprising.

[1] Marsh was recommended to Ormonde, the lord-lieutenant by Dr. Fell of Christ Church: H.M.C. (Ormonde), new series, vol. IV, pp. 166–7.

[2] T.C.D. Library Loan Book: e.g. see under Thewles, May, 1685; Jan., 1687; Mossom, Feb., 1695/6; Gilbert, July, 1695; Browne, Nov., 1697: It is only fair to say that some of the fellows took out Gassendi, Descartes, Hobbes and Cudworth from the library as well as Aquinas, Peter Lombard on the sentences, Ptolemy and

As at Oxford, a Dublin Philosophical Society came into existence in 1683, but its members were few and it proved a short-lived, though interesting, phenomenon.[1] Locke's *Essay Concerning Human Understanding* was read by some students, though far too much has been read into this by historians anxious to demonstrate the modernity of the general intellectual atmosphere within the college. It does not seem likely that a volume which aroused such suspicions of heterodoxy in Oxford should have been accepted without demur in Oxford's Irish offshoot.

The most significant fact about the social and intellectual position of Trinity was its function as a colonial-style institution. The task of the college was to educate an Anglo-Irish ruling *élite* in both Church and state, which would rule Ireland in the interests of the mother country. Its curriculum was of necessity influenced by this and tended to emphasize subjects and disciplines which were suited to a leisured class. These were not to be despised. They acted, for example, as a nursery for the rhetoric of Burke. In time, with the rise of the Dublin hospitals and the foundation of new chairs during the eighteenth century, medical studies became important at Trinity, though with a Protestant, upper-class tone to them.

Restoration Scotland remains something of an enigma. There was no obvious line of social change, such as the Cromwellian confiscation of Ireland, but it seems clear that some movement did take place towards 'social conservatism'. The return of the bishops and the principle of hierarchy cannot be seen merely as an ecclesiastical phenomenon, but as a change with wider social implications. The same must also be said of the bloody repressions which followed the rising of the Covenanters in 1666 and 1679. It seems reasonable to assume that these rebellions were seen as a social threat by the aristocratic establishment of Church and state. Unfortunately, until the social bearings of Scottish history have been worked out, all the historian of universities can do is to make a number of tentative suggestions.[2]

Bellarmine. It was perhaps this dialectical situation which produced George Berkeley, the critic of Locke.

[1] See Dr. T. Hoppen's forthcoming study of the Dublin Philosophical Society.

[2] The excellent study by T. C. Smout, *A History of the Scottish People* (1969), appeared unfortunately after this chapter was in type.

The Scottish universities even during this period, were scarcely influenced by the social ideal of the gentleman, with the exception perhaps of St. Andrews. Their position in the towns provided them with a ready supply of urban, *bourgeois* students, a phenomenon which became the more marked as the commercial side of Scottish life began to take on a new importance. The clerical orientation of the Scottish universities remained, and with it the role which the universities played as avenues of social mobility. The better-off sections of society turned to a legal career, which by-passed university studies in favour of what amounted to a legal apprenticeship. In contrast, the university was the high road to the manse, the route offering high prestige but a low income.

The Scottish clergyman was not a gentleman like his English counterpart, the parson. Intellectual consequences flowed from this simple fact. The universities followed quasi-professional courses which kept literary culture to a minimum and concentrated instead upon clerical subjects—logic, metaphysics, physics—in a more professional, perhaps more rigid mould, than was the case in England. There was all the difference in the world between the haphazard appearance of an English student's notebook and a Scottish student's, the one deriving from an informal tutorial system, the other systematically laid out, following the dictates of a lecturer, the 'regent'.

The philosophical emphasis of the Scottish universities had obvious limitations. It goes some way, for example, to explaining the absence of a strong literary culture in Scotland. But the students' notebooks of the Restoration period reveal an impressive concern to come to grips with the problems presented by the 'new philosophy' and their range of reference was much wider than any English equivalent during the period.

At Aberdeen, the older generation had been Aristotelian. Robert Forbes, for example, presided in 1660 over a deputation in which Aristotle was praised as 'princeps philosophorum'.[1] But other winds were now blowing. At Marischal College by 1669, the names of the new philosophers were dominating discussion, Descartes and Gassendi, as well as Charleton and Henry More.[2] The chief enemy was Thomas Hobbes. There were references to

[1] Aberdeen University Library MS The M 643 (3).
[2] Aberdeen University Library MS The M 669.

Bramhall's attack on Hobbes and Hobbesian scepticism was clearly felt to be the main topic of academic debate. In 1675, under the chairmanship of George Middleton, scepticism was attacked as a 'monstrous delirium', but Aristotle was no longer seen as the answer.[1] Instead, Middleton turned to Cartesian method as the basis of certainty. In 1681, John Buchan referred constantly to such 'moderns' as Boyle, Bacon, Gassendi, Kenelm Digby and Clauberg, the German Cartesian, and praised Cartesianism as a philosophy most serviceable for theology, defending it against the charge of atheism.[2] Robert Forbes was still preaching Aristotelianism in 1680 but he seems to have been a lone voice.[3] Clearly the new philosophy entered Aberdeen earlier than the other Scottish universities.

Edinburgh offered a contrast to all this. In 1661, Thomas Crawford was still offering his students a diagram of the spheres on Ptolemaic lines and stating that the heavens were incorruptible. His fellow regents, James Pilan and John Wishart were equally conservative. Wishart in 1668 praised Aristotelianism as the pinnacle of human intellectual achievement and denounced Descartes and Hobbes as fools. He was still critical of Descartes in 1680. William Tweedy, another regent, attacked the Copernican view as contrary to the Scriptures—'Mundi centrum esse Terram'. His colleague, William Patterson, attacked Descartes as an apostate.[4]

In 1683 a change took place. The Regent Andrew Massic praised 'the most happy imagination' of Descartes and his students took down notes entitled, 'Institutiones Physicae Generalis secundum Principia D. Renati Descartes'. David Gregory, the great mathematician, was also lecturing at the same time in optics and mechanics.[5]

The intellectual trend at Glasgow during the Restoration period resembled that at Edinburgh. The famous Glasgow Regent, John Tran, for example, was an admirer of the metaphysics of Suarez.[6] His fellow Regent, Gilbert Maxwell, was still making use of the

[1] Edinburgh University Library Small Bequest, Da. Theses (4).
[2] Aberdeen University Library MS Df.9 138 (7); Edinburgh University Library also has a copy.
[3] Edinburgh University Library Small Bequest, Da. Theses (11).
[4] Edinburgh University Library MS Dc.5.55; Dc.6.4; Dc.6.5.   [5] *D.N.B.*
[6] Edinburgh University MS La.III.715. Tran praised Suarez for his acumen and subtlety but criticized those who followed him in a servile manner.

neo-scholastics in 1681, and in 1684 discussed equally the Ptolemaic, Copernican and Tychonic world systems, though not the Cartesian.[1] By 1687, however, a Glasgow student was taking notes on metaphysics and ethics, according to the principles of Descartes,[2] and even John Tran was coming round to accept the Copernican hypothesis as presenting fewer difficulties than Ptolemy and Tycho, and this in the same year, 1687, that Newton published his *Principia*.[3]

The Revolution of 1689 was marked in Scotland by a return to Presbyterianism and the abolition of episcopacy. This led to changes within the universities. Most of the regents were removed and an attempt was made to establish some form of philosophical orthodoxy throughout the universities, by devising a common set of textbooks. David Gregory was forced to seek refuge in England and the whole episode may well have been marked by a recrudescence of anti-intellectualism and conservatism. At Aberdeen, for example, James Gilchrist in 1690 presided over a disputation at which a diagram of the Ptolemaic universe was used,[4] but the trend towards the new philosophy continued, despite this temporary setback. Notebooks belonging to students at Glasgow and elsewhere of about 1700 show that the ideas of Descartes and Locke were being sympathetically discussed.[5]

[1] Glasgow University Murray Collection.
[2] Glasgow University Murray Collection.
[3] Glasgow University MS 2-1933; 1-a14.
[4] Aberdeen University Library King's MS K.156.
[5] E.g. A notebook at Glasgow belonging to James Dick. Edinburgh University Library MS Dc.8.57.

CHAPTER X

1700: Ancients and Moderns

The political changes of the last decades of the seventeenth century had little effect upon the intellectual life or the social position of the English universities. James II's attempt to install Roman Catholic nominees at Oxford was merely a temporary episode. (In practice if not legally, he was doing what his predecessors had done as a matter of course.) The Glorious Revolution and its aftermath led to the resignation of a small number of non-jurors, more numerous at Cambridge than Oxford. This donnish refusal to swear allegiance to Dutch William had an admirable dramatic quality about it, but it cannot be said to have led to radical changes.

The chief interest of these years lies first in the continued decline of the universities as a social force, and secondly, in the reaction of the universities to the challenge of the 'Moderns'. For the historian, the major fact to note is that the universities were no longer the major social and intellectual force in English life but merely one among several. Oxford and Cambridge found it difficult to counter the attraction of London. It was London which provided the material basis for the growing number of professional openings in medicine, law, commerce, insurance and related occupations. Almost as important were the new intellectual centres of the provinces, at Liverpool, Manchester, Birmingham and elsewhere. New institutions appeared based upon the model of the Royal Society, in which considerable attention was paid to questions of practical utility in industry and agriculture.

The declining significance of the universities was reflected in falling student numbers which represented a smaller proportion of the relevant age group. In a generation which saw the foundation of the Bank of England, the establishment of the National Debt and the rise of the City to power, the universities remained essentially what they had been, the organs of the landed gentry and the clergy, both of them declining social groups. In addition, the passing of the Toleration Act in 1689 and the creation of a limited public tolerance of dissent, undermined the political function of the universities as guarantees of orthodoxy. In the age of dissent, Oxford and Cambridge lost their central position within the state. At the same time the social values for which they stood were losing ground rapidly in the face of merchant wealth.

The tone of the university curriculum, and its relationship to the social function of Oxford and Cambridge, is brought out clearly in Obadiah Walker's *Of Education*, which had gone into six editions by 1699. Walker, who was a fellow of University College until ejected in 1648, Master of his college in 1676, and a convert to Catholicism under James II, defended the traditional pre-occupation with logic and rhetoric. He thought that young gentlemen should learn to write, speak and read the Latin tongue as well as modern languages. He criticized the modern tendency to exaggerate the significance of science:

> In these parts of the world, we seem to run after sciences, and think them to be all things, whereas the great and universal business of our life . . . is wisdom, prudence, nobleness and liberty of spirit.[1]

In these words, Walker was expressing his opposition to the contrary ideal which we may identify broadly with the world of commerce.

Walker recommended the study of scholastic theology, partly on the grounds that it showed up the limitations of physical and mathematical studies and provided an effective answer to the materialism and atheism of the day. He also defended Aristotelianism on the basis of its empirical content. He spoke vehemently in favour of disputation, as the best method of bringing a problem to a point, and discovering the truth, even in natural philosophy. 'Indeed in Natural Philosophy, what is there that is not disputable?' The universities in Walker's view were 'the best place' to follow this kind of education, in contrast to Locke who thought that a tutor was sufficient.

Walker's treatise was the most influential manifesto of the traditionalists against the radicals. In it we can see the alliance of

[1] Obadiah Walker, *Of Education* (Oxford, 1673).

gentlemanly values ('nobleness and liberty of spirit') with the Latin language, the disputation, scholasticism and the ancillary disciplines of logic and rhetoric. This was the traditional gentleman's curriculum. Against it was ranged the new model provided by Locke in his treatises, *Essay concerning Human Understanding* (1690) and *Some Thoughts concerning Education* (1693), in which Locke provided a programme for intellectual and educational change. Locke saw himself as putting a match to the superstructure which had been built up on Greek foundations from Aristotle to Descartes. He doubted, like Descartes, the relevance of conclusions, which thousands of academics had taught, and the methods which had been used for reaching them. But where Descartes had doubted, only to seek reassurance in a vast quasi-scholastic synthesis, Locke refused to follow. If Locke's views were accepted, the wisdom of the Ancients was so much hocus-pocus and a fresh start had to be made.

A challenge from such a source could no more be ignored by the academic world, than one from Darwin a century and a half later. Locke could not be dismissed on grounds of social inferiority, as the critics of the 1650s had been. He was no tradesman or artisan, but a distinguished product of the university of Oxford. He was the author of *Two Treatises of Civil Government*, the political Bible of the post-1688 generation. Locke was not a marginal eccentric, but a central figure of the Williamite régime, and his criticisms were made in the plainest English prose, which could be digested, superficially at any rate, by any gentleman.

But the strength of Locke's position rested upon more than his social status and his intellectual arguments. It depended essentially upon the appeal which he made to the new social groups of eighteenth-century England. During the last years of his life, Locke was closely linked with the financial policies of the Whig government and hence with the 'City'. His views were sought upon the Great Recoinage and upon the details of commercial policy. After his death in 1704, Locke's views continued to appeal to the merchants and the financiers of London, with whom the future was largely to lie. In the 1650s, criticism of the universities had come from much the same social groups, but then they were no match for the gentry. By 1700, victory had gone to the 'monied interest'.

Locke expressed the Baconian message for a generation which was ready to hear it. Education should be useful in the sense of increasing the sum of human happiness. For this purpose, mathematics and ethics were essential, all else was secondary. Mathematics could replace logic as a more efficient method of teaching human beings to reason well. Ethics were capable of mathematical demonstration to a trained mind. The rest of accepted human knowledge Locke regarded with the greatest scepticism. He doubted whether a true science of causes was possible, given the limitations of human understanding. This ruled out natural philosophy, and *a fortiori* metaphysics. All men could hope for was the limited illumination of a few successful experiments. Reason was 'the candle' of the Lord, and not much more.

Locke's philosophy, if accepted, assigned the ancients a minor role in education. Cicero was useful in rhetoric. Aristotle deserved as much praise as a practical countrywoman for her knowledge of the weather. But in general, a philosophy deriving from Aristotelian doctrines was worse than useless. He told Edward Clarke 'if you would have your son reason well, let him read Bacon'. Boyle he also recommended as 'fittest for a gentleman', and Descartes's *Principles* was a system 'the most intelligible and most consistent with itself than any yet to be met with'. In his *Essay*, Locke referred to the moderns, Bacon, Boyle and Sydenham as his models.

The educational implications for the arts curriculum were vast, as they were also for theology. The universities of Oxford and Cambridge were after all institutions in which theology had reigned without challenge from the thirteenth century. Established methods of disputation and argument had been built up which seemed part of the natural order and though critics like Milton had attacked them, they had survived and flourished until the present day. Locke's *Essay* implied that the vast tones of scholastic theology which had been an essential part of the diet of Protestant divines, were now so much waste paper—'rubbish' in Locke's words, 'to be cleared away by a humble day labourer'.

In his *Some Thoughts concerning Education* Locke made clear his contempt for the universities and the type of education which they stood for. A gentleman's son should be educated at home by a tutor under his father's eye. Locke saw such a tutor not as a learned academic full of Latin and logic but a man who appreciated 'the ways of carriage and measures of civility'. The criterion of a young man's education was to be what 'will be of most and frequentest use to him in the world'.

> Seneca complains of the contrary Practice in his time; and yet the Burgersdicius's and the Scheiblers did not swarm in those days as they do now in these. What would he have thought, if he had lived now, when the Tutors think it their great business to fill the studies and heads of their pupils with such Authors as these?[1]

These remarks about Burgersdicius and Scheibler bring out clearly the contrast between Locke and Obadiah Walker (a contrast made all the more piquant because Walker had been a zealous supporter of James II in Oxford, at a time when Locke had been in exile). Locke also criticized the method of disputing which Walker went to such pains to defend. Perhaps the most revealing difference between the two was Locke's insistence that a gentleman should learn a manual trade. Locke also thought another skill absolutely necessary, the ability to keep accounts:

> Merchant's Accompts, though a Science not likely to help a Gentleman to get an estate, yet possibly there is not any thing of more use and efficacy, to make him preserve the Estate he has . . . I would therefore advise all Gentlemen to learn perfectly Merchant's Accompts, and not to think it is a skill, that belongs not to them, because it has received its Name, and has been chiefly practised by by Men of Traffick.[2]

In all this Locke may be said to have adapted the traditional idea of a gentleman's education to suit an age in which commerce was increasingly dominant. He criticized tradesmen for sending their sons to learn Latin, a skill which would be useless to them in his view, while, at the same time, upbraiding gentlemen for failing to acquire mercantile skills. In such an educational *schema*, the values represented by scholasticism and humanism did not count. Locke dismissed the schoolmen and restricted the classical

[1] *The Educational Writings of John Locke*, ed. J. L. Axtell (Cambridge, 1968), p. 199.
[2] Ibid., pp. 319–20.

authors to a very narrow utilitarian range, for example his recommendation of Cicero's *Epistles* as a model for letter-writing.
He considered music unimportant, and he did not mention poetry.
This was a far cry from Milton's essay *On Education* and much
more in the tradition of Hartlib and Petty.

The novelty of Locke's approach to universities is also implied
in his views on religious toleration. Locke, the spokesman for
toleration, opposed by implication the function which Oxford
and Cambridge had performed as bastions of orthodoxy. He
specifically criticized, in *Some Thoughts concerning Education*, those
dons who were ready 'to Cry out Heresie' against anyone who
criticized traditional methods of teaching. In contrast, Obadiah
Walker stood for the old pattern in which universities formed
part of the defences of true religion against heresy and scepticism.

The differences between Walker and Locke foreshadowed the
course which the English universities were to take in the eighteenth
century. The universities saw their function as the bulwarks of
intellectual tradition. This implied an emphasis upon the values
of the classics and of scholasticism which was unfashionable by
the standards of Locke. It also implied an orthodoxy which led
the university authorities at Oxford to forbid the circulation of
Locke's *Essay concerning Human Understanding*. Such conservatism,
however, cannot be considered merely in the abstract. It formed
part of a social picture in which the universities drew their support from the two declining social groups of clergy and gentry.
The universities 'reflected' the hostility which these social groups
felt towards the menace of commerce and dissent.

The picture was never a static one and there was considerable
variation from college to college. But the two universities retained their gentlemanly tone even when they tended to diverge
from one another. 'Pure' mathematics flourished at Cambridge, as
a form of intellectual activity, which was as socially acceptable as
the classical studies of Oxford. The impure forms of mathematics,
including political arithmetic, did not gain entrance into the curriculum, which though it changed, kept a strictly anti-practical
and anti-commercial frame of reference. Those sciences with a
utilitarian implication developed outside the universities.

This conservative mentality is revealed in the students' notebooks of the late seventeenth century. To judge from this evi-

dence, the old philosophy still dominated the curriculum. At Wadham, Charles King's notebook provides detailed information about his undergraduate studies.[1] He studied logic and metaphysics in three months (November, 1681 to January, 1682) and physics in six months (January to June, 1682). A short course in ethics followed (9th June to 16th June) and then courses in 'economics', politics, cosmography, geometry and optics. The old and the new mingled in King's university studies. In physics he still discussed the four elements and the planetary spheres, but optics brought him into touch with new thought.

At Queen's, the centre of traditionalism, change was slow to come, but even here during the 1680s, the correspondence of the Fleming brothers reveals that the new philosophy was having some effect. The classics kept their place side by side with Heerebord and LeGrand. Henry Hooton, who took his M.A. in 1689, kept copies of the Latin proses and verses which he wrote regularly during almost the whole of his undergraduate career.[2] The old philosophy may be seen in the textbooks by Burgersdicius which another Queen's student, Thomas Brockbank, received in 1687 from his father.[3] Five years later a friend of his was trying to sell his undergraduate textbooks, all of them of conservative flavour, including Scheibler's *Metaphysics*.

Other colleges seem to have been more conservative than Queen's. At St. Edmund Hall, in 1683, Francis Cherry, the prominent non-juror, kept a notebook which shows him to have been completely oblivious of Descartes or anything else connected with the new philosophy.[4] The same is true of Pembroke where Thomas Dickinson in 1690 was still studying scholastic metaphysics in the light of Suarez, Aquinas, Bradwardine, Scotus and the rest of the schoolmen.[5]

Magdalen was something of an exception. There in 1684, Robert Strickland in his post-M.A. years, took notes of lectures on the senses by Dr. Thomas Smith, President of the college, on 9th May, 5th June, 6th June and 4th July, 1684.[6] These were up-to-date in the sense of being anatomical in character and dealt with the

---

[1] Bodleian MSS Rawlinson D.1442.　　[2] Bodleian MSS Lat. Misc. e. 38.

[3] *The Diary and Letter Book of the Rev. Thomas Brockbank*, Chetham Society (Manchester, 1930), pp. 42–3.

[4] Bodleian MS Cherry 45–6.　　[5] Bodleian MSS Top. Oxon. e. 287.

[6] Bodleian MSS Smith 128.

theories propounded in Descartes' *Principia*. The lectures were given on the contrasting views of Gassendi, Descartes and More, on the intellect. Smith himself had been an undergraduate at Queen's during the Commonwealth and a Fellow of Magdalen from 1662. He was a Tory in politics who had attacked Shaftesbury in 1681 and was later to be a non-juror. He lectured regularly in the hall at Magdalen and seems to have kept an open mind about Descartes.

But the most revealing piece of evidence is that provided by the collection-book of Christ Church, which shows what books undergraduates were required to read for their collections (vacation exercises).[1] This shows clearly how the alliance between scholasticism and the classics survived until the mid-eighteenth century. Burgersdicius's *Metaphysics* did not drop out of the reading-lists until 1744. Eustachius's *Ethics* and Baronius's *Metaphysics* were still being read in the early decades of the century. Locke's *Essay concerning Human Understanding* was eventually recommended only in 1744. Christ Church was a college, which, more than any other, combined social tone and Anglican orthodoxy, and it is tempting to see in this collection-book a small but decisive example of the way in which the characteristic intellectual position taken up by the universities was closely linked up with their social connections.

This conservative position did not mean complete stagnation. Guides to students drawn up at Oxford in about 1700 suggest that some tutors at least tried to bring changes into the traditional curriculum.[2] If we compare these guides with Barlow's *Directions*, the balance of subjects is still much the same. Logic, ethics, metaphysics and physics cover the first four years. Along with these, classical literature was studied. But the combination of philosophy and humanism was altered. The scholastic authors no longer had the philosophical field to themselves. In logic, Stierius, Brerewood and Smith were still recommended, but so also was the 'Socratic Method' and the new logic exemplified in Descartes's *De Methodo*, the *Ars Cogitandi*, and Duhamel's *De Mente Humana*. In ethics also, Eustachius remained but along with it was found Henry More's *Enchiridion Ethicum*.

[1] Lambeth Library MSS, Christ Church Collection Book.
[2] Bodleian MSS Rawlinson D.40.

Metaphysics survived in spite of all Locke's criticisms. In this section the names of Baronius, Scheibler, Suarez and Burgersdicius inevitably appeared, along with Locke's chapter 'Of Ideas' from the *Essay concerning Human Understanding*, with answers to it by Bishop Stillingfleet, and Sergeant's *Sound Philosophy Asserted*. Henry More and Cudworth were also recommended. Finally, in physics, the peripatetic system of Aristotle and his commentators was still to be read, but reference is also made to the 'more ancient Corpuscular Philosophy' of Epicurus, Lucretius and Gassendi, and to the modern philosophy of Descartes and More. Modern authors are also recommended for cosmology (Whiston, Woodward, Boyle, Digby), anatomy, astronomy, geometry and geography, and Bacon and the Royal Society figured prominently. The difficulty about drawing conclusions from this list is that it may have been drawn up as a piece of hopeful reform which was never put into practice.

In contrast with Oxford, Cambridge had been consistently more open to the new ideas. The Cartesian tradition continued to flourish there. At Trinity, for example, in the 1680s, Jonathan Cotton studied first 'Principia Cartesiana Tyronum Captibus Accomodata', then 'Prolegomenon Philosophiae Naturalis Principia' and then 'Quaestiones in Cartesii Passionibus'.[1] Clearly Cartesianism was prominent right up to 1687 when Newton's *Principia* was published, and even afterwards.

At St. John's in the same decade, John Allsopp studied Descartes's *Principia* and took notes of experiments on the lines of the Royal Society. These included 'An experiment whereby to prove the air have vis elastica' and 'An experiment whereby 'tis proved if air is necessarily required to the making of sound'. Allsopp's notebook also indicates that he studied history via Raleigh's *History of the World*, and an *Epitome of Roman History*. His books included Baronius's *Metaphysics*, Gassendus's *Astronomy*, Grotius, Erasmus and Hobbes.[2] At Pembroke, a decade later, the notes of Roger Long show him to be well acquainted with the new philosophy and to have taken notes from the Italian scientist Borelli. He also took notes on 'An attempt to prove the motion

---

[1] Cambridge University Add. MS 3307.
[2] St. John's, Cambridge MS S.17 (James 411). See also an article by Miss K. M. Burton in *The Eagle*, (vol. LIV, 1951), pp. 248–58.

of the earth from observations made by Robert Hooke, Fellow of the Royal Society'.[1]

Cambridge notebooks of this date are scarce, but taken together they do suggest that the university as a whole from undergraduates upward, was more scientifically minded than Oxford. It is also confirmed by the 'Guide to Students' drawn up by Robert Green of Clare and by the printed text of Whiston's lectures on astronomy given in 1701.[2]

Robert Green's 'Guide' represents an extraordinary change from the advice to students given by Merryweather and Sterry in the 1650s. Some elements of the old curriculum keep their place but they are relegated entirely to the first year and the first part of the second. By the third year, the undergraduate had passed on from arithmetic and algebra to optics, cosmic sectors, fluxions, infinite logarithms, hydrostatics and other scientific subjects. Well over half the recommended reading came from the works of Newton, Huygens, Boyle and many others. Unfortunately, this picture is not backed up by evidence from students' notebooks and may well have been sketched as wish more than reality.

It may well be that a less adventurous picture suggested by a new version of *Holdsworth's Guide* [sic], re-edited late in the seventeenth century, provides a sounder basis than Green's 'Guide' for making an assessment of the general character of the Cambridge curriculum.[3] The editor left in place most of the books recommended earlier. The students' mornings, as in the 1650s, were to be devoted to philosophy, a good deal of it Aristotelian, though now to be augmented by Descartes, Le Grand, Heerebord and Sergeant. The editor was much concerned about the growth of scepticism and free thought, and he obviously saw the scholastics as a means of defence, taken in conjunction with suitably-chosen 'moderns'. Indeed, his views have a good deal in common with those of Barlow, whose *De Studio Theologiae* he recommended. His reference to reason as 'the Candle of God in the Soul' may indicate sympathy for the Cambridge Platonists, and he did in

[1] Pembroke, Cambridge MSS L.C.II 169, L.C.II 169.1.
[2] C. Wordsworth, *Scholae Academicae* (Cambridge, 1877), Appendix IV; W. Whiston, *Astronomical Lectures read in public schools at Cambridge* (London, 1715).
[3] Emmanuel MS 3.1.11.

fact recommend More's *Ethics*. Though the editor was sympathetic to the scholastics, it is obvious from his comments that the traditional curriculum on natural philosophy was being modified. He wrote in the section on natural philosophy:

> With the aforesaid Books of Aristotle, or if you will, instead of him (because the course of philosophical study is now altered) you may make use of Descartes . . . and other Cartesians.

An illuminating section of the 'Guide' is provided by editorial additions to the list of books drawn up for the gentry, i.e. 'those who came to university not intending to make scholarship their profession'. This social tone of the list is shown by the inclusion of *The Gentleman's Calling* and the works of Sir Robert Filmer as well as works on horsemanship and fencing. The classics were recommended (in translation) and modern authors such as Shakespeare and Jonson. Though Boyle and Bacon were on the list, the general character of this 'Guide' was nearer to Obadiah Walker than to Locke. It was a reading-list which excluded all utilitarian considerations.

Conclusion

In this book, I have tried to discuss the relationship between university education and society during the period 1500–1700. I have shown, I hope, that the universities were exposed to political and social pressures, which affected the shape and content of the curriculum. Clearly, this is not the only possible approach to the history of universities. There is obviously a sense in which universities have been communities of scholars working within a general European tradition, and this perhaps is the 'ideal' university, which has survived over the centuries, and been reinforced in the modern period by the rise of modern science and the growth of an international community of scientific research workers. To discuss political and social factors in the history of universities is, in effect, to draw attention to the ways in which universities have diverged from the ideal, perhaps inevitably so.

In the period under discussion, the universities of the British Isles produced many scholars who made a contribution to their particular discipline. From this point of view, the universities were centres for 'the advancement of learning' (or, in our terms, research). Such scholars, however, were few in relation to the great mass of students, for whom the universities were institutions designed to inculcate a set of political or social values. The university curriculum which these students encountered was, in part a changing social construct, which owed its existence to social pressures as much as intellectual conventions.

Some historians would be tempted to go further and see university curricula as reflecting the dominant values of a society. But this, in my view, is to go too far and to allow too little room for the role of chance, compromise and personal idiosyncrasy in the creation of curricula. In an ideal, unchanging, society, there would, no doubt, be a simple correlation between it and the curriculum. But the societies under discussion were complex and changing. The term 'society' itself in my view refers to an 'aggregate of social relationships', not a unified entity, and the curriculum itself varied from time to time, and from college to college.

With this caveat in mind, what social relationships may the universities be said to have reinforced? So far as England was concerned, the dominating fact of the sixteenth century was the division of society into a leisured class and an agricultural labouring population. The universities strengthened this division in many ways, not least by their insistence upon Latin. High fees acted as a further social sieve, and from the passing of the Clarendon Code onwards, religious tests acted as a further social barrier, by keeping out dissenters belonging to the lower social groups. During the period 1550–1650 more people went to Oxford and Cambridge, and relatively a higher proportion of the appropriate age-groups, but the rise benefited the *élite*, not the non-*élite*. Those who went up to universities from outside the ranks of the *élite*, normally entered its ranks by the clerical door, a form of 'sponsored' mobility. The poor student looking for a Church living, depended upon patronage either from his college, his bishop, a gentleman or the Crown. In this system, the odds were weighted heavily against the independent-minded.

The universities also acted as the instrument by which the medieval division of society into clergy and laity was perpetuated. The image of the scholar which the universities fostered was that of the clerical scholar. Scholarship itself was associated with

theology, and even classical studies fell into place in their presumed relationship to divinity. The clerical aura which sur-
rounded this view of learning meant that criteria of orthodoxy
were never far away. University scholarship was 'guided' scholarship, always liable to be called to account by authority. From this
point of view, the universities may be seen as controlling the
supply of learning, in the presumed interests of government and
society.

In fact, the universities failed in this particular function. The
seventeenth century witnessed the rise of the lay scholar, especially
in the politically sensitive field of legal history. Laymen also
entered philosophical studies. But perhaps the decisive factor was
the rise of scientific studies, which were overwhelmingly in lay
hands. The seventeenth century saw the relative decline of the
influence of the clergy and the rise of the lay intellectual.

In England, the restriction of higher education to two academic
centres meant that the Crown had a ready-made instrument for
political centralization. Education at Oxford and Cambridge broke
down the local differences of outlook between gentry from the
outlying parts of the kingdom. The universities thus helped to
create a single community of gentry which was so marked a
feature of the seventeenth century. The Great Rebellion, unlike
the local rebellions of the sixteenth century, was a national conflict.

The centralization of university life meant that gentry from all
over England and Wales were exposed to the same system of
élitist social values. This no doubt played a crucial part in the
creation of a gentry class. But we may also argue that it accounts
in large measure for the intense degree of social discontent among
non-gentry groups, which was revealed in England during the
crisis of 1640–60, especially during the Barebone Parliament. The
universities in confining their attention to the powerful few
aroused the hostility of the excluded majority.

The role of the universities in creating the conditions which led
to the Puritan Revolution is very much a matter for debate. Professor Curtis attributes a good deal of importance to 'alienated
intellectuals' who were excluded from the patronage system, and
there is certainly something to be said for his argument. To my
mind, however, the crucial fact in the Puritan Revolution was the

division of the *élite* into two contrasting and eventually opposed groups. Messrs. Brunton and Pennington, some years ago, drew attention to the age difference between Royalists and Parliamentarians, the Royalists being appreciably younger than their opponents. Clearly a generation gap can be important, but by itself it is not enough to explain a civil war, or else there would be a civil war in every generation. But against the background of the history of the universities, the age difference becomes intelligible. The leaders of the Parliamentarian gentry, Pym, Hampden, Cromwell and the rest, went up to Oxford and Cambridge before the scholastic reaction had set in in full force. They went, indiscriminately, to either Oxford or Cambridge, but within the universities they attended colleges with a 'godly' tutor or a 'godly' reputation. This was the generation which went up to college in the 1590s. John Pym, for example, went to Broadgates Hall (1599–1602) where the Carnsew brothers had been a decade earlier and which was undoubtedly a Puritan institution. Hampden went to Magdalen, Humphrey's old college, from 1609–13. The next generation were not exposed to the same intense Puritan influences during their years at the university. By the 1620s, as we have seen, scholasticism was very much in the ascendant and the influence of the universities was thrown on the conservative side, even before the coming of Laud.

Thus, the age-gap between Royalist and Parliamentarian, to which Brunton and Pennington drew attention, was perhaps more specifically a difference of intellectual generations. The Oxford and Cambridge of Pym and Cromwell were places in which a more Puritan form of education was possible than was the case twenty years later. The Parliamentarians were in large measure the age-group which had been exposed to the influence of Humphrey and Rainolds at Oxford, or Whitaker and Perkins at Cambridge. The Royalists belonged to the next generation, when less intense voices were dominant in the universities. In broad terms, we may suggest that the difference lay between a generation reared on the Bible and one reared on the schoolmen. For a time they were forced together in a common enmity to Laud but fell out when it came to discussing what form the future was to take.

The crisis after the Civil War re-united the gentry. In a world where so many landmarks had shifted and in which open and bitter criticism of social and religious *élites* was expressed, the attractions of hierarchical values, as defended in scholasticism, seemed very great indeed. Within the universities, this social and intellectual reaction took the form of a renewed emphasis upon scholasticism and classical learning, which was to be seen at Oxford in Barlow's 'Directions for younger schollers' and at Cambridge in the Holdsworth [*sic*] 'Guide to Students'. The appearance of medical studies within the universities also had a social significance by reinforcing the gentlemanly aura of the medical profession. This intellectual reaction, if it may be so termed, continued after the Restoration. The universities stood for the 'eternal verities', social and intellectual. A gentry, which had witnessed the execution of the King, found these more than acceptable.

It was precisely at this moment of time that the traditional intellectual position came under attack, first from Descartes and the Cartesians, and then from John Locke and his followers. The work of Tawney and others, however, should prevent us from seeing this too clearly as a clash of the forces of darkness and light. The scholastic synthesis may well have acted as a brake against too violent economic change by its insistence upon the values of an organic society. Norman O. Brown in his book *Life Against Death* (1959) regards Descartes as a source of 'the insane delusion that the true essence of man lies in disembodied mental activity'. Without pressing either of these points closely, we must surely assume that there was loss and gain in the decline of scholasticism and the victory of Moderns over Ancients.

By and large the English universities stood for the Ancients, duly modified by acceptable and refined modern doctrines. The new England went forward with the Whigs and the City of London. Oxford and Cambridge adhered to the gentlemanly ideal, when commercial wealth and social mobility created a society in which this became increasingly unfashionable. They stood out on the whole against the revival of religious emotion in the form of methodism. There were some evangelicals to be found within the universities but on the whole Oxford and Cambridge, like Harvard, preserved an intellectual approach in theology, once more against the dictates of fashion. The universities turned their face against this new commercial civilization. The values inculcated by the curriculum were those of classical civilization in which the merchant had counted for very little. Classical scholarship flourished and 'pure' mathematics, but the new discipline of 'political arithmetic' was excluded.

It would be foolish, however, to ignore the influence of classical values upon eighteenth-century English culture. The architecture of the English country house is sufficient reminder, if one were needed, of this. The universities were the main instrument by which a classical, aristocratic tradition, with its virtues as well as drawbacks, was preserved, at a time when the trend was almost all the other way.

The social function of Trinity College, Dublin, was as clear cut as that of the English universities. By the end of the seventeenth century Trinity College had become the intellectual institution of the new ruling *élite* created by Elizabeth and reinforced, if not re-created, by Oliver Cromwell. The crucial religious tests at the college had a social effect in excluding the Catholic majority and the dissenting Presbyterian minority of Ulster. The Anglo-Irish gentleman and the Church of Ireland minister, both educated at Trinity, were as much social allies as the English gentleman and the Anglican parson, both educated at Oxford or Cambridge. Those outside the Church of Ireland were forced to seek higher education abroad either in the colleges of Spain, France, Italy and the Spanish Netherlands or in the universities of Glasgow and Edinburgh.

Almost inevitably, the privileged social position of the college tied it to conservatism. The only possible intellectual justification for its existence was as a citadel of civilization against Papist superstition on the one hand and Presbyterian bigotry on the other. The college which produced Swift, Berkeley, Molyneux, Burke and Grattan in the eighteenth century could lay a strong claim to being a civilizing influence. But this achievement need not obscure the social price which was demanded, and which influenced the curriculum. The college placed its influence upon the side of the *status quo*, even though in later centuries it could boast of having produced its share of rebels.

Trinity, to some extent, suffered from the same social isolation as Oxford and Cambridge, in the sense that the rise of a new middle class, Catholic in the South, Presbyterian in the North, changed the economic balance of power within the country. Trinity, in fact,by turning the attention of its graduates away from mundane commercial pursuits helped to undermine the economic foundations of the Ascendancy.

The position of the Scottish colleges is much more difficult to sum up succinctly. Scotland was a poor country and its six colleges were small and locally based; (England boasted over thirty colleges at Oxford and Cambridge, most of which were richer and larger than any college in Scotland.) This made for the emergence of what G. E. Davie has called 'the Democratic Intellect' but what might be more accurately termed 'the Professional Intellect'. The defects of this were more obvious than its virtues in the seventeenth century. The Scottish colleges were narrow in their curriculum and utilitarian in emphasis. The students' dictates show that great emphasis was placed upon following the course laid down by particular lecturers (regents) whose notes were purchased in immaculately copied form by many students.

The emphasis upon dictation was most marked after the departure of Melville, if we may judge by the large numbers of notebooks for the periods of episcopalian control, 1606–40 and 1660–90. This points to a concern on the part of the authorities that a common line should be followed within the colleges for the purpose of censorship, during a period when governments were preoccupied with questions of security. The need became much less after 1690, after the victory of the Presbyterian majority and an accompanying self-confidence provided the universities with a greater freedom than they enjoyed in the seventeenth century, along with a broad social base. The professional system which had been created as a measure of greater control formed the basis of more liberal arrangements.

When all is said, however, all universities of this period were institutions, which aimed at social and political control by confirming higher education to a small minority, and providing a curriculum whose values reinforced the *status quo*. If this situation changed, it was partly because governments changed, or because an *élite* became divided, or finally because society itself underwent a radical shift, in which the city merchant became more important than the country gentleman.

CHAPTER XI

A Comparative Postscript:
The Nineteenth Century

I.

To provide a wider perspective in time, I propose, in a concluding chapter, to examine the social implications of the curriculum in the universities of nineteenth-century England, Ireland and America.

For a member of the English upper class during this period, going to university meant going to Oxford or Cambridge. This was the 'done thing'. Any other course was almost unthinkable, and it was better to go straight into business or the army than suffer social degradation in the provincial universities. Going to Oxford and Cambridge was part of a social code, which became all the more important in a society undergoing considerable social change. The upper social groups were no longer landed gentlemen with country estates. To own an estate certainly made a gentleman, but this was no longer a practical criterion for large sections of the urban-based, industrial upper middle class. Increasingly, the criterion of a gentleman became membership of certain professions, the established church, law, medicine, the army, the higher civil service and the Indian civil service, banking and 'the City', and not least, politics. Entrance into these professions was largely governed by a public school education and the possession of an Oxbridge degree.[1]

Much of the tone of the two universities derived from this. Undergraduates were not 'students' but 'gentlemen'. From the mid-nineteenth century teaching was on a tutorial basis, one pupil at a time, and tutorials were as much social occasions as intellectual confrontations. Indeed, admission to some colleges depended less

[1] Asa Briggs has noted the change from 'hierarchy' to 'class' as the basis of English society. A. Briggs, 'The Language of Class in early nineteenth-century England', in A. Briggs and J. Saville, *Essays in Labour History* (London, 1960). This undoubtedly affected the universities.

upon academic ability than social 'background'. Certain colleges were thought to have a higher social tone than others, which suggests that an appropriate analogy should be with a London club, as much as with an educational institution. The ideal of some colleges was to have a 'balanced' admission, in the sense of a mixture of scholars, sportsmen and others. The university admitted a wider set of values than academic ones by tolerating the existence of a pass degree, which few were likely to fail. A master's degree could be acquired for a small fee, three years after graduation as bachelor. For most undergraduates, the formal course of studies was a minor element in their lives and serious 'honours' courses were the concern of a minority.

But it would be a mistake to underestimate the amount of social and intellectual change which took place within the ancient universities. At each university, the number of matriculations more than doubled, from 200 to 500 by 1850. The role of landed gentleman declined and a new academic seriousness made head way. From the mid-nineteenth century, reformers like Jowett, Pattison and T. H. Green at Oxford, and Sidgwick, Jebb and Jackson at Cambridge, revived the idea of the college as a responsible teaching institution. The college tutor replaced the extra-collegiate crammer as the chief instrument of teaching within the universities, and the college themselves took greater responsibility for the moral and physical welfare of their members. The college boat, coached by one of the dons, became a symbol of muscular Christianity.[1]

Formal changes were also made in the university curriculum. At Oxford, new schools of study were set up in *Literae Humaniores* (or 'Greats' based on the classics), law, modern history and natural science. At Cambridge, mathematics was the oldest tripos but a new tripos in classics was founded in 1824 and triposes in moral sciences and natural sciences in 1848. Throughout the century, new professorships were added including the chair of experimental physics in 1871. The Oxford 'Schools' and the Cambridge 'Triposes' were honours courses which attracted a growing proportion of undergraduates.[2]

[1] For Oxford, see M. Richter, *The Politics of Conscience* (London, 1964), chap. 3; for Cambridge, S. Rothblatt, *The Revolution of the Dons* (London, 1968), chap. 7.
[2] D. A. Winstanley, *Later Victorian Cambridge* (Cambridge, 1947), chap. 5.

In spite of all this, the tradition of the gentleman survived, albeit in a different form. In 1900, the number of pass men at Cambridge was still half the undergraduate population.[1] Even in the honours courses, prestige throughout the nineteenth century rested with classics at Oxford, and pure mathematics and classics, at Cambridge.[2] The triumphs of the reformers, if anything, accentuated this emphasis. At Balliol, Jowett threw his weight on the side of *Literae Humaniores* and it was taken for granted that a 'Greats' man could get up any other subject without difficulty.[3] At Cambridge, most fellowships went to those who excelled in mathematics or classics, and the election of a scientific fellow to Downing, one of the smaller colleges, was an exceptional event. Prestige rested with the disciplines without a direct practical significance, and when history came to be studied emphasis was often laid on the need to study the past for its own sake.

At both universities, the revival of serious educational interest brought its triumphs, in philosophy and history at Oxford, in mathematics and physics at Cambridge. Disciplines with a practical bent were kept at arm's length, and sometimes pure scholarship and pure snobbery combined to create a sublime compound of which Montagu Butler, Master of Trinity, struck Bertrand Russell as a particularly fine example. Russell, who was an undergraduate at Trinity in the 1890s, described Butler as a figure 'straight out of Thackeray's Book of Snobs!'.

> He generally began his remarks with 'Just thirty years ago today' or with 'Do you by any chance remember what Mr. Pitt was doing one hundred years ago today?' and he would then proceed to relate some very tedious historical anecdote to show how great and good were all the statesmen mentioned in history. . . .

In June, 1893, Butler wrote to Russell,

> I cannot tell you how happy this grand victory has made us. Just 33 years have passed since I placed the Fifth Form prize for Latin prose in the hands of your dear Father at Harrow, and

[1] Rothblatt, op. cit., p. 185.
[2] Winstanley, op. cit., pp. 209, 211.
[3] Richter, op. cit., p. 62: Roy Harrod in *The Prof in Two Worlds* (London, 1961), p. 116, describes the reaction of F. A. Lindemann to classical dominance in Oxford.

now I am permitted to congratulate his son and his own Mother on a remarkable Mathematical success which will be much appreciated in the College. . . .[1]

As Professor Rothblatt has shown, even the reformers perpetuated a suspicion of business and commercial dealing. The Church of England provided the universities with a third of their students, and the established Church was traditionally associated with the landed classes, and not with commerce. But the crucial factor seems to have been a growing acceptance of the idea that certain professions were more 'liberal', and hence more suited for gentlemen than others. The rise of the professions in England still awaits its historian, but its 'class' basis seems beyond doubt. The liberal professions were socially exclusive institutions, which maintained their exclusiveness by a variety of methods, including high entrance fees and expensive academic qualifications. The ancient universities placed themselves at the heart of this social system. Only one-tenth of the undergraduates at Cambridge in the 1890s came from families associated with business, whereas half came from professional or clerical (i.e. Anglican) backgrounds. The number of working-class students was, of course, negligible.[2]

There was another social shibboleth built into the system. It was taken for granted that Latin and Greek were necessary for admission into the university. This intellectual requirement acted as an effective social bulwark in restricting entry.[3] It meant that only the products of a comparatively small number of schools were eligible for admission. In addition, the content of the classics themselves did nothing to undermine the notion of an educational *élite*, since there were assumptions (e.g. the desirability of a leisured class) built into the study of such classical authors as were selected, which implied that such an *élite* was a normal way of governing society. Jowett, for example, introduced Plato's *Republic*, the classical defence of government by *élites* as a philosophical textbook.[4] Another source of *élitism* was the influence of Cole-

---

[1] Bertrand Russell, *Autobiography* (London, 1967), pp. 87-8.
[2] Rothblatt, op. cit., chaps. 1-2.
[3] Cf. Lawrence Stone, 'Education and Modernisation in Japan and England', in *Comparative Studies in Society and History* (1966), p. 225.
[4] W. Abbot and L. Campbell, *Life and Letters of Benjamin Jowett* (London, 1897), vol. I, p. 132. I am indebted for this reference to C. A. Kent's unpublished Ph.D. thesis (Sussex), July, 1968, 'Academic Radicalism in mid-Victorian England.'

ridge, Carlyle and Comte.[1] Hence, the literary and sociological study of classical authors was neglected. Their direct political relevance was thought more important.

This *élitist* mentality also exercised an indirect influence upon other disciplines, if only for the reason that they were taught, more often than not, by classical dons. The tone of history teaching, for example, was directed towards the decision-making which future leaders of the nation would have to make. The emphasis fell upon political or constitutional history. In its normal form, history was the history of the English ruling class seen in idealized terms through the medium of its main institution—Parliament. To most historians no other form of history seemed worth studying—labour history, economic history, American history.[2]

Constitutional history in particular was a topic which rested upon *élitist* assumptions about the nature of English society.[3] Historians reared in 'the Whig Interpretation of History' took for granted the truth of Tennyson's judgment, that freedom slowly broadened down from precedent to precedent. This gave a comforting re-assurance that rebellions had been justly, if bloodily, repressed in earlier centuries, because they were out of due time. The historians of Wales, Scotland and Ireland were comfortably ignored. More attention was paid to European history, studied on the grand scale, as part of the necessary background for a politically-minded gentleman.

The gentlemanly tone resulted in gentlemanly scholarship, in both complimentary and critical senses of the phrase. At its best, a work of learning emerged as the unhurried product of several decades, undertaken for its own sake without regard for career advancement or modish prestige. At its worst, Oxbridge scholarship was the regurgitation of out-of-date lectures by a 'good college man'. These were the virtues and vices of a particular social milieu.

2.

In the provinces the new educational institutions of the second half of the nineteenth century provided a markedly different cur-

---

[1] Kent, op. cit., chap. 1.   [2] Thorold Rogers was an exception.

[3] The teaching of constitutional history in Cambridge has been largely in conservative hands. A distinguished line of constitutional historians included Kenneth

riculum. Where Oxford and Cambridge mirrored the social values and sometimes the social conscience of a ruling *élite* in the form of 'liberal' education, the provincial universities reflected the predominantly practical orientation of their students and their patrons. At Manchester the university, though founded in 1851, looked back to the tradition of the dissenting academies of the late eighteenth century. Arthur Thomas Barnes, Presbyterian minister at Cross Street Chapel, described a 'plan of liberal education for young men designed for civil and active life, whether in trade or in any of the professions.' Barnes wrote of the education of the commercial community:

> I shall imagine to myself a system of education for a commercial man which shall contain all the parts of science proper for him to know, as much as possible in practical form and which amidst all the other objects of study shall keep this point continually in view.[1]

Local magnates, when they put their money into the local university, did so with a practical end in view, while the students themselves shied away from classics and philosophy and turned towards engineering, as at Liverpool, or textile technology, as at Leeds. The arts degree was more often than not a passport to teaching, especially after the demand for teachers rose in the wake of the Education Act of 1870.

But there was loss and gain at Manchester as well as Oxbridge. T. H. Green decided to stay at Oxford to teach philosophy because, as he wrote,

> In the teaching I suspect I can do more here. Manchester clerks would want some shorter cut than my Hegelian philosophy, whereas here I anticipate increasing success with pupils.[2]

Green was probably right in thinking that the need to get out and earn one's living limited intellectual horizons.

In the urban universities, the 'professor' and the department

---

Pickthorn, Conservative M.P. an fellow of Corpus. It is no accident that the most eloquent exposition of conservatism has been written by a former Cambridge don, Michael Oakeshott—see *Rationalism in Politics* (London, 1962).

[1] H. B. Charlton, *Portrait of a University* (Manchester, 1951), pp. 16–17.

[2] Richter, op. cit., p. 93.

made their appearance and with them the notion of academic hierarchy. This again was in marked contrast with the egalitarianism of the Oxbridge colleges. The need to climb a ladder of success, the search for professional qualifications, low salaries, lower fees, evening students, poor facilities, all gave university education a different tone outside Oxbridge.

This practical orientation emerged in the kind of emphasis which history received. Manchester eventually produced a new school of social and economic history, or a type of medieval history which concentrated upon practical administrative issues —the tradition of Tout's *Chapters in Administrative History*. Practical interests were also discernible in the type of science studied in the provincial universities. The most popular sciences were the practical ones—engineering, electrical and civil and technological sciences, geology, architecture, metallurgy. Above all, medicine counted as a practical science. It was no accident that the universities of Liverpool and Manchester were next-door to important civic hospitals.[1]

The B.Comm. (Bachelor of Commerce) illustrates another difference between the two types of institution. The B.Comm. set up at Manchester in 1903[2] was essentially practical economics. The contrast here lay with the type of economics at Cambridge in the tradition of Marshall and Keynes, in which a high degree of abstract thought was achieved. At this level, economics almost counted as one of the 'moral sciences'. There was no B.Comm. at Oxford or Cambridge. The equivalent was the pass B.A. for the pass gentleman, whereas the B.Comm. was for the pass businessman.

3.

In Ireland, analogous relationships may be discerned between universities and society.[3] Trinity College, Dublin, was the Irish

---

[1] At Manchester the most important subjects were medicine ,education (sc. teacher-training courses) and commerce. Ibid., p. 112. Manchester University was associated with the already existing medical school and infirmary from 1866. On the university scene generally, see W. H. G. Armytage, *Civic Universities* (London, 1955).

[2] Charlton, op. cit., p. 112.

[3] I have taken most of my evidence for this section from the *Reports of the Royal Commission on Trinity College, Dublin* (Dublin, 1906–7), cited here as *First Report* and *Final Report*.

equivalent of Oxbridge and the organ of the Protestant Ascendancy. The Queen's Colleges, founded by Peel in 1845, at Belfast, Cork and Galway, and the Catholic University, founded by Newman in 1854 (later called University College, Dublin), were the impoverished counterparts of an English civic university. For a member of the Anglo-Irish ruling *élite*, going to university meant going to Trinity, or in the case of some of the gentry, to Oxbridge (as did Parnell). Rooms and servants were provided in college. Sport and the pass degree went together in Trinity as in Oxbridge. Classics and mathematics were dominant and the main courses of study, divinity, medicine and law, had a professional rather than a practical relevance. By Oxbridge standards the college was large, with over a thousand students at the end of the century.

The Queen's Colleges and the Catholic university catered for the needs of the lower middle classes. At Belfast, the majority of the students were Presbyterian and were sons of small farmers, shopkeepers, ministers and country doctors.[1] At Cork, about half the student body was Catholic, at least at the end of the century.[2] At the Catholic university, it seems likely that the students were drawn from the Catholic equivalent of the social group which supplied Queen's, Belfast.[3] None of these colleges rivalled Trinity in size. At Belfast, the numbers of students fluctuated between four and five hundred in the second half of the century. University College, excluding medical students, had about 300 students, Cork about 200 and Galway an insignificant 40.[4] Endowments and salaries were also much lower than at Trinity.

Another key difference between Trinity and the other Irish institutions of higher education was the size of the fees involved. At Trinity, the student could expect to pay a minimum of £83 for examination and tutorial fees, and in most cases well over £100. The fees at University College were ten guineas.[5] There

[1] T. W. Moody and J. C. Beckett, *Queen's Belfast* (London, 1959), vol. I, pp. 133–4.
[2] *Final Report*, p. 228.
[3] On the social differences which exist even today between Trinity College and the other colleges of the National University see an important paper by Monica Nevin to be published by the Irish Statistical Society (1969).
[4] *Parliamentary Papers* (1903), vol. XXI, p. 190; it should be noted that, in 1900, Maynooth with 700 students was by far the largest Catholic institution of higher education in the nineteenth century. The rise of University College, Dublin, from 300 in 1900 to 8,000 today indicates a social shift of great significance.
[5] *Ibid.*, p. 278.

was an additional financial hurdle at Trinity, in that the course of undergraduate studies stretched over four years, as compared with three elsewhere. The total cost of four years' residence at Trinity was estimated to be £400. Even the course of medicine was more expensive there than elsewhere, since a medical student was obliged to graduate in arts before passing on to medicine. The medical fees at Trinity were £230, at Belfast £100.[1]

Like Oxford and Cambridge, Trinity was affected by social and intellectual change during the course of the nineteenth century. Around 1800, the influence of the gentry and the 'bloods' was strong. By 1900, the tone was set by the higher professional groups, especially the Church of Ireland and medicine. Most of the 'plums' in the Church went to Trinity men. The rise of the professions, at the expense of the gentry, was also to the benefit of Trinity graduates. In banking, in insurance, in the higher positions of the civil service, in most of the Dublin hospitals, and in the managerial side of Arthur Guinness, the prizes went to this small social group.[2]

Trinity also benefited from Ireland's position within the United Kingdom, and the Empire. The Church of Ireland looked as much to Canterbury as Armagh, and many Trinity men found livings in England and the colonies.[3] Trinity graduates went to administer British law in India and elsewhere.[4] Inevitably, the tone of the curriculum was affected by Trinity's place in the unionist sun. Trinity played down its Irish connections and emphasized its links with England. There was little or no hint in the curriculum that this was an Irish university. Indeed, Irish history was conspicuous by its absence, and the Professor of History in 1900, J. H. Wardell, stated that he was the first to give a lecture on Irish history within the college.[5] There was a chair of Irish, founded in 1840, but it had been staffed from its foundation by Protestant clergymen and seems to have been largely connected with the divinity school. The Kyle prize in Irish was presented

[1] Ibid., p. 173.
[2] Ibid., pp. 181, 287.
[3] Ibid., pp. 368–9. There were 1,500 Trinity graduates serving in the Church of England in 1905–6 and 150 in the colonies.
[4] First Report, pp. 41, 79.
[5] First Report, p. 72. Provost Mahaffy and Professor Dowden were closely associated with unionist politics during the first Home Rule crisis of 1886 and afterwards.

by 'The Irish Society', a Protestant organization dedicated to the evangelization of the Gaelic-speaking peasantry.[1]

The link of Trinity with the Empire was implied in the existence of several lectureships in Indian studies, including Hindustani. There were also special courses for those wishing to enter the Indian civil service.[2] In addition, there were classes aimed at students taking a commission in the army or navy, both of them careers in which a private income was essential. (The Professor of History described himself as a lieutenant in the Rifle Brigade.)[3] Critics of Trinity pointed out that there were no courses with a practical content, for example agriculture, commerce or 'education'. The Trinity curriculum was directed towards the socially 'higher' professions of medicine, law, the army, navy and the I.C.S. Such experimental science as there was was geared largely to the needs of the medical students.[4]

At Trinity, income, power and status were weighted heavily on the side of the fellows, and hence of classics and pure mathematics. Fellowships were awarded on the basis of competitive examination in these disciplines, college prizes existed largely for them, and the fellows who ran the college lectured and examined in them. A number of professorships in modern sciences had been established in the later half of the nineteenth century, but they were university appointments and carried little weight in the running of the college. Most professors had no permanency of tenure, whereas a fellow once appointed was fellow for life. Professorial salaries were lower than those of the fellows.[5] In the other Irish colleges, the professor ruled his little roost, dominating an entourage of anxious 'assistants'.

When university education was investigated by a Royal Commission at the beginning of the twentieth century, plans for a unified university of Dublin brought out into the open the social differences between Trinity and University College, and the implications of these for the curriculum. It was the Catholic middle class which demanded a more practical emphasis in university studies.

Father Delany, S.J., President of University College, Dublin, and others, pressed for a university in which agriculture, com-

[1] *Final Report*, p. 210.   [2] *First Report*, p. 79.   [3] Ibid., p. 73.
[4] *Final Report*, p. 303.   [5] Ibid., pp. 156, 165, 176.

merce and applied sciences could be studied and where education in the sense of teacher training would have a place.[1] The Trinity pass degree included such 'liberal' subjects as astronomy, logic, psychology, ethics and hydrostatics.[2] The 'reformers' pressed for a practical curriculum with due weight given to modern languages. They had their way when the National University of Ireland was set up in 1908 with colleges in Dublin, Cork and Galway. The B.Comm. now came into its own. Indeed Austin Clarke, a student at the Dublin college in its early years, describes its interior as resembling 'one of the commercial colleges around it in St. Stephen's Green . . . our philology and Old English classes were held around a deal table in the attic of the main building and we climbed to knowledge by dirty back-stairs'.[3]

The practical nature of studies at University College had not formed part of the original concept of its founder, John Henry Newman, who founded his university as a college for the sons of Catholic gentlemen, English as well as Irish. He wrote to a correspondent in 1857:

> You cannot have a university till the gentlemen take it up. I wrote a very strong letter on this subject two years ago; since which time no Irish gentleman has been added, I think, but More O'Ferrall.[4]

His lectures on the 'Idea of a University' given in Dublin in 1852 were in effect an attempt to project the concept of liberal, sc. gentlemanly scholarship against academic utilitarianism. In fact, however, his ideal soon collapsed in the face of the inexorable social facts of Ireland. Newman found to his dismay that the Catholic hierarchy on whom he depended for financial backing were uneasy in the presence of the upper or middle classes.

> They do but feel awkward [he wrote] when a gentleman is converted, or shows himself a good Catholic; and in fact . . . they think that then only Ireland will become again the Isle of Saints, when it was a population of peasants ruled over by a patriotic priesthood patriarchally.[5]

---

[1] *Final Report*, p. 271. [2] Ibid., p. 40.
[3] A. Clarke, *A Penny in the Clouds* (London, 1968), p. 2.
[4] F. McGrath, *Newman's University: Ideal and Reality* (London, 1951), p. 436.
[5] Ibid., p. 398.

Newman resigned his rectorship in 1859. The college then numbered just over a hundred students.

The only faculty to flourish at Newman's university was the medical school. In its successive refoundations, the university took on a resolutely practical orientation, though all this was rather lost to sight in 1954, when the college celebrated the centenary of its 'foundation' by Newman.

Both Dublin colleges were sectarian, but religious belief was tantamount to being the ideology of a particular social group. The tradition of the Church of Ireland at Trinity, and the exclusion of Catholics from fellowships, set a tone in the college, which if it did not exclude Catholics entirely, deprived them of effective influence on the curriculum and other aspects of policy. The few Catholic students at Trinity were usually upper-middle class products, who accepted the values of the college as part of their own social environment.

The link between religious belief and social affiliation at University College was more subtle. The college, run by the Jesuit order, from 1883 had its own middle-class allegiance. In the hands of the Christian Brothers, if such a thing were possible, it might have opened its doors to a broader social entry in a less fashionable quarter of Dublin, north of the Liffey. Under the Jesuits, the college set up a resolutely middle-class course, which its later history did nothing to alter.

This was the college which James Joyce attended. When in due course it became part of the National University, Joyce thought of applying for the Chair of Italian, but the practical nature of the course deterred him. He wrote to his brother Stanislaus in 1909:

There will be no professorship of Italian in the new National University . . . only a lectureship to mixed (evening) classes in commercial Italian. £100 a year. No literature or philology.[1]

The difference between the two types of University also emerged in their approach to history. The characteristic historical emphasis at Trinity was upon the importance of the English connection. In medieval history, this implied concentrating attention upon the Anglo-Norman period after 1169. The Norman con-

[1] R. Ellman (ed.), *Letters of James Joyce* (London, 1966), vol. II, pp. 234–5.

querors were seen as bringing civilization, government and law to a backward people, the twelfth-century equivalent of the role of the British Empire. Orpen's *Ireland Under the Normans* (1911–20) was both a classic of scholarship and a defence of the aristocratic assumptions of the Protestant Ascendancy. So also was Provost Mahaffy's history of the college, *An Epoch in Irish History* (1906), in which he wrote:

> From that day [1660] to the close of the nineteenth century this many-sidedness has been the peculiar fashion of the College, and has produced men whom specialists have acknowledged as masters in each of their studies. This quality was originally stimulated by the circumstances of a small staff being compelled to teach many subjects; but its strange success in avoiding superficiality must be due to some deeper cause than this, or the many and stringent requirements of the Fellowship Examination. The real cause seems to be the versatility of the Anglo-Irish intellect, that type represented all over the world in so many successful soldiers, traders, lawyers, statesmen, that it may fairly be regarded as the most valuable strain in the very composite Anglo-Saxon race. Trinity College has been from the beginning the College of this Anglo-Irish breed, and that is the reason why it has flourished and produced great results in the face of great obstacles, in spite of many rebellions and revolutions.[1]

Similar social assumptions lay behind Lecky's interest in the eighteenth century. This for him was the Golden Age of Irish history when landlord and peasant worked together in harmony.

> The Irish character is naturally intensely aristocratic; and when gross oppression was not perpetrated, the Irish landlords were, I imagine, on the whole very popular, and the rude, good-humoured depotism which they wielded was cordially accepted. Their extravagance, their lavish hospitality, their reckless courage, their keen sporting tastes, won the hearts of their people, and the feudal sentiment that the landlord should command the votes of his tenants was universal and unquestioned.[2]

[1] Mahaffy, *An Epoch in Irish History* (London, 1903), pp. 323–4.
[2] W. E. H. Lecky, *Leaders of Public Opinion in Ireland* (London, 1871), p. 252. On Lecky, see an illuminating article by D. McCartney, *Irish Historical Studies* (Sept., 1964), pp. 119 ff.

The tradition was carried on by Professor Constantia Maxwell in her writings on Georgian Ireland. At Trinity, learning went hand-in-hand with a particular social outlook, in which the values of a ruling *élite* were accepted.

In contrast, the historians of University College, under the influence of the Gaelic Revival, rejected the notion of an aristocratic society of lord and peasant. To them, the eighteenth century marked the most bitter period of Irish history, when the great majority of Irishmen were excluded from political and cultural life. They looked back to a truly Irish society in the eighth century, a period, as they saw it, of general equality among the social orders. This assumption lies behind Professor Eoin Mac-Neill's study *Phases in Irish History* (1919), in which he wrote of Orpen:

> When I see the eulogist of Anglo-Norman feudalism in Ireland sitting in judgment upon the political institutions of a people which he has never studied and does not at all understand, I call to mind the estimate formed by 'the ancient philosophers of Ireland' about Victorius of Aquitaine—that he was deserving of compassion rather than of ridicule. A barbarous people in 'the tribal stage'—every item culled out that might suggest comparison with the head-hunters of New Guinea and the Hottentot—and beside this and in the midst of it schools everywhere, not schools but universities—books everywhere, 'the countless multitude of the books of Eire'—yes, we can still use the scrapings of our Irish vellum as a cure for the foreign snake-bite—and on the other hand, the pomp and circumstance of Feudalism, with its archiepiscopal viceroys, its incastellations and its sub-infeudations, its charters and its statutes, its registers and its inquisitions, but during four centuries not one school of note, not even one, and one abortive university, no literature except the melancholy records of anti-national statecraft, and whatever learning there was for the most part suborned to the purposes of a dominating officialdom, just as in our own day we have seen the highest achievements of science and invention suborned to the service of the war departments.[1]

Each institution had its own intellectual achievement. At Trinity,

[1] E. MacNeill, *Phases of Irish History* (Dublin, 1919), p. 240.

the classical scholarship of Mahaffy and Tyrell, the work of Dowden in English literature and Lecky in English, Irish and intellectual history, stood for a particular style of scholarship.[1] At University College, the introduction of Celtic studies bore fruit in the gifted generation of Bergin and Binchy. (Celtic archaeological studies under Sean P. Ó. Riordáin also came to flourish in this atmosphere later on.) These differences in scholarship may be related at least in part to distinctive social and political assumptions, which provided the tone of each institution. It goes without saying that the revolution of 1916 and the creation of an Irish Free State brought a change in the balance of social power in Ireland, as a result of which Trinity made radical adjustments, which fifty years later are still working themselves out.

4.

Finally, another example of the way in which the social function of the university interacts with its intellectual tone, is provided by the United States during the second half of the nineteenth century. Here, there was an almost exact parallel with the social changes in England and Ireland, albeit on a much grander scale. In the United States during the period after the Civil War, society was transformed by the overwhelming onset of industrialism. Urbanization took place on the grand scale, new sources of commercial and industrial wealth were created, and the balance of social power shifted irrevocably to the great cities.

The existing institutions of higher education in the United States—the colleges—were ill prepared to meet this challenge. Essentially they were small sectarian institutions, committed to supporting the religious beliefs of higher social groups. Unitarianism at Harvard, and Presbyterianism at Princeton had nothing in common with the Catholicism of the immigrant Irish or the Judaism of the immigrant Russian and German Jews, to say nothing of the evangelical beliefs of other Protestant sects.

Religion as in England and Ireland acted as an effective social bulwark. It was reinforced in the colleges by an insistence on Latin as a requirement for entry and by the generally unprofessional

[1] Strictly speaking, Lecky was never a professor but his name cannot be dissociated from the college.

content of the curriculum. The American college carried on the English tradition of educating its students for the career of a gentleman or what amounted to the same thing, a learned clergyman. High fees added to the strength of the defences. In a sea of rising democracy, the colleges were 'citadels of privilege'.

Harvard was the only Eastern college to go any way towards adapting itself to the new conditions of social revolution. The *élitist* traditions of Princeton and Yale remained unchanged well into the twentieth century. The same social phenomena observable at Oxford and Dublin were to be observed here. Princeton concentrated its attention upon undergraduate studies and when graduate studies were finally reorganized, a graduate *college* was built on Oxford lines and a mile from the main undergraduate campus. Dining clubs for the undergraduates were a prominent feature of Princeton, with a pronounced atmosphere of social cliquishness combined with a lack of intellectual endeavour. Woodrow Wilson, President of the college, though critical of the 'clubs' saw the Princeton tradition as providing education for men who would take a high place in the counsels of the nation.[1]

Again, as at Oxford and Dublin, social influences played their part in setting the tone of the curriculum. English history had obvious attractions, as part of the defences of which the Anglo-Saxon Protestant Ascendancy, to draw perhaps too crude a parallel with Ireland, came to stress its Anglo-Saxon heritage. The English elements in the American heritage, from Magna Carta to Puritanism, were singled out for special emphasis. Tocqueville had seen the legal profession as the American equivalent of a European aristocracy, and it was perhaps no accident that Anglo-Saxon values were held to be the foundation of the American common law.

Without doubt, this tradition made enduring contributions to scholarship. From it came the endowments for the Folger Shakespeare Library in Washington, the Newberry Library in Chicago and the Huntington Library in California, each of them dedicated to some aspect of Renaissance culture, when the ideal of the gentleman was dominant. The great American editions of Burke, Coleridge, Walpole and other English conservatives, were part of the same picture, as was the Yale tradition of constitutional history,

[1] L. Veysey, *The Emergence of the American University* (Chicago, 1965), p. 244.

culminating in Wallace Notestein's impressive edition of the diaries of the 1621 Parliament. In contrast, American scholars made little direct contribution towards understanding the new industrial Britain of the nineteenth and twentieth centuries. Their interest was concentrated upon what in a sense was the myth of 'Renaissance' or 'Puritan' England.

The new state universities provided a marked contrast with all this. They were in fact the American equivalent of the English provincial universities and of University College, Dublin. Their students came from the urban middle class of the great cities of the mid-West, and from the beginning they had a professional orientation. The student was allowed to choose which courses he found most useful to him, which meant that the 'old-fashioned' cultural subjects tended to go by the board. Latin and Greek studies almost disappeared. Graduate schools proliferated, most of them offering a direct professional qualification. The arts degree was downgraded to being an introductory course at an elementary level, and a university department without graduate studies had no prestige. Undergraduate teaching itself became a matter of routine lecturing to large classes with little or no contact between lecturer and student. The new university in short attempted mass education on the grand scale.

Financial patronage was given to subjects with a practical, useful bias. The highest salaries were paid to professors in the medical fields, but others, like engineering, were close behind. Schools of Business Studies were created. Law Schools became an essential feature of any university worthy of the name. The status of the arts professor and his salary slumped. Redemption was seen to be in developing arts graduate schools offering a higher research degree analogous to those of medical schools. The Ph.D. was created as a defence of the arts.

It was in the new universities that a new emphasis on American history made itself felt. F. J. Turner, Professor at Wisconsin, put forward the 'Frontier Thesis' as his explanation of the American character. His emphasis upon the West began a trend away from the 'Anglo-Saxon heritage', towards the use of quasi-sociological concepts in which due weight could be given to the mass of the American people, and not least the immigrant. Presidents like Lincoln were placed against a general background of frontier virtues and were regarded as exceptional, but also typical, Americans. The great success which Turner's thesis enjoyed showed that it met an emotional as well as an intellectual need. In its democratic and American emphases, it was the answer to the *élitist* Anglo-Saxon interpretation of American history. The mid-West had created its own mystique which the new universities helped to foster.

A new tone of historical scholarship was also set at Johns Hopkins by Herbert Baxter Adams in the 1890s. The new historians, 'tended to regard history as a branch of industry rather than of art, laying great stress on the exploitation of raw materials, the importance of production and the scientific method'. Adams himself was praised as 'a great Captain of Industry'.[1]

The latent social function of the new universities was to assimilate the great mass of new Americans. The state foundations were non-sectarian and thus helped to break down the social distinctions which sectarianism helped to foster. They were also instruments of social mobility, and their professional graduate schools provided training for new generations of would-be middle-class Americans. They also played their part in strengthening the new social ideal of the American businessman. Businessmen replaced clergymen as a majority among the trustees of these new institutions, sometimes with the deplorable results that Thorstein Veblen outlined in *Higher Education in America*. A concern for conformity and respectability could be as deadening an influence as the gentlemanly ideal of the colleges.

These generalizations do not include all that could be said about the social aspect of university education in England, Ireland and the United States. But they do provide further illustration for the main theme of this book, the relationship between the intellectual aspects of universities and social pressures. Clearly one distinction between the seventeenth century and the nineteenth century is that between pre-industrial and industrial societies. But this distinction, though helpful, is not enough. There are societies within societies. Pre-industrial values survive amid industrialization. And universities may play their part as the educational organs of sub-societies. The essential question is, what does going to university mean?

[1] C. Vann Woodward, *Origins of the New South 1877–1913* (Baton Rouge, 1951), pp. 441–2.

The answer is not always obvious or easy to come by, and it may change from generation to generation. But it offers an important means of understanding the intellectual attitudes of particular societies and the social implications of intellectual traditions.

Bibliography

I MANUSCRIPT MATERIAL

A. *Student Notebooks*

ENGLAND

1. Oxford

(All MSS are in Bodleian Library unless otherwise stated)

Balliol
> Balliol MS 438   1616
> B.M. Harl. MS 1779   1637
> Balliol MS 399   1656
> Balliol MS 318/319   1676

B.N.C.
> Rawl. D.985   1582
> B.N.C. MS 23   1619

Broadgates Hall
> Carnsew Brothers' Notebook
> P.R.O. SP 46/15

Christ Church
> Rawl. D.273   1576
> B.M. Harl. MS 4048   1581
> MS Lat. misc. e.32   1625–40
> Add. MS B.109   1635–46
> Rawl. D.233   1650
> Rawl. D.258   1658
> Locke MS 'Hortus Siccus'   1660
> Locke MS F.11   1661
> Rawl. D.256   1663
> Rawl. D.286   1663
> Rawl. D.1371   c. 1665
> B.M. Lansdowne MS 695   1665–70
> Lambeth Palace MS, Christ Church
> Collection-Book

Corpus
    Rawl. D.47   1606
    Savile MS 89   1655
Exeter
    B.M. Harl. MS 977   1615
    MS Top. Oxon. f.39   1624
    B.M. Sloane MS 1472 1659
Jesus
    Add. MS B.109   1635–49
    Nat. Lib. of Wales MS 30–31 1651–2
Lincoln
    Rawl. D.1110   1662
    B.M. Add. MS 29305   1683
Magdalen
    MS Smith 128   1680
    Rawl. Q.e.21   1684
    MS Top. Oxon. f.61   1693–7
Oriel
    Rawl. D.274   1589
    Rawl. D.947   1620
    B.M. Add. MS 16, 171   c. 1635
Pembroke
    MS Top. Oxon. e.287   1690
Queen's
    T.C.D. MS D.3.5   1600
    Queen's MS 147   1613
    Queen's MS 437   1617
    Queen's MS 196   1623
    Queen's MS 200   1625
    Queen's MS 423   1643–7
    Camb. Univ. MS Dd.12.57 1643–7
    Smith MS 21   c. 1650
    Bodl. fol. θ 659   1651
    B.M. Harl MS 5043   1675–6
    Queen's MS 376   1685
    MS Lat. misc. e.38   c. 1680
    Queen's MS 425–32   c. 1700
St. Edmund Hall
    St. Ed. Hall MS 16   1659

Worcester College MS 4.17   1672–3
MS Cherry 45–6   1683
St. John's
  Rawl. D.1423   1601
  Rawl. D.237   1690s
  Rawl. D.954
  Rawl. D.1178   1700
  Rawl. D.40
Trinity
  MS Aubrey 10   (Aubrey's reminiscences)
University College
  B.M. Harl. MS 5247   1596
Wadham
  Queen's MS 438   1622
  Rawl. D.1452   1650
  Rawl. D.32   1653
  Rawl. D.254   1657
  Rawl. D.1111   1658
  Corpus Christi College MS 289   1662
  Essex Record Office D/DB/L11   1672
  Add. MS A.65   1677
  Eng. misc. sf.4   1680
  Rawl. D.1442   1681

                    2. Cambridge
Caius
  B.M. Sloane MS 3308   1638
  Camb. Univ. Add. MS H.2640   1681
Christ's
  Pembroke (Camb.) MS LC II 164   c. 1565
  B.M. Harl. MS 3230   c. 1590
  Camb. Univ. MS Dd.6.46   1668
Clare
  Bodl. MS Top. Camb. e.5   c. 1652
  Camb. Univ. Add. MS H.2640   1681
Emmanuel
  Bodl. Sancroft MSS 25,80,87   1630–40
  Bodl. Tanner MS 8,467   c. 1636–8

Bodl. Rawl. D.1104   1640
Bodl. Smith MS 21   *c.* 1640
T.C.D. MS   1644
Camb. Univ. Add. MS 6160   1644–5
Emmanuel MS 3.1.11   *c.* 1700

King's
Bodl. Rawl. D.318(6)   *c.* 1597
Lincoln Coll., Oxford, Latin MS 123
  (deposited in Bodleian)   *c.* 1612

Pembroke
Bodl. MS Rawl. D.1414   1634
Pembroke MS L.C. II 5
Pembroke MS L.C. Z. 8   *c.* 1676
Pembroke MS L.C. II 169.1   *c.* 1698

Peterhouse
Durham Univ. Lib. MS 31   (Notebook of Thomas
                           Carr *c.* 1609–13)
Camb. Univ. Add. MS 84

Queens'
Unclassified MSS   (Notebooks *c.* 1610)

St. John's
B.M. Harl. MS 7039   (List of students
                           1577–87)
Harl. MS 191   (D'Ewes notebooks
                           1619)
Bodl. MS Sancroft 107, 111   *c.* 1630
Bodl. Rawl. D.24
Durham Univ. Hunter MS 9(272)   1688/9
St. John's MS S.17 (James 411)   (see article by K. M. Bur-
                           ton, *The Eagle*, 1951)

Sidney Sussex
Samuel Ward MSS Notebooks 13–24
Durham Univ. Hunter MS 106   *c.* 1650

Trinity
B.M. Harl. MS 5356   *c.* 1605
B.M. Harl MS 7033
Bodl. Eng. misc. c.13
Bodl. Rawl. D.1041   *c.* 1643
B.M. Sloane MS 586   1646

B.M. Sloane MS 600
Camb. Univ. Add. MS 3996 (Isaac Newton *c.* 1661)
Bodl. Rawl. D.1453   1677/8
Bodl. Rawl. D.3307   1683
Camb. Univ. Add. MS 3455 1700

3. Cartesian Notebooks
('Principia Cartesiana')

Camb. Univ. MS Dd. 6.46
B.M. Sloane 2613
Camb. Univ. Add. MS 2640
Camb. Univ. Add. MS Dd.12.33
Bodl. MS Top. Oxon. e.344
Camb. Univ. Add. MS 3307

SCOTLAND

There are too many Scottish student notebooks to be listed here.

The main collections of Scottish students' notebooks are to be found in the manuscript collections of the universities of Glasgow, Edinburgh, Aberdeen and St. Andrews, and the National Library of Scotland. There is a small collection at Worcester College, Oxford (MS 4.30) and odd examples in some other college libraries, e.g. Jesus, Cambridge (MS Q.B.20). I have come across over two hundred Scottish notebooks, including 35 for St. Andrews, 25 for Glasgow, 100 for Edinburgh and 50 for Aberdeen covering the period 1600–1700.

IRELAND

Trinity College, Dublin
(T.C.D. MSS unless otherwise stated)

MS D.1.9   Luke Challoner's Book-list 1595
D.3.12 ⎤
D.3.20 |
D.3.16 | Ussher's notebooks 1600–10
D.1.3 ⎰
D.1.9 |
D.3.18 ⎦

D.2.10	John Travers 1610
C.3. 1–6	Ambrose Ussher's notebooks
Marsh's Library MS Z.3.5.28	Caesar Williamson
F.1.22	Michael Ward's Library Catalogue *c.* 1678
Q.3.31	List of books of Josiah Haydock *c.* 1680
MS T.C.D.	Library Loan Book 1687
MS E.6.7	James Stopford 1711
Camb. Univ. Add. MS 1952	1662–82: Disputations, etc.

B. *Guides to Study*

'Dr. Reynolds his letter touching the method of study in Divinitie', Corpus Oxon. MS D.21 (Coxe 303) ff.167ff.

Thomas Cartwright, 'Directions in the study of divinity' in A. Peel and L. H. Carlson (eds.), *Cartwrightiana* (London, 1951).

James Ussher, 'De modo studii', Queen's College, Oxford, MS 217.

N. Sterry, 'A direction for a good and profitable proceeding in study', Bodl. Tanner MS 88. f. 5.

'Short Directions for a student by John Merryweather B.A. late of M.C. in Cambridge 1651/2', Bodl. Rawl. D.200. (Another copy is Emmanuel MS 48 (pressmark I.2.27), usually known as Holdsworth's 'Directions for a Student in the university'.)

'Advice for students from the Bishop of Down', 1660, Camb. Univ. Add. MS 1452/711.

Barlow's 'Directions', Durham Univ. Hunter MS 66 (two copies); St. John's, Cambridge, MS K.38; Worcester College, Oxford; MS 4.19. (E. Jacobsen in *Jnl. of English and Germanic Philology* (July, 1964) shows that only the first two sections are by Barlow, part of the remainder being by Richard Baxter.)

'Letters of advice to a young gent coming to Oxford' (1684), Bodl. MS Top. Oxon, d.344.

John Aubrey, 'An idea of the education of young gentlemen', Bodl. MS Aubrey 10.

'Some short hints at a method of study in the university for the first eight years', *c.* 1700, Bodl. Rawl. D.1178; another copy, Rawl. D.40.

'Directions for a method of study' (Oxford, 1696), Bodl. Rawl. D.1178. f. 9.

'Green's Guide' (Clare, 1707), printed in Wordsworth, *Scholae Academicae*, Appendix IV.

II PRINTED MATERIAL

A. *Pamphlets, etc.*

(See F. W. Bateson, *Cambridge Bibliography of English Literature* (Cambridge, 1940), under 'Education'.)

Francis Bacon, *Of the Advancement of Learning* (1605).

J. Beaumont, *Some observations upon the Apologie of Dr. Henry More for his Mystery of Godliness* (Cambridge, 1665).

Robert Boreman, *The Triumph of Learning over Ignorance* (1652).

William Dell, *The Stumbling Stone* (1653).
The Tryal of Spirits both in Teachers and Hearers (1653).

Thomas Elyot, *The Boke Named the Governour* (1531), ed. H. H. S. Crofts (London, 1883).

L. Humphrey, *The Nobles* (1563).

George Kendall, *A Fescue for a Home book or an Apology for University Learning* (1654).

Edward Leigh, *A Treatise of Religion and Learning* (1656).

J. Milton, *Of Education* (1644).

Sir William Petty, *The Advice of W.P. to Mr. S. Hartlib for the Advancement of Some Particular Parts of Learning* (1648).

Joseph Sedgwick, *A Sermon Preached at Cambridge May 1st 1653 or An Essay to the discovery of the Spirit that disturbs and strikes at the universities* (1653).

John Sturmius, *A Rich Storehouse or Treasure for Nobilitye and Gentlemen* (1570).

Obadiah Walker, *Of Education* (1673).

Seth Ward, '*Vindiciae Academiarum* containing some briefe animadversions upon Mr. Webster's Book stiled the Examination of Academies' (1654).

Edward Waterhouse, *An Humble Apologie for Learning and Learned Men* (1653).

J. Webster, *Academiarum Examen* (1654).

199

B. *General*

H. G. Aldis, *A List of Books Printed in Scotland before 1700* (see items listed under 'Theses') (Edinburgh, 1904).

Sears Jayne, *Library Catalogues of the English Renaissance 1500–1640* (California, 1956).

W. Matthews, *British Diaries* (Cambridge, 1950).
British Autobiographies (Cambridge, 1955).

L. W. Riley, *Aristotle Texts and Commentaries to 1700* (Philadelphia, 1961).

F. Wormald and C. E. Wright, *The English Library before 1700* (London, 1958).

C. *Historical Background*

W. H. G. Armytage, *Civic Universities* (London, 1955).

E. Ashby, *Technology and the Academics* (London, 1958).

P. Dibon, *La philosophie neerlandaise au siècle d'or* (Amsterdam, London, 1954).

W. H. Dunham and S. Pargellis, *Complaint and Reform in England 1436–1714* (New York, 1938).

James E. Farnell, 'The Usurpation of Honest London Householders: Barebone's Parliament', *Eng. Hist. Rev.* (January, 1967).

W. Haller (ed.), *Tracts on Liberty in the Puritan Revolution* (New York, 1934).

N. Hans, *New Trends in Education in the Eighteenth Century* (London, 1951).

S. d'Irsay, *Histoire des universités* (Paris, 1933).

M. Johnson, 'Bibliography of registers (printed) of the universities, inns of court, colleges and schools of Great Britain and Ireland', *Bull. Inst. Hist. Research*, IX (1931).

B. D. Karl, 'The power of intellect and the politics of ideas', *Daedalus* (summer, 1968).

H. M. McLachlan, *English Education under the Test Acts* (Manchester, 1931).

Hastings Rashdall, *The Universities of Europe in the Middle Ages*, new edition edited by F. M. Powicke and A. B. Emden, 3 vols. (Oxford, 1936).

G. H. Sabine (ed.), *The Works of Gerrard Winstanley* (New York, 1941).

L. Stone, 'Literacy and education in England 1640–1900', *Past and present* (February, 1969).

'Education and modernisation in Japan and England', *Comparative Studies in History Society* (1966).

W. A. L. Vincent, *The State and School Education 1640–60* (London, 1950).

C. Wordsworth, *Scholae Academicae: some account of the studies at the English universities in the eighteenth century* (Cambridge, 1877).

M. Wundt, *Die deutsche Schulmetaphysik des 17 Jahrhunderts* (Tubingen, 1939).

D. *Social and Intellectual Background*

P. Allen, 'Scientific Studies in 17th century English Universities', *Jnl. Hist. Ideas* (April, 1949).

H. Baron, *The Crisis of the Early Italian Renaissance* (Princeton, 1955).

F. Caspari, *Humanism and the Social Order in Tudor England* (Chicago, 1954).

K. Charlton, *Education in Renaissance England* (London, 1965).

M. Curtis, *Oxford and Cambridge in Transition* (Oxford, 1959).

'The alienated intellectuals of early Stuart England', *Past and Present* (November, 1962).

A. Everitt, 'Social mobility in early modern England', *Past and Present* (April, 1966).

A. B. Ferguson, *The Articulate Citizen and the English Renaissance* (Durham, Duke U.P., 1965).

Olive M. Griffiths, *Religion and Learning. A study in English Presbyterian thought from the Bartholomew Ejections (1622) to the foundation of Unitarian movement* (Cambridge, 1935).

J. H. Hexter, 'The education of the aristocracy in the Renaissance', *Re-appraisals in History* (London, 1961).

R. Hooykaas, *Humanisme, Science et reforme: Pierre de la Ramée (1515–72)* (Leyden, 1958).

W. S. Howell, *Logic and Rhetoric in England 1500–1700* (Princeton, 1956).

M. James, *Social Problems and Policy during the Puritan Revolution* (London, 1930).

R. F. Jones, *Ancients and Moderns* (St. Louis, 1961).

R. Kelso, *The Doctrine of the English Gentleman in the Sixteenth Century*, University of Illinois Studies in Language and Literature, vol. XIV, nos. 1 and 2 (1929) (contains a good bibliography).

J. K. McConica, *English Humanists and Reformation Politics* (Oxford, 1965).

J. E. Mason, *Gentlefolk in the Making* (Philadelphia, 1935).

R. K. Merton, 'Puritanism, Pietism and Science', *Sociological Rev.* (January, 1936).

P. Miller, *The Puritans* (London, 1938).

W. J. Ong, S.J., *Ramus: Method and the Decay of Dialogue* (Harvard, 1958).

Stuart E. Prall, 'Chancery reform and the Puritan Revolution', *American Jnl. of Legal History*, vol. VI, pp. 28–44.

W. Prest, 'The legal education of the gentry at the Inns of Court', *Past and Present* (December, 1967).

R. Schlatter, 'The higher learning in Puritan England', *Historical Magazine of the Protestant Episcopal Church* (1954).

J. Simon, *Education and Society in Tudor England* (Cambridge, 1966) (contains a good bibliography).

G. Smith, 'The reform of the laws of England 1640–60', *Univ. Toronto Quarterly* (1941).

Leo J. Solt, 'Anti-intellectualism in the Puritan Revolution', *Church History* (1956).

L. Stone, 'The educational revolution', *Past and Present* (July, 1964).

The Crisis of the Aristocracy 1558–1641 (Oxford, 1965).

'Social mobility in England 1500–1700', *Past and Present* (April, 1966).

M. Walzer, *The Revolution of the Saints* (Cambridge, Mass., 1965).

L. B. Wright, *Middle Class Culture in Elizabethan England* (Univ. N. Carolina, 1935).

E. *More Specialized Studies*

ENGLAND

1. Oxford

C. W. Boase and A. Clark (eds.), *Register of the University of Oxford* (Oxford Hist. Soc., 1884–9).

M. Burrows (ed.), *The Register of the Visitors of the University of Oxford* (Oxford, 1881).

E. H. Cordeaux and D. H. Merry, *A Bibliography of Printed Works Relating to the University of Oxford* (Oxford, 1958).

A. B. Emden, *An Oxford Hall in Medieval Times* (Oxford, 1927).

J. M. Fletcher, 'The teaching and study of Arts at Oxford *c.* 1400–1520' (Oxford D. Phil. thesis, 1962).

Strickland Gibson (ed.), *Statuta Antiqua Universitates Oxoniensis* (Oxford, 1931).

A. de Jordy and H. F. Fletcher (eds.), 'A guide for younger schollers' (Illinois, 1961) (cf. review article by E. Jacobsen, *Jnl. of English and Germanic Philology* (July, 1964).

W. von Leyden (ed.), *Locke's Essays on the Law of Nature* (Oxford, 1954).

J. R. McGrath, *The Flemings in Oxford* (Oxford Hist. Soc., 1904–24).

F. Madan (ed.), 'The daily ledger of John Dorne, 1520', C. R. L. Fletcher (ed.), *Collectanea, First Series*, Oxford Historical Society (Oxford, 1885).

Rough List of Manuscript Materials Relating to the History of Oxford (Oxford, 1887).

Oxford Books: a bibliography of works relating to the university and city of Oxford (Oxford, 1895–1931), 3 vols.

C. E. Mallet, *A History of the University of Oxford* (London, 1924–7), 3 vols.

M. Richter, *The Politics of Conscience* (London, 1964).

Anthony à Wood, *The History and Antiquities of the Colleges and Halls in the University of Oxford*, ed. J. Gutch, (Oxford, 1786–90).

Athenae Oxonienses, ed. P. Bliss, (London, 1813–20), 4 vols.

2. Cambridge

E. Cassirer, *The Platonic Renaissance in England,*

R. L. Colie, *Cambridge Platonists and Dutch Arminians* (Cambridge, 1957).

W. T. Costello, S. J., *The Scholastic Curriculum in Early 17th Century Cambridge* (Cambridge, 1958).

H. F. Fletcher, *Intellectual Development of John Milton* (Urbana, 1956–).

R. T. Gunther, *Early Science in Cambridge* (Cambridge, 1937).

J. O. Halliwell-Phillipps, *College Life in the Time of James I as Illustrated by an Unpublished Diary of Sir Symonds d'Ewes* (London, 1851).

J. Heywood and T. Wright, *Cambridge University Transactions during the Puritan Controversies of the 16th and 17th centuries* (London, 1854).

J. Lamb (ed.), *Cambridge Documents* (London 1838)

S. R. Maitland (ed.), 'Original papers relating to Whitgift', *The British Magazine*, vols. XXXII–XXXIII (October, 1847 to February, 1848).

J. E. B. Mayor (ed.), *Cambridge under Queen Anne* (Cambridge, 1911).

J. B. Mullinger, *The University of Cambridge from the Earliest times to the Decline of the Platonist Movement* (Cambridge, 1873–1911), 3 vols.

M. Nicolson (ed.), *The Conway Letters* (London, 1930).

'Christ's College and the Latitude-men', *Modern Philology* (1929–30), vol. XXVII, pp. 35–53.

'Early stages of Cartesianism in England', *Studies in Philology* (1929), vol. XXXVI, pp. 356–74.

J. A. Passmore, *Ralph Cudworth* (Cambridge, 1951).

H. C. Porter, *Reformation and Reaction in Tudor Cambridge* (Cambridge, 1964).

F. J. Powicke, *The Cambridge Platonists* (London, 1926).

S. Rothblatt, *The Revolution of the Dons* (London, 1968).

E. J. L. Scott (ed.), *Letter book of Gabriel Harvey 1573–80* (Camden Society, 1874).

Joan Simon, 'The social origins of Cambridge students 1603–1640', *Past and Present* (November, 1963).

H. S. Wilson and C. A. Forbes, *Gabriel Harvey's Ciceronianus* (Univ. Nebraska, 1945).

D. A. Winstanley, *Later Victorian Cambridge* (Cambridge, 1947).

3. Other Colleges

C. Hill, *Intellectual Origins of the English Revolution* (Oxford, 1965).

R. Holdsworth, *Praelectiones Theologicae Habitae in Collegio Greshamensi*, ed. R. Pearson (London, 1661).

F. R. Johnson, 'Gresham College, precursor of the Royal Society', *Jnl. Hist. Ideas*, vol. I.

H. McLachlan, *Warrington Academy* (Manchester, 1943).

G. H. Turnbull, 'Oliver Cromwell's college at Durham', *Research Review* (London, 1952).

J. Ward, *Lives of the Professors of Gresham College* (London, 1741).

SCOTLAND

P. J. Anderson, *Collections towards a Bibliography of the Universities of Aberdeen* (Edinburgh, 1907).

J. H. Baxter, *Collections towards a Bibliography of St. Andrews* (St. Andrews, 1926).

R. G. Cant, *The University of St. Andrews* (London, 1946).

G. E. Davie, *The Democratic Intellect* (Edinburgh, 1961).

W. C. Dickinson, *Two Students at St. Andrews 1711–1716* (London, 1952).

J. Durkan, 'The beginnings of humanism in Scotland', *Innes Rev.* (1953), IV, pp. 5–24.

Fortuna Domus, a series of lectures delivered in the university of Glasgow in commemoration of the fifth centenary of its foundation (Glasgow, 1952).

A. Grant, *The University of Edinburgh during its First Three Hundred Years* (Edinburgh, 1884).

D. B. Horn, *A Short History of the University of Edinburgh 1556–1889* (Edinburgh, 1967).

C. Innes and J. Robertson (eds.), *Monumenta Almae Universitatis Glasguensis* (Glasgow, 1854).

D. Laing (ed.), *Letters and Papers of Robert Baillie* (Edinburgh, 1841–2).

T. McRie, *Andrew Melville* (Edinburgh, 1856).

D. Mathew, *Scotland under Charles I* (London, 1955).

W. M. Mathew, 'The origins and occupations of Glasgow students, 1740–1839', *Past and Present* (April, 1966).

G. S. Pryde, *The Scottish Universities and the Colleges of Colonial America* (Glasgow, 1957).

J. B. Salmond, *Veterum Laudes. Being a tribute to the achievements of the members of St. Salvator's College during five hundred years* (London, 1950).

H. R. Trevor-Roper, *George Buchanan and the Ancient Scottish Constitution*, *E.H.R.*, supplement 3 (London, 1966).
'Scotland and the Puritan Revolution', *Religion, Reformation and Social Change* (London, 1967).

IRELAND

[Compiled by the Jesuit Fathers] *A Page of Irish History* (Dublin, 1930).
F. McGrath, *Newman's University* (London, 1951).
J. P. Mahaffy, *An Epoch in Irish History* (London, 1903).
(ed.), *The Particular Book of Trinity College, Dublin* (London, 1904).
C. E. Maxwell, *A History of Trinity College, Dublin 1591–1892* (Dublin, 1946).
T. W. Moody and J. C. Beckett, *Queen's Belfast 1845–1949* (London, 1959).
W. O'Sullivan, 'Ussher as a collector of manuscripts', *Hermathena* (1956).
W. B. Stanford, 'Classical studies at T.C.D.' *Hermathena* (1941).
J. W. Stubbs, *The History of the University of Dublin* (London, 1889).
M. Tierney (ed.), *A Struggle with Fortune* (Dublin, 1954) (history of University College, Dublin, by various contributors).

AMERICA

B. Bailyn, *Education in the Forming of American Society* (New York, 1960).
E. Battis, *Saints and Sectaries* (Chapel Hill, 1962).
P. Miller, *The New England Mind* (New York, 1939).
Roger Williams (New York, 1953).
S. E. Morison, *The Founding of Harvard College* (Cambridge, Mass., 1935).
Harvard College in the 17th century (Cambridge, Mass., 1936).
L. Veysey, *The Emergence of the American University* (Chicago, 1965).

Index

Abbott, John, 146
Aberdeen, colleges of, 53, 54, 55, 89, 130, 132, 154
Adams, Herbert Baxter, 191
Alvey, Henry, 61, 62, 67
Ames, William, 61–2, 136
Angus, Earl of, William Douglas, 55
Anti-intellectualism, 74–6
Apprentices, Statute of, 32
Aquinas, Thomas, 62, 136, 163
Argyll, Earl of, Archibald Campbell, 129
Aristotle, 81 ff., 96, 105, 125, 131–2, 147, 149, 150
   Ethics, 38, 53
   Topics, 69
   Attacks upon, 49–50, 72
Arriaga, Rodrigo, 136
Ascham, Roger, 48

Bacon, Francis, 61, 98–9, 124–6, 155
Bacon, Nicholas, 27
Baillie, Robert, 88, 107, 129 ff.
Bancroft, Richard, 59, 62
Banks, Sir John, 142
Barebone Parliament, 116
Barebone, Praise-God, 119
Barlow, Thomas, 78, 124–5, 146–7, 149, 167
Barnes, Arthur Thomas, 179
Baron, Hans, 34

Barron, Robert (Baronius), 89, 90, 164–5
Barrow, Henry, 71–5
Battis, E., 114
Baxter, Richard, 149
Baylie, Richard, 64, 94
Beale, William, 95
Beaumont, Joseph, 150
Becon, Thomas, 72
Bedell, William, 95, 69
Bedford, Earl of, Francis Russell, 44
Belfast, Queen's College, 181–2
Bellarmine, Robert, 77, 91, 136, 149
Bergin, Osborn, 188
Beurhusius, Friedrich, 60, 63, 68
Beza, Theodore, 44
Bilson, Thomas, 83
Binchy, Daniel, 188
Blair, Robert, 89
Bodley, Thomas, 43
Booth, Robert, 62, 84
Borelli, Giovanni Alfonso, 165
Boyd, Robert, 88
Boyle, Richard, Earl of Cork, 32
Boyle, Robert, 127, 155, 165, 166–7
Boyle, Roger, Lord Broghill, 138
Bradwardine, Thomas, 163
Brahe, Tycho, 137
Braithwait, Thomas, 107
Bramhall, John, 95, 155
Brent, Nathaniel, 107, 108

Brerewood, Edward, 164
Bretton, Lawrence, 84
Briggs, Henry, 65
Bright, Timothy, 60
Brockbank, Thomas, 163
Brooke, Lord, Robert Greville, 92
Browne, Robert, 73-4
Brudenell family, 27
Buchanan, George, 132, 149
Burgersdijk, Franz (Burgersdicius), 78, 104, 107, 133, 147, 161, 163-5
Burke, Edmund, 153, 189
Butler, James, Earl of Ormonde, 146
Butler, Montagu, 176

Caesar's *Commentaries*, 38, 44
Calvin, John, 44, 131
Cambridge, University of, *passim*; *see also* Bibliography
  Colleges:
  Caius, 94, 151
  Christ's, 61-2, 151
  Clare, 166
  Corpus (Benet Hall), 72, 94
  Emmanuel, 28, 61, 63, 66, 94, 103, 114
  Jesus, 95
  King's, 61, 63
  Magdalene, 104
  Pembroke, 95
  Peterhouse, 21, 37, 95
  Queens', 95
  St. John's, 61-2, 66, 79, 95, 143
  Trinity, 21, 35, 37, 62, 79, 94, 105, 151
  Trinity Hall, 94
Cambridge Platonists, 150
Campbell, Archibald, Earl of Argyll, 129

Canon law, 16, 18, 19
Cant, Andrew, 136
Cardano, Girolamo (Cardanus), 138
Carlyle, Thomas, 178
Carnsew brothers, 44
Cartesianism, 150-1, 155
Cartwright, Thomas, 44, 52, 53, 60, 61, 68, 71, 109
Cary, Valentine, 62
Case, John, 64
Castiglione, Baldassare, 38
Catholic University, *see* Dublin, University College
Cecil, Thomas, 25
Cecil, William, 25
Challenor, Luke, 67
Chappell, William, 95
Charleton, Walter, 154
Cheke, Sir John, 21, 36-7
Cheynell, Francis, 107, 108
Child, Sir Josiah, 142
Cicero, influence of, 38, 48
Clarke, Austen, 184
Classes, Act of, 133
Clauberg, Johann, 155
Clavius, Christopher, S.J., 137
Clergy, 15-22, 24, 28-33
  secular clergy, 29
  seminaries, 29
Clifford, George, Earl of Cumberland, 38
Coker, William, 146
Coleridge, Samuel Taylor, 178, 189
Combachius, Ludovicus, 78
Comenius (Jan A. Komensky), 100
Comte, Auguste, 178
Copernicus, Nicolaus, 137
Corbet, Richard, Bishop of Oxford, 92
Corbett, Edward, 107

Cork, Earl of, Richard Boyle, 32
Cork, Queen's College, 181
Cosin, John, 93, 100
Cotton, Jonathan, 165
Covenant, Solemn League and, 102
Crackanthorp, Richard, 83, 85, 105, 148
Cranmer, Thomas, 21
Crawford, Thomas, 155
Cromwell, Henry, 139–40
Cromwell, Oliver, chap. VII, 134 ff., 146, 170
Cudworth, Ralph, 106, 165
Culpeper, Nicholas, 117
Cumberland, Earl of, George Clifford, 38
Curtis, Mark, 23–4

Davie, G. E., 173
Day, John, 82, 83
Delany, Father, S.J., 183
Dell, William, 112, 118
Descartes, René, 83, 106, 124, 131, 136–7, 154, 155–61, 164–6
Dickenson, Thomas, 121
Dickson, David, 130
Digby, Kenelm, 83, 124, 155, 165
Diggers, the, 111–12
Dillingham, William, 106
Dorne, John, 34
Douglas, William, Earl of Angus, 55
Dowden, Edward, 188
Downham, George, 61–2, 136
Dowsing, William, 102
Dryden, John, 148
Dublin Philosophical Society, 153
Dublin, Trinity College, 139–40, 152–3, 172, 181–8
Dublin, University College, 181–8

Dudley, Robert, Earl of Leicester, 64
Dudley, Thomas, 114
Duhamel, Jean Baptiste, 164
Duncombe, Thomas, 123, 146
Dunster, Henry, 116
Duppa, Brian, 94
Durham, projected college at, 121–2
Dury, John, 100

Eachard, John, 143
Edinburgh, University of, 55, 88, 155
Edward VI, 23
Ejectors, 121–2
Elyot, Sir Thomas, 23, 35, 37, 38, 39–44
English, John, 64
Epicurus, 165
Erasmus, Desiderius, 48, 165
Eustachius of S. Paulo, 105, 147, 150, 164

Fairfax, Sir Thomas, 122
Fayreclough, Daniel, 64
Featley, Daniel, 93
Fell, John, 146–7
Fenner, Dudley, 61
Field, John, 43–4
Field, Richard, 83
Fitzwilliam family, 27–8
Fleming, Henry, 147
Floyd, Nicholas, 124, 146
Flynt, Josiah, 116
Folger Library, Washington, D.C., 189
Fonseca, Petrus de, 82, 88, 105
Foote, Daniel, 105
Forbes, Bishop Patrick, 89, 90, 129
Forbes, Robert, 155

Forbes, William, 88
Fox, George, 121-2
Foxe, John, 39, 44
Freigius, Johann Thomas, 48, 60, 68
Fulke, William, 68
Fullerton, James, 67

Galilei, Galileo, 127, 136
Galway, Queen's College, 181
Gandy, John, 83
Gassendus, Pierre (Gassendi), 83, 124, 154-5, 164-5
Gauden, John, 101
Gentleman's Calling, The, 148
Gentry, rise of, 22-3
    importance of, 26
Gilbert, William, 138
Gilchrist, James, 156
Gillespie, Patrick, 135, 138
Gladstanes, George, 87
Glasgow, University of, 53, 55, 56, 88, 130, 133, 155-6
Glisson, Francis, 145
Goad, Roger, 63
Goddard, Jonathan, 120
Goodwin, John, 112, 119, 149
Gordon, George, Earl of Huntley, 55
Goslette, Benjamin, 123
Gouge, William, 61
Green, Robert, 166
Green, T. H., 175, 179
Greenwood, John, 72
Gregory, David, 155-6
Gresham, Sir Thomas, 65
Gresham College, 65-6
Greville, Robert, Lord Brooke, 92
Grindal, Edmund, 36
Grotius (Hugo de Groot), 165

Hamilton, James, 67

Hampden, John, 170
Harrison, Major-General Thomas, 117
Harrison, John, 152
Harrison, Robert, 71
Harsnett, Samuel, Archbishop of York, 92
Hartlib, Samuel, 100, 102, 162
Harvard, John, 188-9
Harvard College, 115-16
Harvey, Gabriel, 38, 47-8, 62
Harvey, William, 136
Hearne, John, 123, 146
Heerebord, Adrian, 136, 163, 166
Henderson, Alexander, 129-31
Henry VIII, 21
Hesiod, 132
Hexter, J. H., 23
Hildersham, Arthur, 60, 61
Hill, Christopher, 66
Hoar, Leonard, 116
Hobbes, Thomas, 154-5, 165
Hody, Humphrey, 147
Holdsworth, Richard, 66, 85, 103-5
Holywood, John of, 137
Home, John, Lord Home, 55
Homer, 38, 124, 132
Honour, code of, 26
Hooke, Robert, 166
Hooker, Richard, 81, 136
Hooton, Henry, 163
Hope, Sir James, 134
Horace, 132
Hoyle, Joshua, 69
Humphrey, Lawrence, 38-44, 46, 47, 63, 102, 170
Hunne, Richard, 18
Huntington Library, 189
Huntley, Earl of, George Gordon, 55
Hutchinson, Anne, 113-14, 117

Hutton, Matthew, Archbishop of York, 82
Huygens, Christiaan, 166
Hyde, Edward, 92

Inns of Court, 18, 21, 27
Isham family, 27
Isham, Justinian, 101
Isocrates, 132

Jackson, Henry, 175
Jaffray, Alexander, 134
James VI of Scotland, 89
Javellus, Chrysostomus, 82
Jebb, R. C., 175
Jesuits, 78, 185
Jewell, John, Bishop of Salisbury, 52
Johnson, Francis R., 66
Johnston, John, 87
Jowett, Benjamin, 175-6, 177
Joyce, James, 185
Juxon, William, 94

Keckermann, Bartholomew, 133, 138
Kett's rebellion, 36
Keynes, John Maynard, 180
King, Charles, 163
King, Gregory, 141
Kingsmill, Richard, 44
Knollys, Francis, 43

Lambert, Major-General John, 119, 121
Langbaine, Gerard, 127
Lascelles, Colonel Francis, 121
Laud, William, esp. chap. VI, 31, 90
Le Grand, Antoine, 163
Lecky, W. E. H., 186, 188
Leech, David, 89

Leicester, Earl of, Robert Dudley, 64
Leighton, Robert, 135
Levellers, the, 110-11
Locke, John, 141, 146, 153, 156, 158-62, 164-5, 167
Lockhart, Sir William, 134
Loftus, Adam, 67
Long, Roger, 165
Lucretius, 165

MacNeill, Eoin, 187
Magirus, Johannes, 105, 107, 146, 150
Mahaffy, John Pentland, 186, 188
Major, John, 82
Manchester, Earl of, Edward Montagu, 103, 108
Manchester, Owens College, 179
Marprelate Tracts, 71
Marsh, Narcissus, 146, 152
Marshall, Alfred, 180
Martial, 124
Martin, Anthony, 96
Martyr, Peter, 39
Massie, Andrew, 155
Matthew, David, 90
Maxwell, Gilbert, 89, 156
Mede, Joseph, 84
Medicine, 144
Meldrum, George, 137
Melville, Andrew, 53-60, 87, 109, 132
Menzies, John, 135-6
Merchants' charity, 31
Merryweather, John, 104
Mersenne, Marin, 85, 127
Middleton, George, 155
Milton, John, 101, 149, 162
Monasticism, 18, 20
  criticism of, 19
Monson, James, 151

Montague, Richard, 93
More, Henry, 106, 151, 154, 164–5
More, Thomas, 34, 35
Morison, Samuel, 114
Morton, Thomas, 83

Naylor, James, 122
Neville, Thomas, 62
Newberry Library, 187
Newman, John Henry, 184
Newton, Isaac, 106, 150, 152, 166
Notestein, Wallace, 190

O'Riordain, Sean P., 188
Ormonde, Earl of, James Butler, 146
Orpen, G. H., 186
Oughton, Daniel, 147
Ovid, 132
Owen, John, 120–1, 124, 127, 149
Oxford, University of, *passim*
  Colleges:
  Balliol, 45, 84
  Brasenose, 17, 45, 64
  Broadgates Hall, 44
  Canterbury College, 17
  Christ Church, 20, 21, 35, 44–5, 101, 147, 164
  Corpus, 21, 64, 107
  Durham College, 17
  Exeter, 17, 45, 84, 107, 152
  Gloucester College, 17
  Gloucester Hall, 143
  Halls, disappearance of, 20
  Hart Hall, 143
  Jesus, 194
  Lincoln, 45
  Magdalen, 28, 45, 82, 107, 163
  Merton, 17, 64, 107
  New College, 79, 82, 107
  New Inn Hall, 143

Oriel, 64, 82, 83
Pembroke, 163
Queen's, 45, 83, 107, 124, 147, 163–4
St. Edmund Hall, 147, 163
St. John's, 20, 64, 83, 146
Trinity, 195, see Durham College
University, 64
Waltham, 107, 124–8, 143, 147, 163
Oxford, University of, Regius professorships, 21, 35
Oxford Philosophical Society, 150

Pacius, Julius, 105
Paracelsus (Philippus Aureolus Theophrastus), 127–8
Parker, Henry, 123
Parker, Matthew, 36
Patrick, Simon, 106
Patterson, William, 155
Pattison, Mark, 175
Penny, John, 51, 42, 60, 61, 71
Perkins, William, 50–2, 53, 61, 62, 80, 170
Perne, Andrew, 37
Peter, Hugh, 117
Petty, Sir William, 118–19, 127, 149, 162
Pilan, James, 155
Pinke, Warden, 82, 94
Plato, *Laws*, 38
Plautus, 124
Potter, Christopher, 83
Powell, Vavasour, 118
Prideaux, John, 84, 93
Princeton University, 189
Puritanism, 39–44, 47
Pym, John, 170

Rainolds, John, 64, 83, 170

Raleigh, Sir Walter, 69, 165
Ramée, Pierre de la: *for* Ramism, *see* chap. III, 44, 116
Ramus, *see* Ramée, Pierre de la
Rawdon, Edward, 151
Rawdon, John, 151
Resolutioners, 139
Reynolds, Edward, 107
Reynolds, John, 107
Richardson, John, 61
Rimini, Gregory of, 83
Rogers, John, 64
Rogers, Nehemiah, 147
Rooke, Lawrence, 127
Ross, Alexander, 90
Rothblatt, S., 175–7
Russell, Bertrand, 176
Russell, Francis, Earl of Bedford, 44
Rutherford, Samuel, 129–30

St. Andrews, colleges of, 54, 87, 88, 132, 136, 154
Sallust, 38, 44
Savile, Sir Henry, 64
Scaliger, J. J., 138
Scheibler, Christoph, 77, 78, 83, 85, 105, 107, 134, 136, 146–7, 149, 152, 161, 165
Scholasticism, chap. V, 16, 19, 71
Schuler, John, 151
Scotland, social structure, 54–5
  General Assembly, 55
Scotus, John Duns, 147, 163
Scribonius (Gulielmus Adolphus), 60
Sergeant, John, 165–6
Sharp, William, 132
Sheldon, Gilbert, 94
Sidgwick, Henry, 175
Sinclair, George, 236

Smiglecius (Marcin Smiglecki), 147
Smith, John, 151
Smith, Samuel, 164
Smith, Sir Thomas, 21, 24, 37
Smith, Thomas, 163
Social mobility, 71
South, Robert, 123, 146–7
Spencer family, 27
Spottiswood, John, Archbishop of St. Andrews, 90
Stafford, Earl of, Thomas Wentworth, 95, 97
Stanton, Lawrence, 62
Stearne, John, 140
Sterry, Nathaniel, 105
Stierius, Joannes, 164
Stillingfleet, Edward, Bishop of Worcester, 165
Stone, Lawrence, 23–4, 97
Strang, Principal of Glasgow, 130–1, 137
Strickland, Robert, 163
Sturm, John, 39
Suarez, Francesco, 77, 78, 82, 83, 91, 105, 124, 136, 152, 163, 165
Supremacy, Act of, 19
Swinton, Sir John, 134

Temple, William, 61, 63
Terence, 132
Thomkinson, Thomas, 151
Throgmorton, Sir Nicholas, 25
Thurloe, John, 139
Tillotson, John, 106
Timpler, Clemens, 85, 88
Tithes, 110
Torricelli, Evangelista, 83, 127
Tout, T. F., 180
Tran, John, 155–6
Travers, John, 69

Travers, Walter, 52, 61, 67
Tresham family, 27
Trevor-Roper, Hugh, 133
Triers, 121-2
Trinity College, Dublin, 62, 66-70
Turner, Edward, 123
Turner, Frederick Jackson, 190
Tutors, 22
Tweedy, William, 155
Twyne, Brian, 64

Ussher, James, 67-70, 96
Ussher, Robert, 95
Utrecht, University of, 131

Vane, Sir Henry, 'the younger' 114
Veblen, Thorstein, 191
Veitch, James, 135
Virgil, 124, 132
Voetius, Gisbert, 121, 133

'Wadham Group', 125-8, 146
Wake, William, 148
Walker, Obadiah, 158, 167
Walpole, Horace, 189
Walwyn, William, 111, 117
Walzer, Michael, 52
Ward, Samuel, 69
Ward, Seth, 124-8
Wardell, J. H., 182
Webster, John, 128
Wentworth, Thomas, Earl of Stafford, 95, 97

Westminster Assembly, 106
Whichcote, Benjamin, 106
Whiston, William, 165
Whitaker, William, 62, 170
Whitgift, John, 28, 31, 37, 59, 61, 79
Widdrington, Ralph, 150
Wigginton, Giles, 51
Wilcox, Thomas, 44
Williams, John, Bishop of Lincoln, 101
Wilkins, John, 108, 125
Wilkinson, Henry, 107, 108
Wilkinson, John, 107
Wilson, Thomas, 33 n., 141
Wilson, Woodrow, 189
Winstanley, Gerrard, 111, 117
Winter, Samuel, 139
Winthrop, John, 114-15
Wishart, John, 155
Wolsey, Cardinal Thomas, 15, 18
Woodward, John, 165
Worcester, diocese of, 31
Wren, Christopher, 127

Xenophon, 38

Yale University, 189
Young, Thomas, 103

Zabarella, Giacomo, 62, 88, 89, 105, 146